# THE BLACK GHOST™

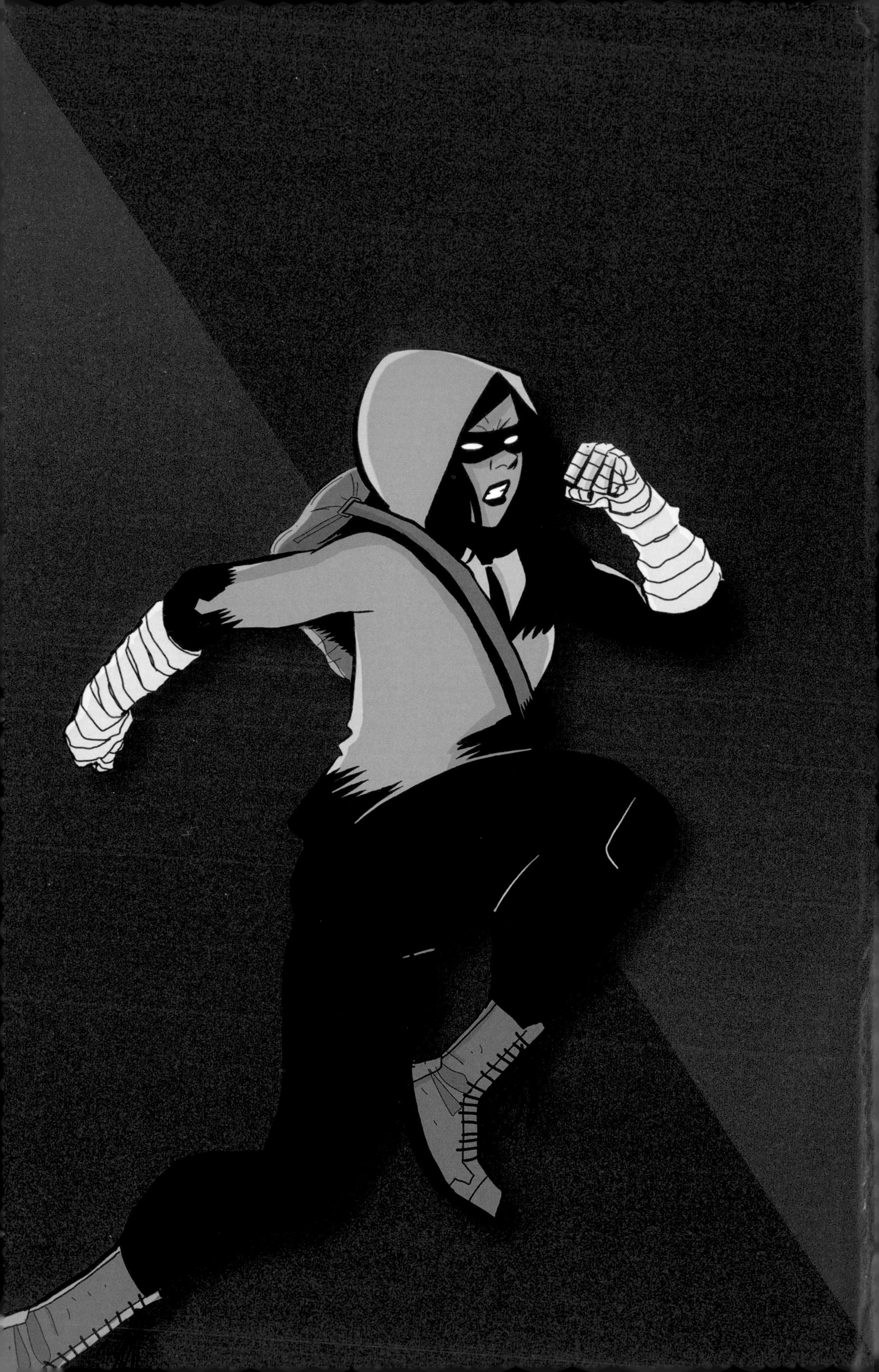

# THE BLACK GHOST

## HARD REVOLUTION

**STORY:** ALEX SEGURA AND MONICA GALLAGHER

**ART:** GEORGE KAMBADAIS

**LAYOUTS (ISSUE 1):** MARCO FINNEGAN

**COLORS:** ELLIE WRIGHT

**LETTERS AND DESIGN:** TAYLOR ESPOSITO OF GHOST GLYPH STUDIOS

**COVER:** GREG SMALLWOOD

**THE BLACK GHOST LOGO:** DYLAN TODD

**ORIGINAL SERIES PROOFREADER:** JAMIE LEE ROTANTE

**ORIGINAL SERIES EDITOR:** GREG LOCKARD

**PUBLISHING CONSULTANT:** J. BETANCOURT

*THE BLACK GHOST* CREATED
BY ALEX SEGURA, MONICA GALLAGHER, AND GEORGE KAMBADAIS

DARK HORSE TEAM

PRESIDENT AND PUBLISHER
MIKE RICHARDSON

EDITOR
DANIEL CHABON

ASSISTANT EDITOR
CHUCK HOWITT

DESIGNER
SKYLER WEISSENFLUH

DIGITAL ART TECHNICIAN
JASON RICKERD

NEIL HANKERSON EXECUTIVE VICE PRESIDENT • TOM WEDDLE CHIEF FINANCIAL OFFICER • RANDY STRADLEY VICE PRESIDENT OF PUBLISHING • NICK MCWHORTER CHIEF BUSINESS DEVELOPMENT OFFICER • DALE LAFOUNTAIN CHIEF INFORMATION OFFICER • MATT PARKINSON VICE PRESIDENT OF MARKETING • VANESSA TODD-HOLMES VICE PRESIDENT OF PRODUCTION AND SCHEDULING • MARK BERNARDI VICE PRESIDENT OF BOOK TRADE AND DIGITAL SALES • KEN LIZZI GENERAL COUNSEL • DAVE MARSHALL EDITOR IN CHIEF • DAVEY ESTRADA EDITORIAL DIRECTOR • CHRIS WARNER SENIOR BOOKS EDITOR • CARY GRAZZINI DIRECTOR OF SPECIALTY PROJECTS • LIA RIBACCHI ART DIRECTOR • MATT DRYER DIRECTOR OF DIGITAL ART AND PREPRESS • MICHAEL GOMBOS SENIOR DIRECTOR OF LICENSED PUBLICATIONS • KARI YADRO DIRECTOR OF CUSTOM PROGRAMS KARI TORSON DIRECTOR OF INTERNATIONAL LICENSING • SEAN BRICE DIRECTOR OF TRADE SALES

PUBLISHED BY DARK HORSE BOOKS
A DIVISION OF DARK HORSE COMICS LLC
10956 SE MAIN STREET
MILWAUKIE, OR 97222

FIRST EDITION: MAY 2021
TRADE PAPERBACK ISBN: 978-1-50672-446-1

10 9 8 7 6 5 4 3 2 1
PRINTED IN CHINA

COMIC SHOP LOCATOR SERVICE: COMICSHOPLOCATOR.COM

THIS VOLUME COLLECTS *THE BLACK GHOST* #1–#5.

**SPECIAL THANKS:**

DARA HYDE

DAVID STEINBERGER

CHIP MOSHER

CHANTELLE AIMEE OSMAN

JUSTIN ACLIN

DAVE WHITE

MICHAEL MORECI

VINCENT LOVALLO

RON CACACE

JON GOLDWATER

PIXIE KOSELA

DAVID HYDE AND
PAMELA MULLIN-HOVARTH
FROM SUPERFAN PRODUCTIONS

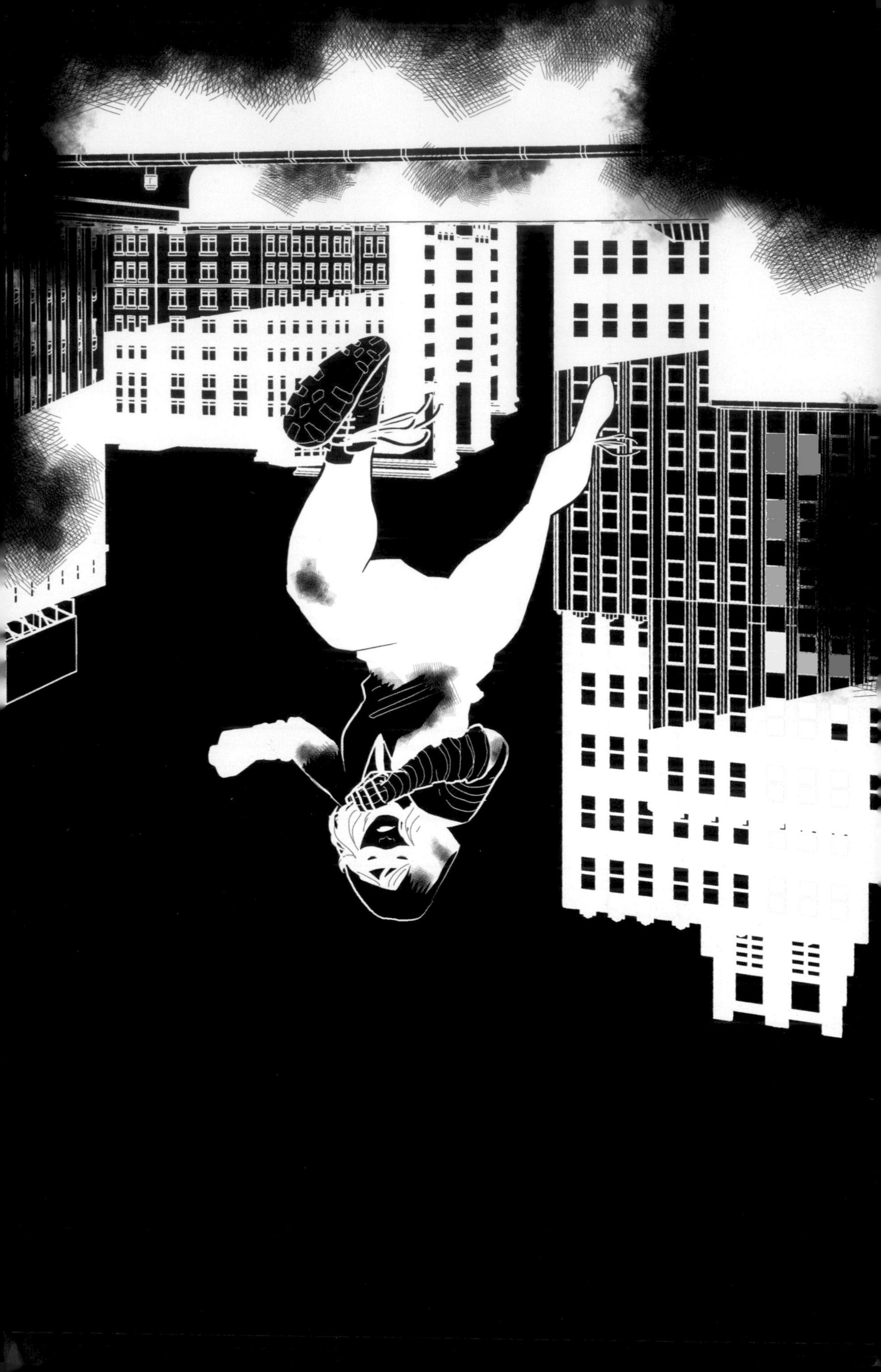

# GHOST OF A CHANCE

If there's one lesson I've learned over the years as a writer and editor, it's that you make your opportunities. You create the lanes for yourself and work within the limits you're given. This is a big reason why you're holding a collected edition for *The Black Ghost* in your hands. This is a project that came from a unified desire for the book to exist. Here's part of the story.

About a year ago, I was at a bit of a creative crossroads. Monica Gallagher and I had just come off a hugely successful run writing/creating *Lethal Lit* for iHeart Media, a crime/YA podcast that garnered fantastic reviews and was routinely in the top ten downloads list for Apple podcasts. More importantly, we'd found in each other a breezy, fun, and engaging creative partnership. In short—when we jammed on something, the end result was unlike anything we'd do alone. It was often better, too. We'd had a blast on *Lit*, but we both came from comics and that's where our hearts were. I'd written a healthy stack of Archie adventures and Monica had done a number of great stories like *Assassin Roommate*. It made sense to collaborate.

In addition to Archie, I grew up a fan of street-level heroes, specifically those told with an edgier twist, like Annie Nocenti and John Romita Jr.'s *Daredevil*, Denny O'Neil and Denys Cowan's *The Question*, or Matt Wagner, Steve Seagle, and Guy Davis's *Sandman Mystery Theater*, to name a few. My shorthand was "proto-Vertigo"—books that retained some of the absurdity of superheroics but also pushed elements forward in an adult, realistic way without being overly gritty. I'd had the idea for a female vigilante hero bouncing around in my head for years, but I could never drill down and take it from rough concept to realized pitch—there was always something else going on. But as Monica and I tried to figure out what was next for our partnership, it came up—"I have this idea for a female vigilante—kind of like an alcoholic private eye that dresses up like a superhero and has an Edward Snowden-type sidekick." Monica's response, if I'm recalling correctly, was an enthusiastic "Um, yes!"

That's the thing about Monica—she's always bursting with enthusiasm and energy, and she brings so much to the project that I find myself really challenged in summing it up. She has a fantastic, real ear for dialogue and, like me, walks the tightrope between embracing and inventing clichés. Bouncing that initial kernel of an idea back and forth led to something much fuller, and much more interesting, than what was originally there. The end result was Lara Dominguez, a conflicted, smart, defiant, funny, and problematic heroine you loved to root for—a character that felt new but also evoked elements from our favorite kind of private eye and superhero stories. Addiction, legacy, antiestablishment. Most importantly Lara was fun to write, and she surprised us with what she did, which is always the sign of a great idea.

But that's all we had at that point. A fleshed-out story and idea. We needed a team to help bring *The Black Ghost* to life. Luckily, we ended up with a dream team.

George Kambadais, our artist, was actually the final piece of the puzzle, and I think, in many ways, the glue that kept the whole team moving. After we'd found a home with ComiXology Originals, we started racing toward our first, looming, deadline. The artist that we had needed to jump off, and when something like that happens so late in the game, you have to reasonably wonder if the entire project is going under. But my pal Michael Moreci, a fantastic comic book writer in his own right, suggested George. We reached out and were immediately blown away by his enthusiasm. In less than a day, we were getting character designs and excited, positive emails. Not only did George like the idea, he wanted it—and it showed. He brought a dynamic art style that was a bit of *Batman: The Animated Series* and modern Dustin Nguyen. It was an approach that, if we're being honest, we hadn't considered, thinking our book needed a gritty, too-realistic approach. I'm glad we were wrong, and I'm glad George arrived when he did. In many ways, he saved the project and gave it new, exciting life. One of the benefits of working with George has been seeing him evolve and develop as an artist, and the pure passion he brings to every detail. Monica and I crafted the ideas and story, but they wouldn't be alive if not for George.

The rest of the team was of the same caliber. Ellie Wright, a rising star colorist, came in and seamlessly took on our rudimentary color notes ("CAN YOU MAKE IT LOOK LIKE THIS BUT NOT!") and translated them into something stylish, neo-noir, and a perfect complement to George's fluid style. I can't imagine one of them without the other. Letterer and designer Taylor Esposito was, in many ways, the book's MVP—giving the series a cohesiveness that provided the book with a professional and indelible sheen I still marvel over. He's a pro's pro, too. Last, but certainly not least, the book's fearless leader, Greg Lockard just made the whole thing sing—he challenged us, pushed us, and understood us. His knack for story and his positive spirit brought us all together and helped elevate *The Black Ghost* from just another vigilante book to something truly special.

I hope you enjoy your trip through the dark, crime-infested streets of our fictional city, Creighton. I hope you come to love Lara, Ernesto, Maggie, and the idea of the Black Ghost as much as we do. Meet us at Milano's after and we'll raise a glass to what's come to pass and what's next.

Alex Segura, cocreator/cowriter

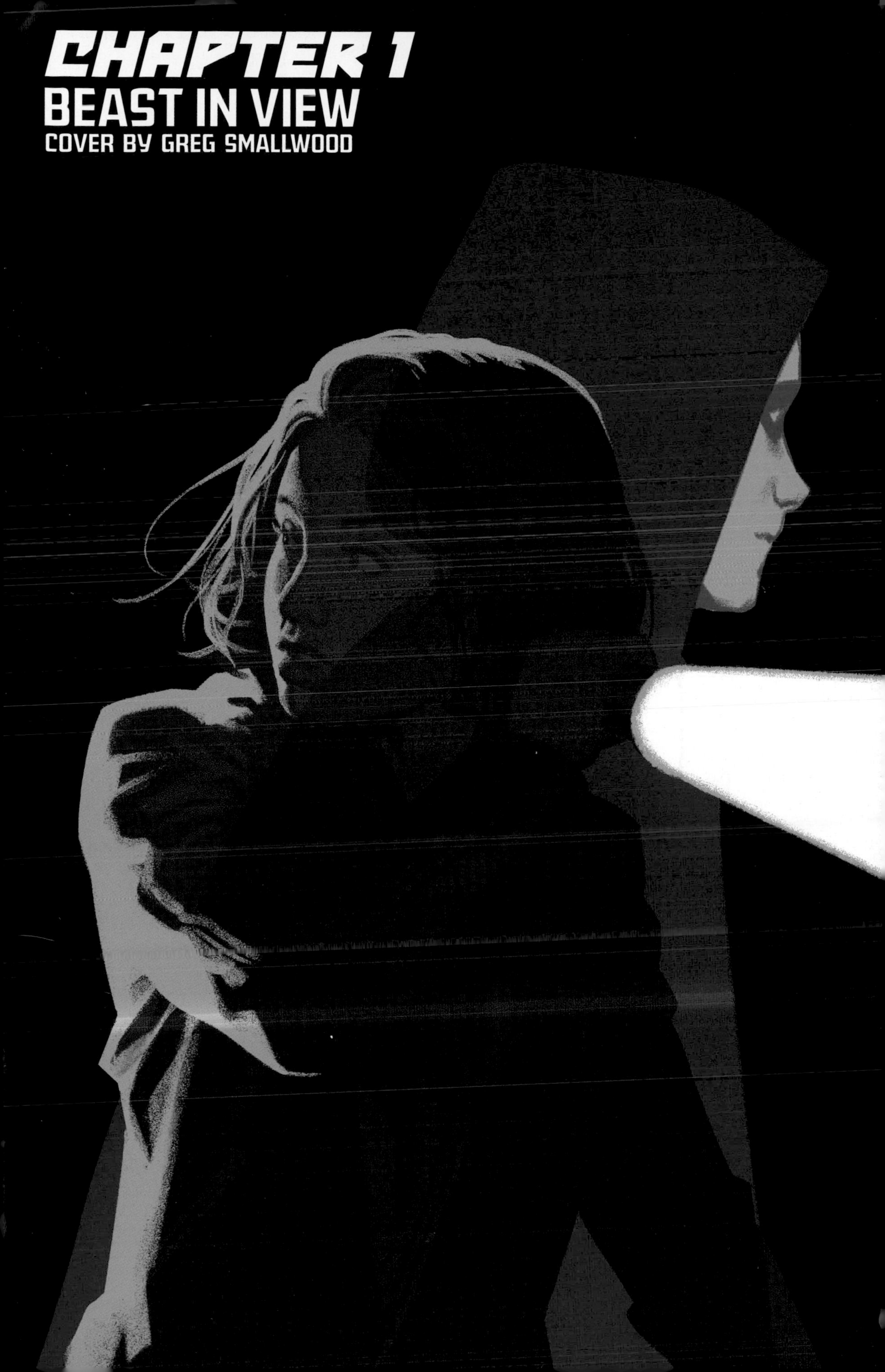
CHAPTER 1
BEAST IN VIEW
COVER BY GREG SMALLWOOD

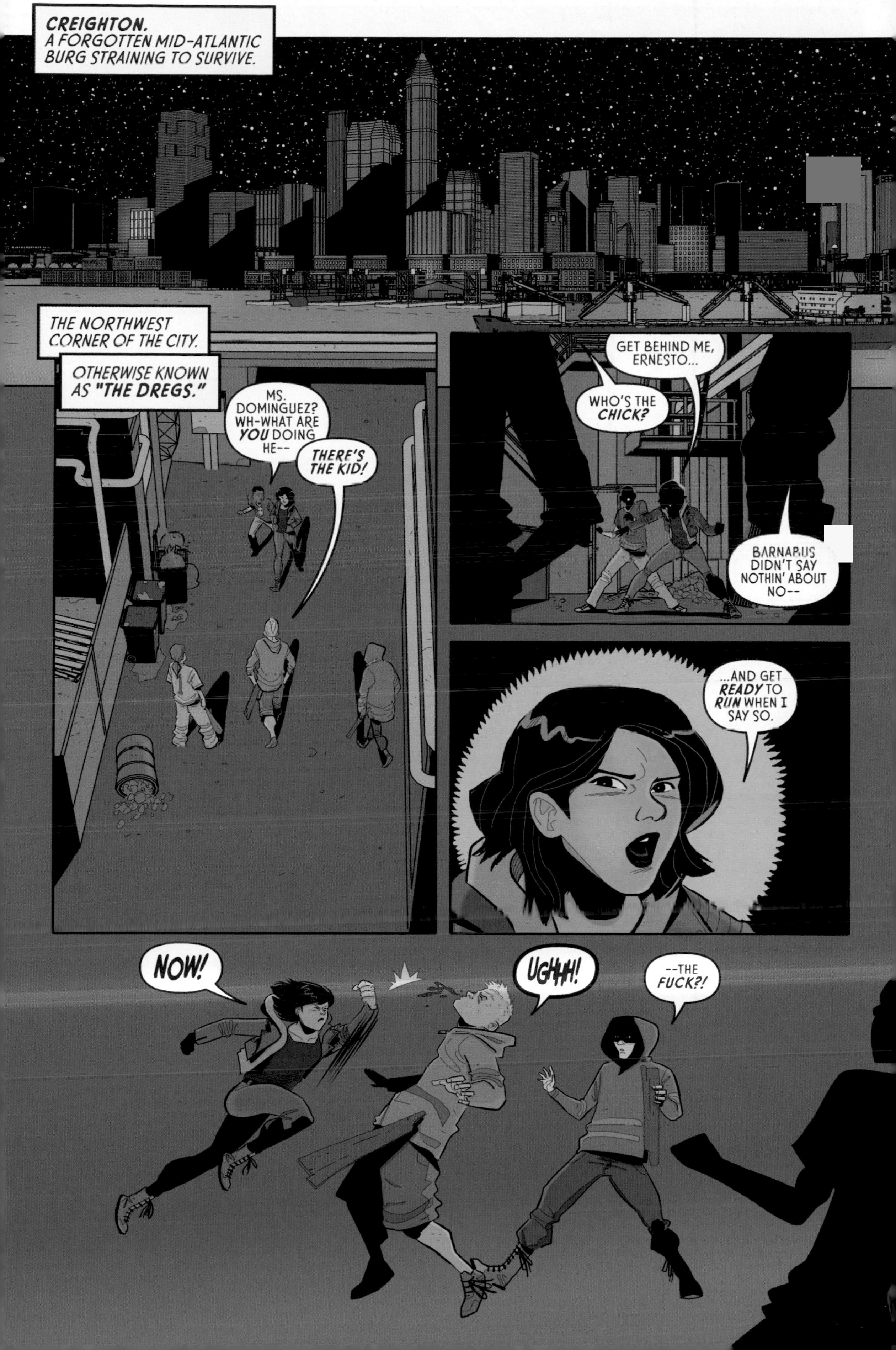
CREIGHTON.
A FORGOTTEN MID-ATLANTIC BURG STRAINING TO SURVIVE.
THE NORTHWEST CORNER OF THE CITY.
OTHERWISE KNOWN AS "THE DREGS."
MS. DOMINGUEZ? WH-WHAT ARE YOU DOING HE--
THERE'S THE KID!
GET BEHIND ME, ERNESTO...
WHO'S THE CHICK?
BARNABUS DIDN'T SAY NOTHIN' ABOUT NO--
...AND GET READY TO RUN WHEN I SAY SO.
NOW!
UGHHH!
--THE FUCK?!

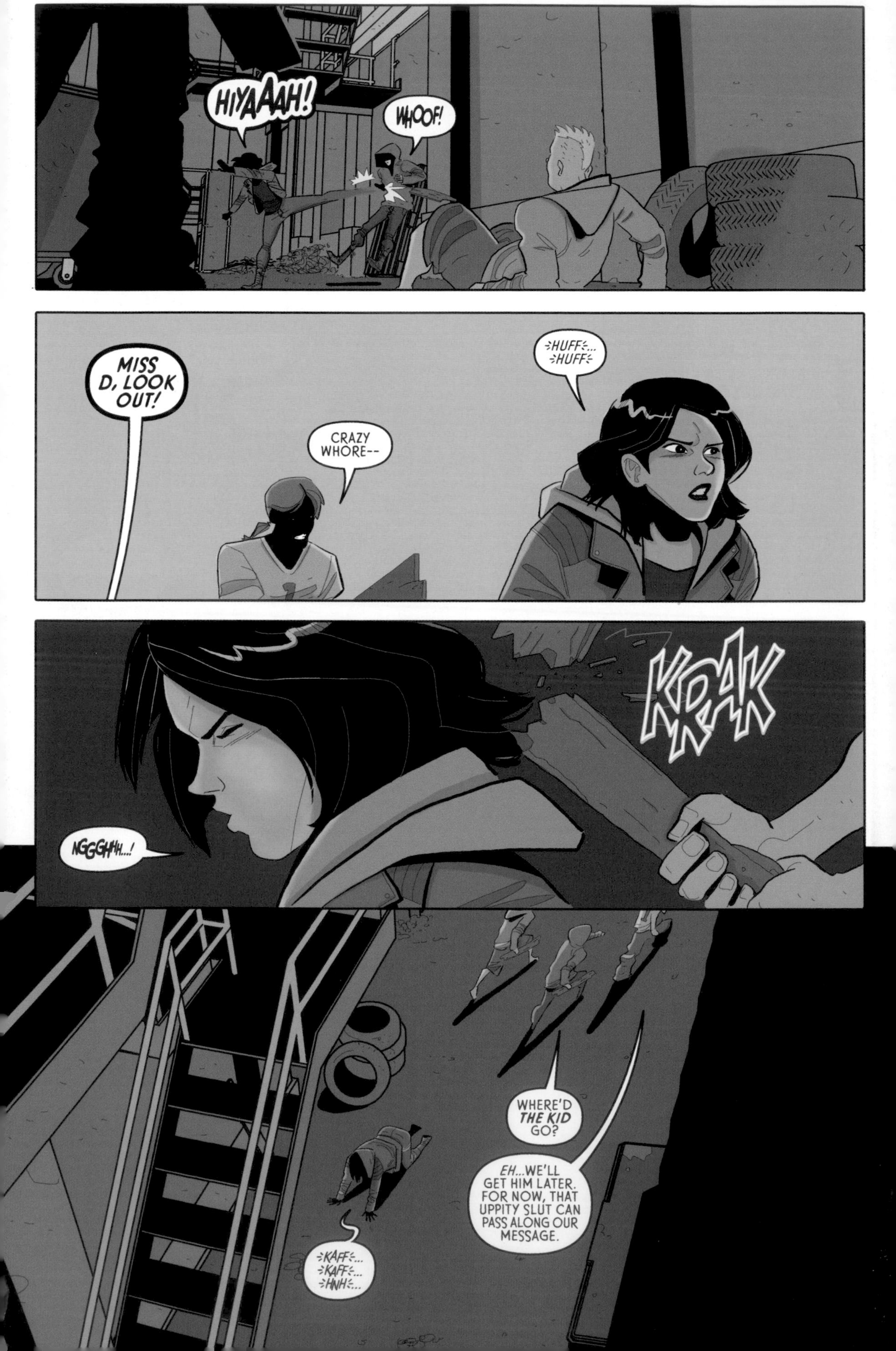
HIYAAAH!
WHOOF!
MISS D, LOOK OUT!
CRAZY WHORE--
HUFF... HUFF
KRAK
NGGGHHH...!
WHERE'D THE KID GO?
EH...WE'LL GET HIM LATER. FOR NOW, THAT UPPITY SLUT CAN PASS ALONG OUR MESSAGE.
KAFF... KAFF... HNH...

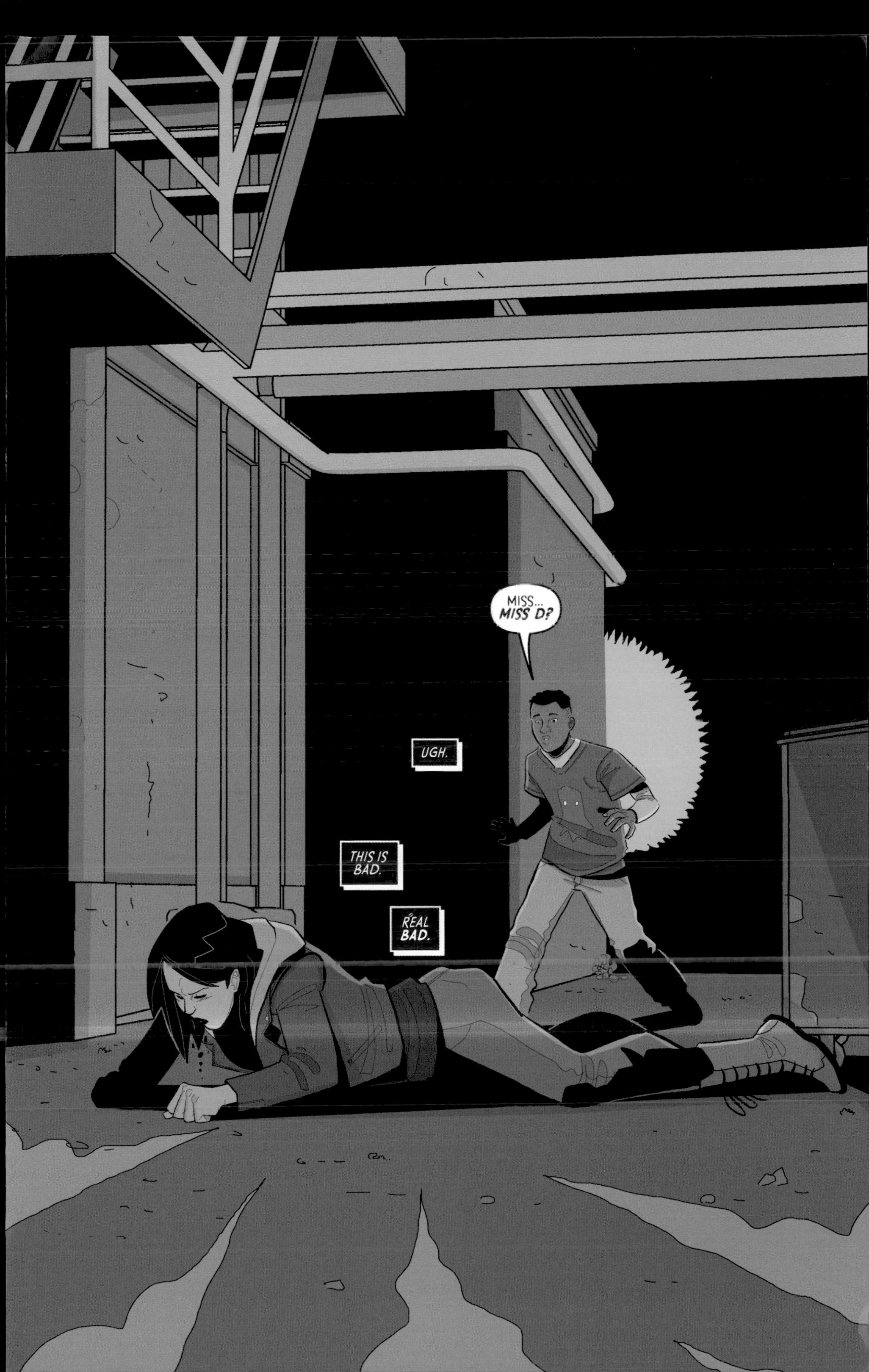
MISS...
MISS D?
UGH.
THIS IS BAD.
REAL BAD.

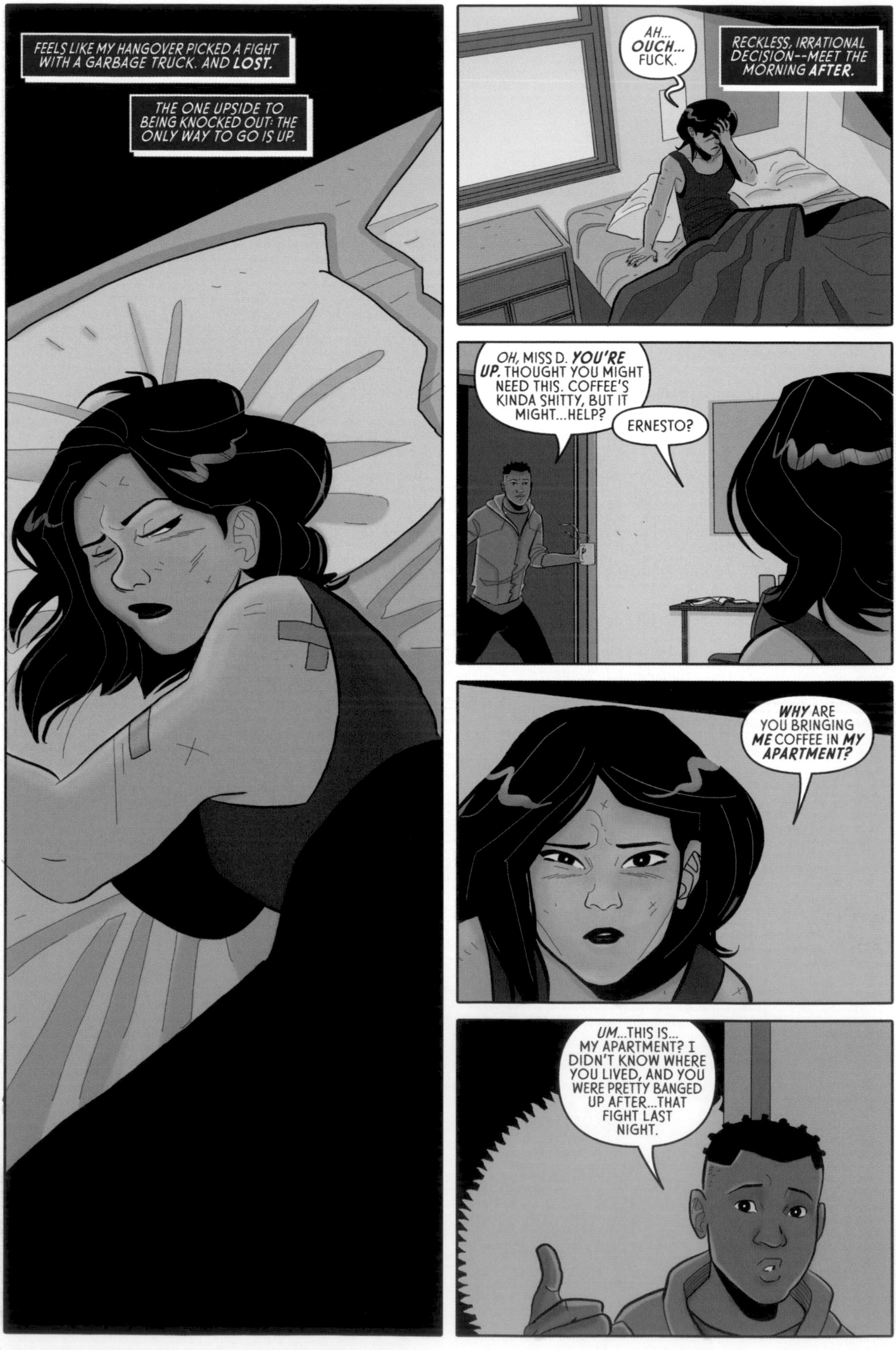
FEELS LIKE MY HANGOVER PICKED A FIGHT WITH A GARBAGE TRUCK. AND LOST.
THE ONE UPSIDE TO BEING KNOCKED OUT: THE ONLY WAY TO GO IS UP.
RECKLESS, IRRATIONAL DECISION--MEET THE MORNING AFTER.
AH... OUCH... FUCK.
OH, MISS D. YOU'RE UP. THOUGHT YOU MIGHT NEED THIS. COFFEE'S KINDA SHITTY, BUT IT MIGHT...HELP?
ERNESTO?
WHY ARE YOU BRINGING ME COFFEE IN MY APARTMENT?
UM...THIS IS... MY APARTMENT? I DIDN'T KNOW WHERE YOU LIVED, AND YOU WERE PRETTY BANGED UP AFTER...THAT FIGHT LAST NIGHT.

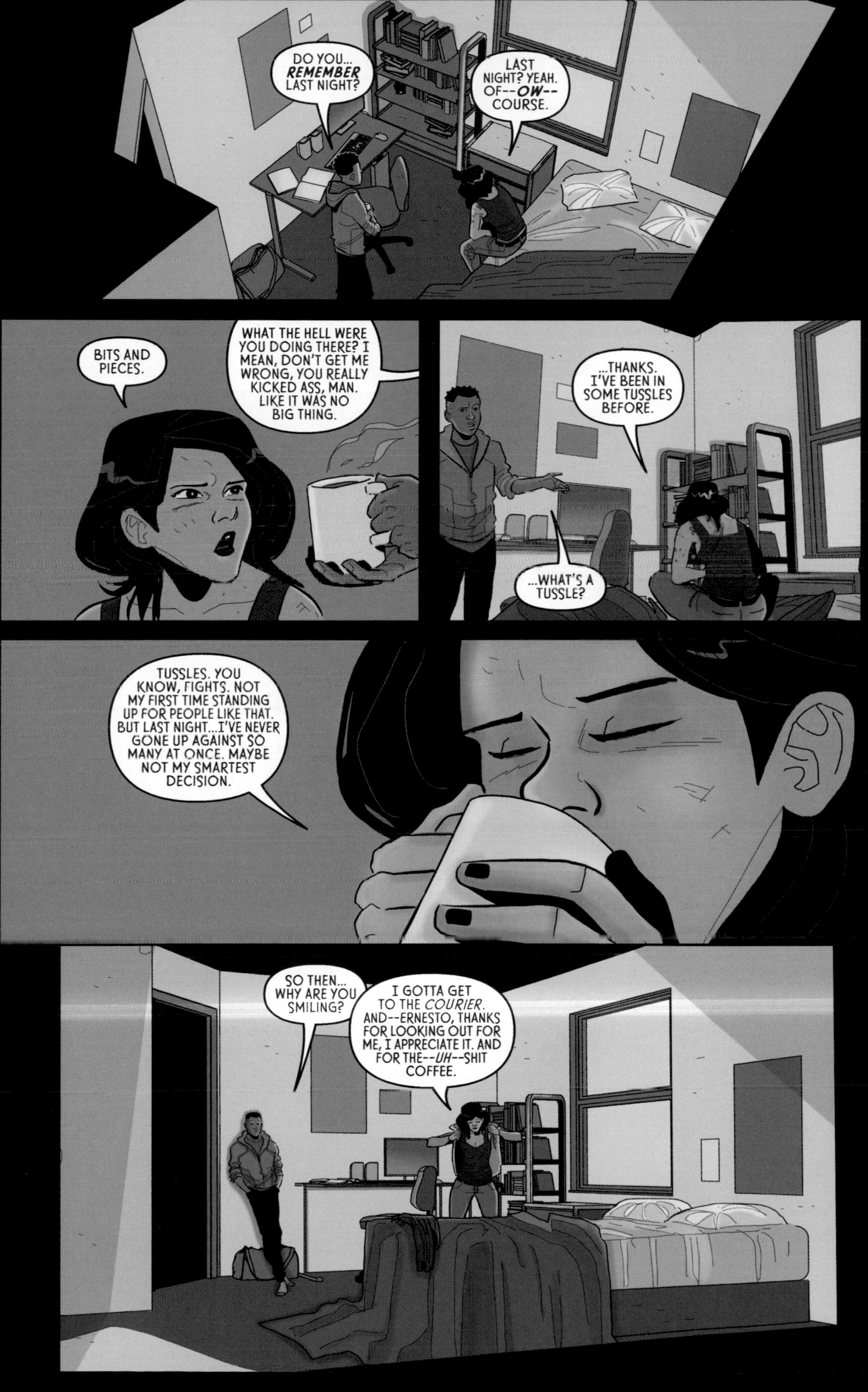
DO YOU... ***REMEMBER*** LAST NIGHT?
LAST NIGHT? YEAH. OF--***OW***--COURSE.
BITS AND PIECES.
WHAT THE HELL WERE YOU DOING THERE? I MEAN, DON'T GET ME WRONG, YOU REALLY KICKED ASS, MAN. LIKE IT WAS NO BIG THING.
...THANKS. I'VE BEEN IN SOME TUSSLES BEFORE.
...WHAT'S A TUSSLE?
TUSSLES. YOU KNOW, FIGHTS. NOT MY FIRST TIME STANDING UP FOR PEOPLE LIKE THAT. BUT LAST NIGHT...I'VE NEVER GONE UP AGAINST SO MANY AT ONCE. MAYBE NOT MY SMARTEST DECISION.
SO THEN... WHY ARE YOU SMILING?
I GOTTA GET TO THE *COURIER*. AND--ERNESTO, THANKS FOR LOOKING OUT FOR ME, I APPRECIATE IT. AND FOR THE--*UH*--SHIT COFFEE.

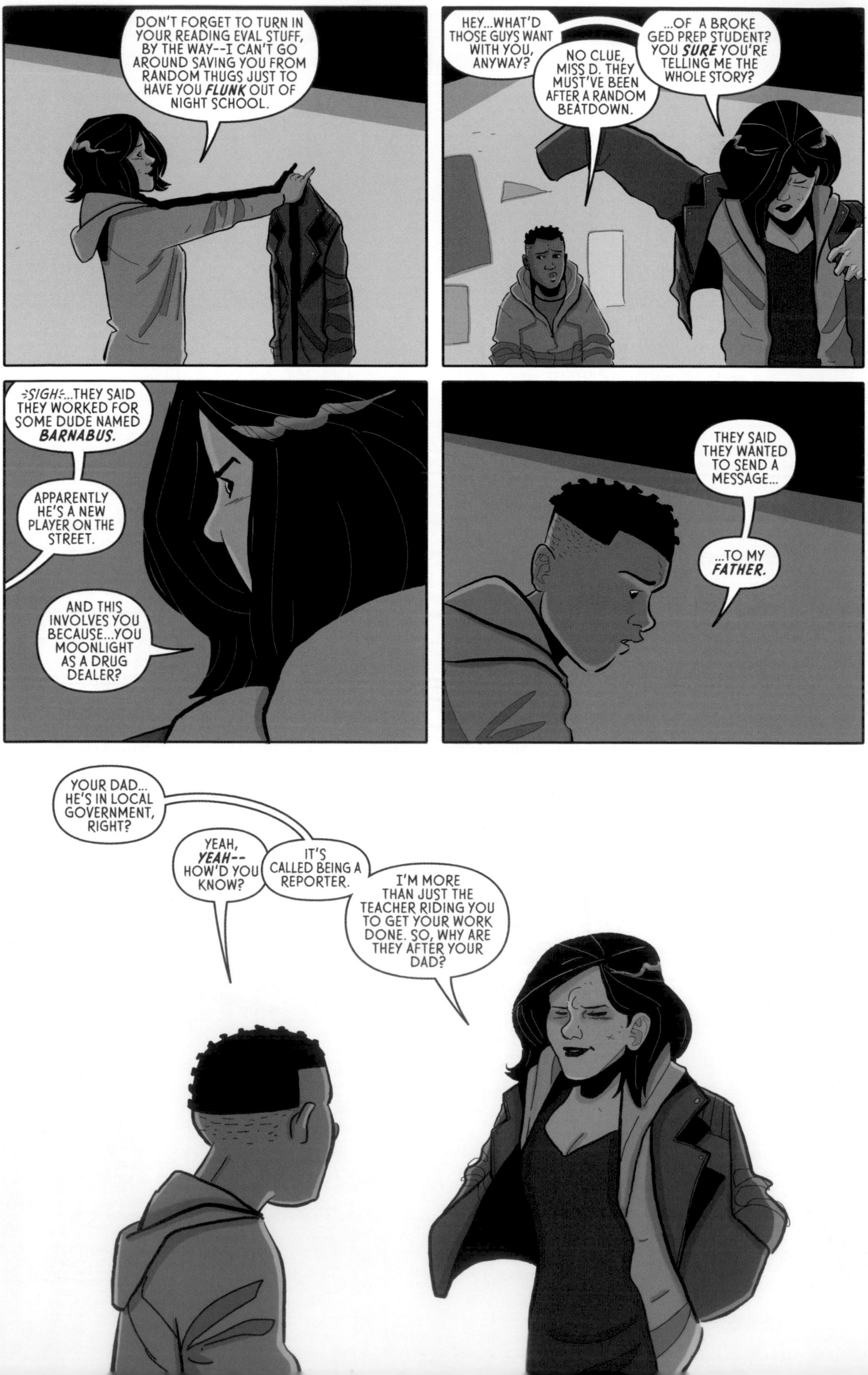
DON'T FORGET TO TURN IN YOUR READING EVAL STUFF, BY THE WAY--I CAN'T GO AROUND SAVING YOU FROM RANDOM THUGS JUST TO HAVE YOU **FLUNK** OUT OF NIGHT SCHOOL.
HEY...WHAT'D THOSE GUYS WANT WITH YOU, ANYWAY?
NO CLUE, MISS D. THEY MUST'VE BEEN AFTER A RANDOM BEATDOWN.
...OF A BROKE GED PREP STUDENT? YOU **SURE** YOU'RE TELLING ME THE WHOLE STORY?
*SIGH*...THEY SAID THEY WORKED FOR SOME DUDE NAMED **BARNABUS.**
APPARENTLY HE'S A NEW PLAYER ON THE STREET.
AND THIS INVOLVES YOU BECAUSE...YOU MOONLIGHT AS A DRUG DEALER?
THEY SAID THEY WANTED TO SEND A MESSAGE...
...TO MY **FATHER.**
YOUR DAD... HE'S IN LOCAL GOVERNMENT, RIGHT?
YEAH, **YEAH--** HOW'D YOU KNOW?
IT'S CALLED BEING A REPORTER.
I'M MORE THAN JUST THE TEACHER RIDING YOU TO GET YOUR WORK DONE. SO, WHY ARE THEY AFTER YOUR DAD?

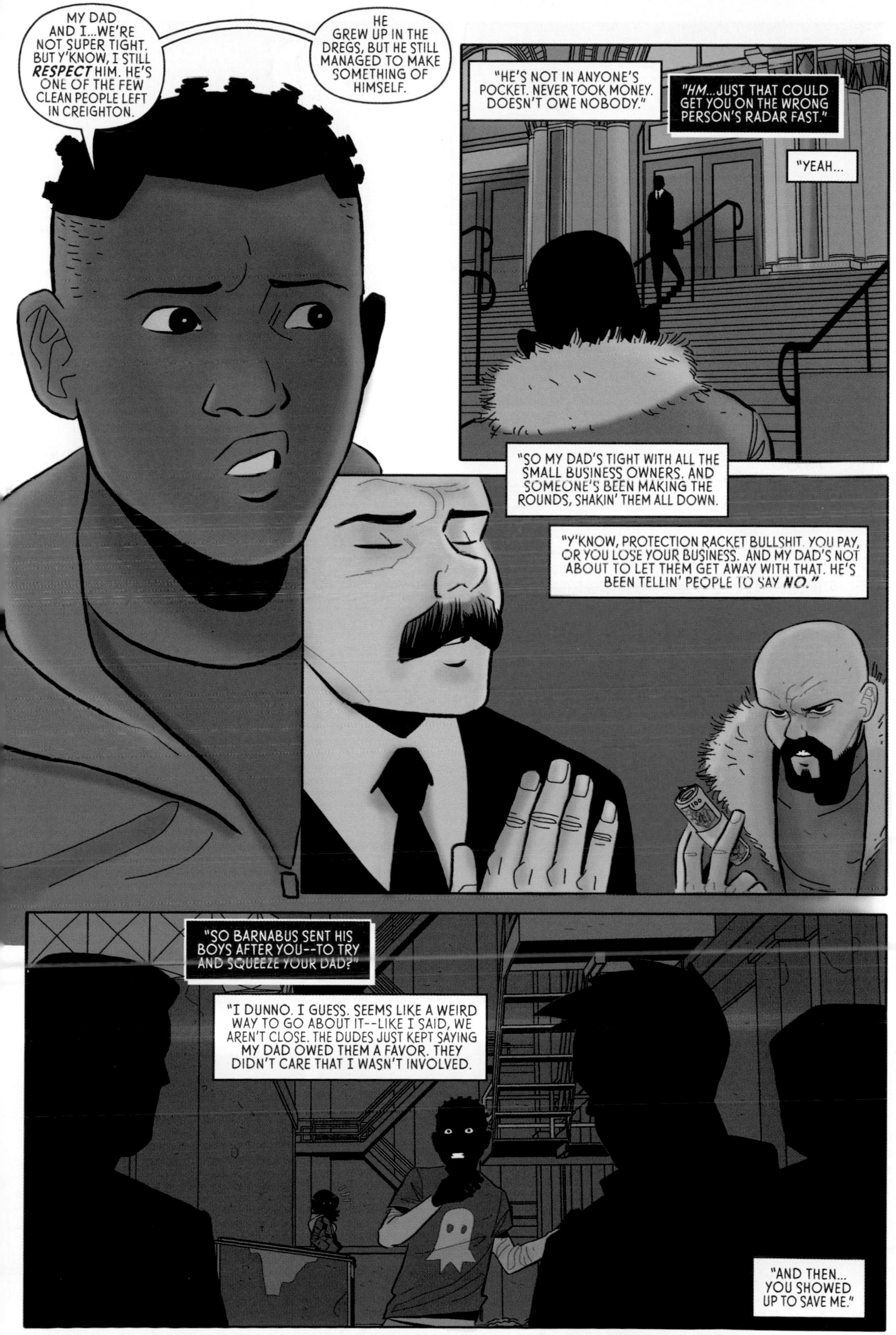

MY DAD AND I...WE'RE NOT SUPER TIGHT. BUT Y'KNOW, I STILL ***RESPECT*** HIM. HE'S ONE OF THE FEW CLEAN PEOPLE LEFT IN CREIGHTON.
HE GREW UP IN THE DREGS, BUT HE STILL MANAGED TO MAKE SOMETHING OF HIMSELF.
"HE'S NOT IN ANYONE'S POCKET. NEVER TOOK MONEY. DOESN'T OWE NOBODY."
"*HM*...JUST THAT COULD GET YOU ON THE WRONG PERSON'S RADAR FAST."
"YEAH...
"SO MY DAD'S TIGHT WITH ALL THE SMALL BUSINESS OWNERS. AND SOMEONE'S BEEN MAKING THE ROUNDS, SHAKIN' THEM ALL DOWN.
"Y'KNOW, PROTECTION RACKET BULLSHIT. YOU PAY, OR YOU LOSE YOUR BUSINESS. AND MY DAD'S NOT ABOUT TO LET THEM GET AWAY WITH THAT. HE'S BEEN TELLIN' PEOPLE TO SAY ***NO.***"
"SO BARNABUS SENT HIS BOYS AFTER YOU--TO TRY AND SQUEEZE YOUR DAD?"
"I DUNNO. I GUESS. SEEMS LIKE A WEIRD WAY TO GO ABOUT IT--LIKE I SAID, WE AREN'T CLOSE. THE DUDES JUST KEPT SAYING MY DAD OWED THEM A FAVOR. THEY DIDN'T CARE THAT I WASN'T INVOLVED.
"AND THEN... YOU SHOWED UP TO SAVE ME."

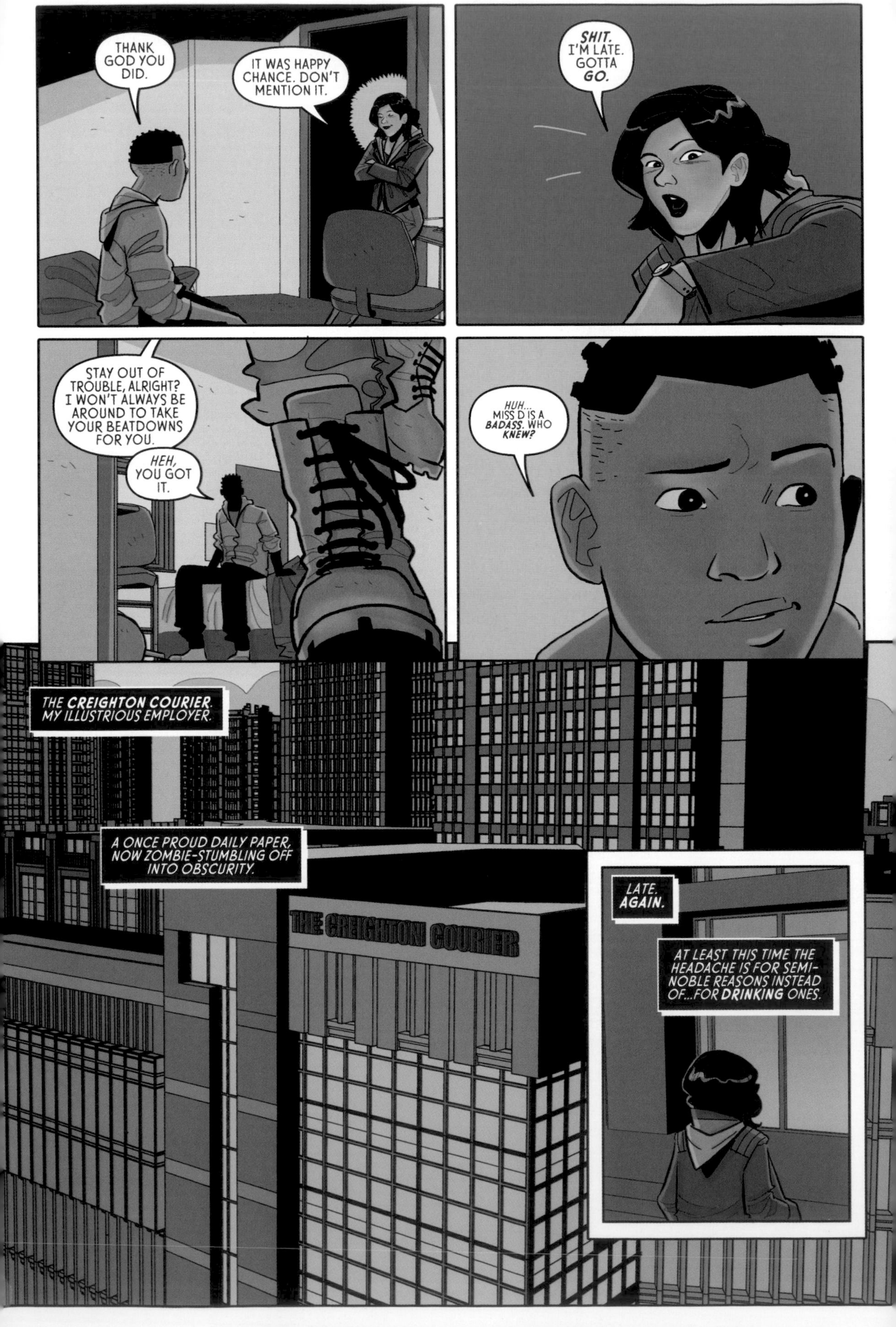
THANK GOD YOU DID.
IT WAS HAPPY CHANCE. DON'T MENTION IT.
***SHIT.*** I'M LATE. GOTTA ***GO.***
STAY OUT OF TROUBLE, ALRIGHT? I WON'T ALWAYS BE AROUND TO TAKE YOUR BEATDOWNS FOR YOU.
*HEH,* YOU GOT IT.
HUH... MISS D IS A ***BADASS.*** WHO ***KNEW?***
*THE* ***CREIGHTON COURIER.*** *MY ILLUSTRIOUS EMPLOYER.*
*A ONCE PROUD DAILY PAPER, NOW ZOMBIE-STUMBLING OFF INTO OBSCURITY.*
THE CREIGHTON COURIER
*LATE.* ***AGAIN.***
AT LEAST THIS TIME THE HEADACHE IS FOR SEMI-NOBLE REASONS INSTEAD OF...FOR **DRINKING** ONES.

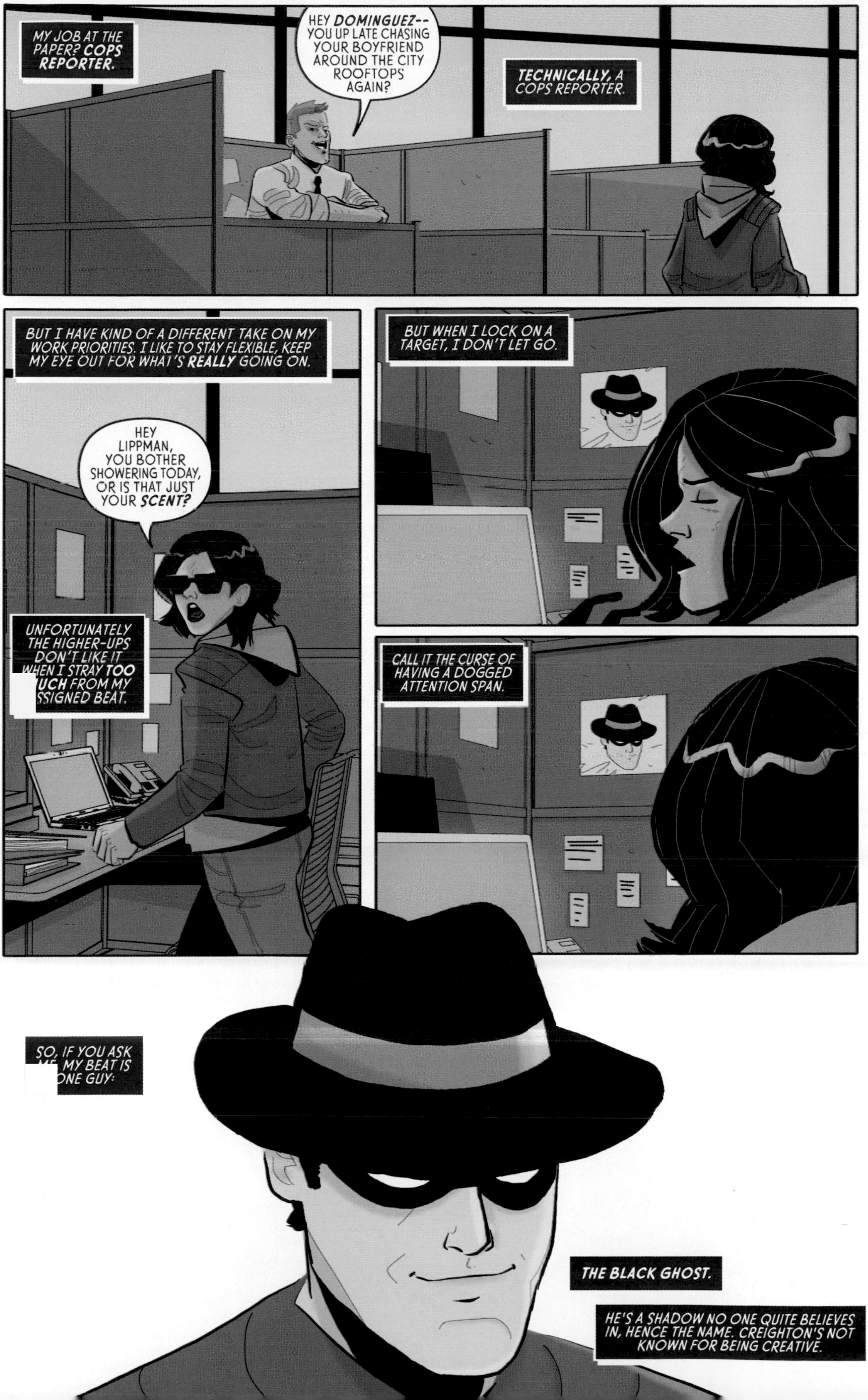
MY JOB AT THE PAPER? **COPS REPORTER.**
HEY **DOMINGUEZ**-- YOU UP LATE CHASING YOUR BOYFRIEND AROUND THE CITY ROOFTOPS AGAIN?
**TECHNICALLY,** A COPS REPORTER.
BUT I HAVE KIND OF A DIFFERENT TAKE ON MY WORK PRIORITIES. I LIKE TO STAY FLEXIBLE, KEEP MY EYE OUT FOR WHAT'S **REALLY** GOING ON.
HEY LIPPMAN, YOU BOTHER SHOWERING TODAY, OR IS THAT JUST YOUR **SCENT?**
UNFORTUNATELY THE HIGHER-UPS DON'T LIKE IT WHEN I STRAY **TOO** UCH FROM MY SSIGNED BEAT.
BUT WHEN I LOCK ON A TARGET, I DON'T LET GO.
CALL IT THE CURSE OF HAVING A DOGGED ATTENTION SPAN.
SO, IF YOU ASK MY BEAT IS ONE GUY:
**THE BLACK GHOST.**
HE'S A SHADOW NO ONE QUITE BELIEVES IN, HENCE THE NAME. CREIGHTON'S NOT KNOWN FOR BEING CREATIVE.

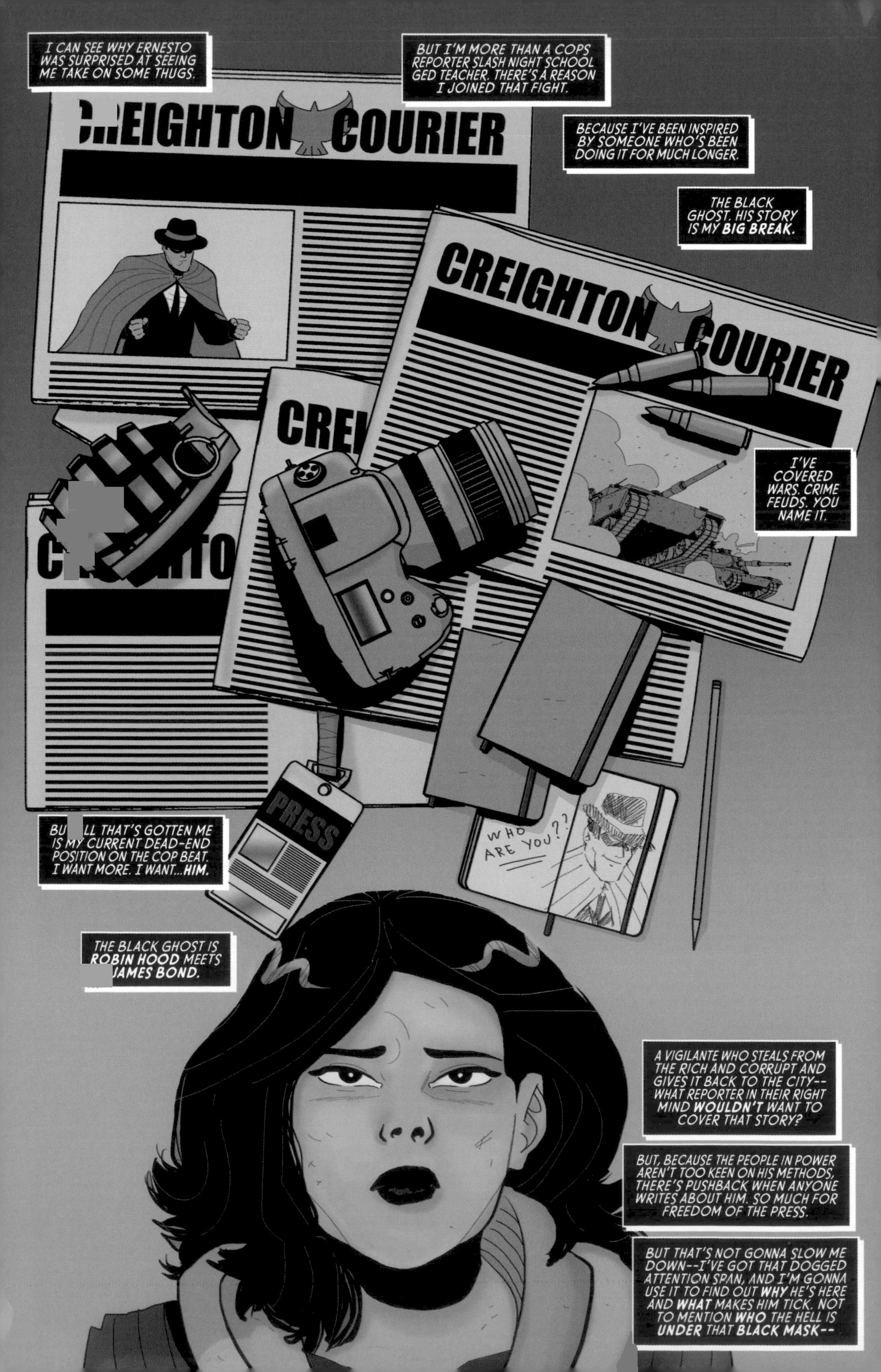
I CAN SEE WHY ERNESTO WAS SURPRISED AT SEEING ME TAKE ON SOME THUGS.
BUT I'M MORE THAN A COPS REPORTER SLASH NIGHT SCHOOL GED TEACHER. THERE'S A REASON I JOINED THAT FIGHT.
BECAUSE I'VE BEEN INSPIRED BY SOMEONE WHO'S BEEN DOING IT FOR MUCH LONGER.
THE BLACK GHOST. HIS STORY IS MY **BIG BREAK.**
CREIGHTON COURIER
I'VE COVERED WARS. CRIME FEUDS. YOU NAME IT.
BU LL THAT'S GOTTEN ME IS MY CURRENT DEAD-END POSITION ON THE COP BEAT. I WANT MORE. I WANT...**HIM.**
PRESS
WHO ARE YOU??
THE BLACK GHOST IS **ROBIN HOOD** MEETS **JAMES BOND.**
A VIGILANTE WHO STEALS FROM THE RICH AND CORRUPT AND GIVES IT BACK TO THE CITY-- WHAT REPORTER IN THEIR RIGHT MIND **WOULDN'T** WANT TO COVER THAT STORY?
BUT, BECAUSE THE PEOPLE IN POWER AREN'T TOO KEEN ON HIS METHODS, THERE'S PUSHBACK WHEN ANYONE WRITES ABOUT HIM. SO MUCH FOR FREEDOM OF THE PRESS.
BUT THAT'S NOT GONNA SLOW ME DOWN--I'VE GOT THAT DOGGED ATTENTION SPAN, AND I'M GONNA USE IT TO FIND OUT **WHY** HE'S HERE AND **WHAT** MAKES HIM TICK. NOT TO MENTION **WHO** THE HELL IS **UNDER** THAT **BLACK MASK--**

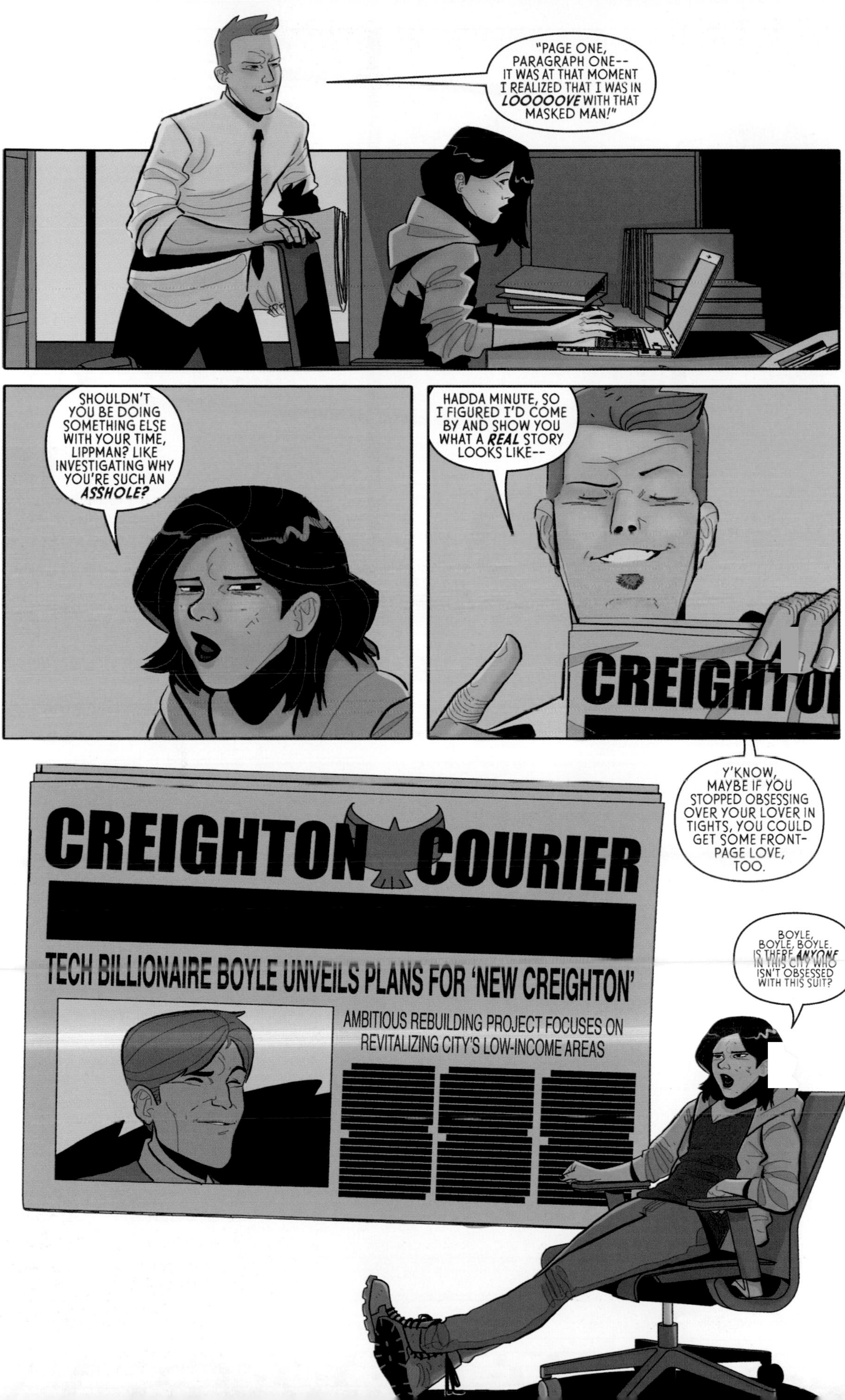
"PAGE ONE, PARAGRAPH ONE-- IT WAS AT THAT MOMENT I REALIZED THAT I WAS IN *LOOOOOVE* WITH THAT MASKED MAN!"
SHOULDN'T YOU BE DOING SOMETHING ELSE WITH YOUR TIME, LIPPMAN? LIKE INVESTIGATING WHY YOU'RE SUCH AN ***ASSHOLE?***
HADDA MINUTE, SO I FIGURED I'D COME BY AND SHOW YOU WHAT A ***REAL*** STORY LOOKS LIKE--
CREIGHTO
Y'KNOW, MAYBE IF YOU STOPPED OBSESSING OVER YOUR LOVER IN TIGHTS, YOU COULD GET SOME FRONT-PAGE LOVE, TOO.
CREIGHTON COURIER
TECH BILLIONAIRE BOYLE UNVEILS PLANS FOR 'NEW CREIGHTON'
AMBITIOUS REBUILDING PROJECT FOCUSES ON REVITALIZING CITY'S LOW-INCOME AREAS
BOYLE, BOYLE, BOYLE. IS THERE ***ANYONE*** IN THIS CITY WHO ISN'T OBSESSED WITH THIS SUIT?

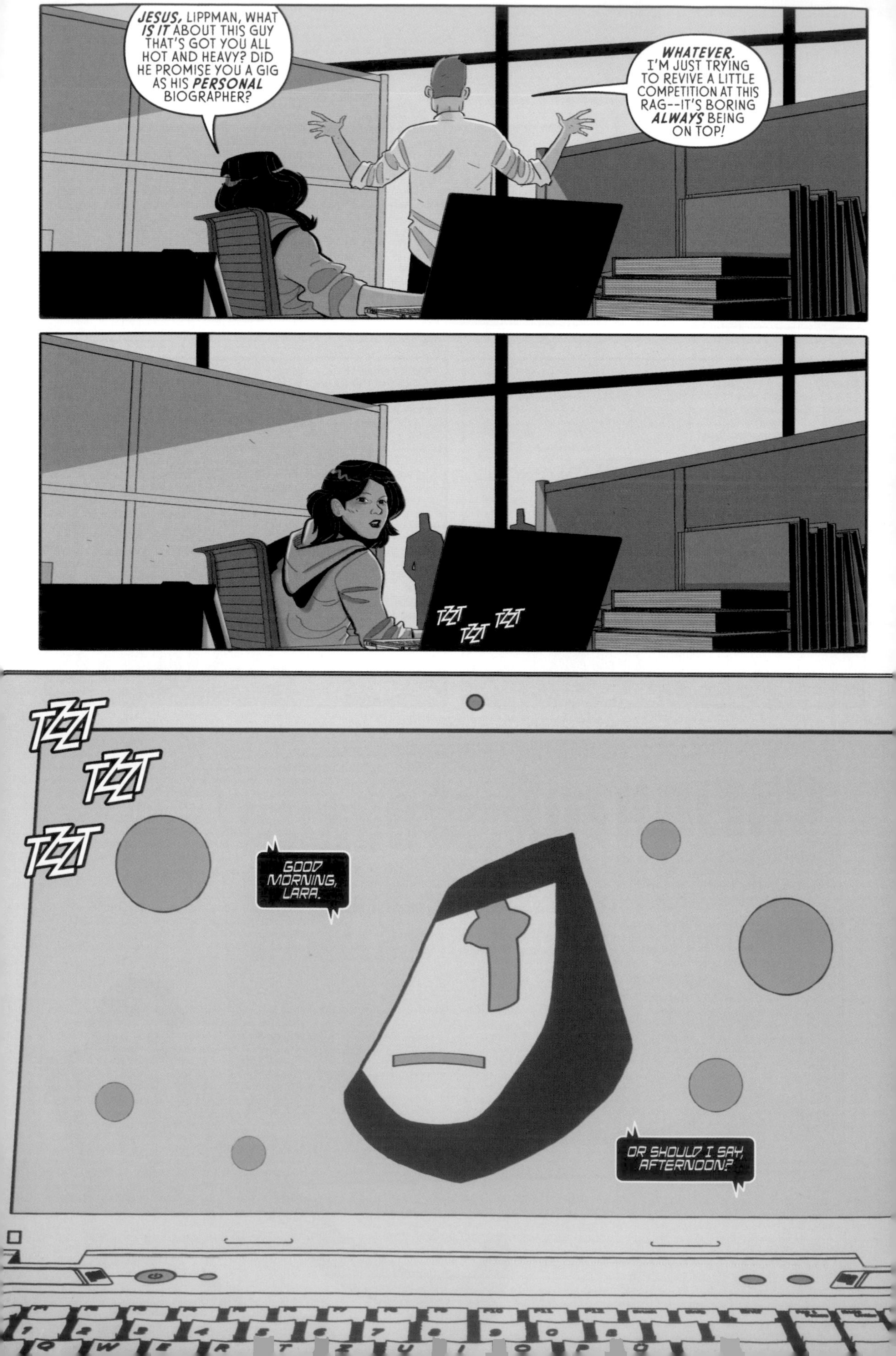

***JESUS,*** LIPPMAN, WHAT ***IS IT*** ABOUT THIS GUY THAT'S GOT YOU ALL HOT AND HEAVY? DID HE PROMISE YOU A GIG AS HIS ***PERSONAL*** BIOGRAPHER?
***WHATEVER.*** I'M JUST TRYING TO REVIVE A LITTLE COMPETITION AT THIS RAG--IT'S BORING ***ALWAYS*** BEING ON TOP!
TZZT TZZT TZZT
TZZT TZZT TZZT
GOOD MORNING, LARA.
OR SHOULD I SAY, AFTERNOON?

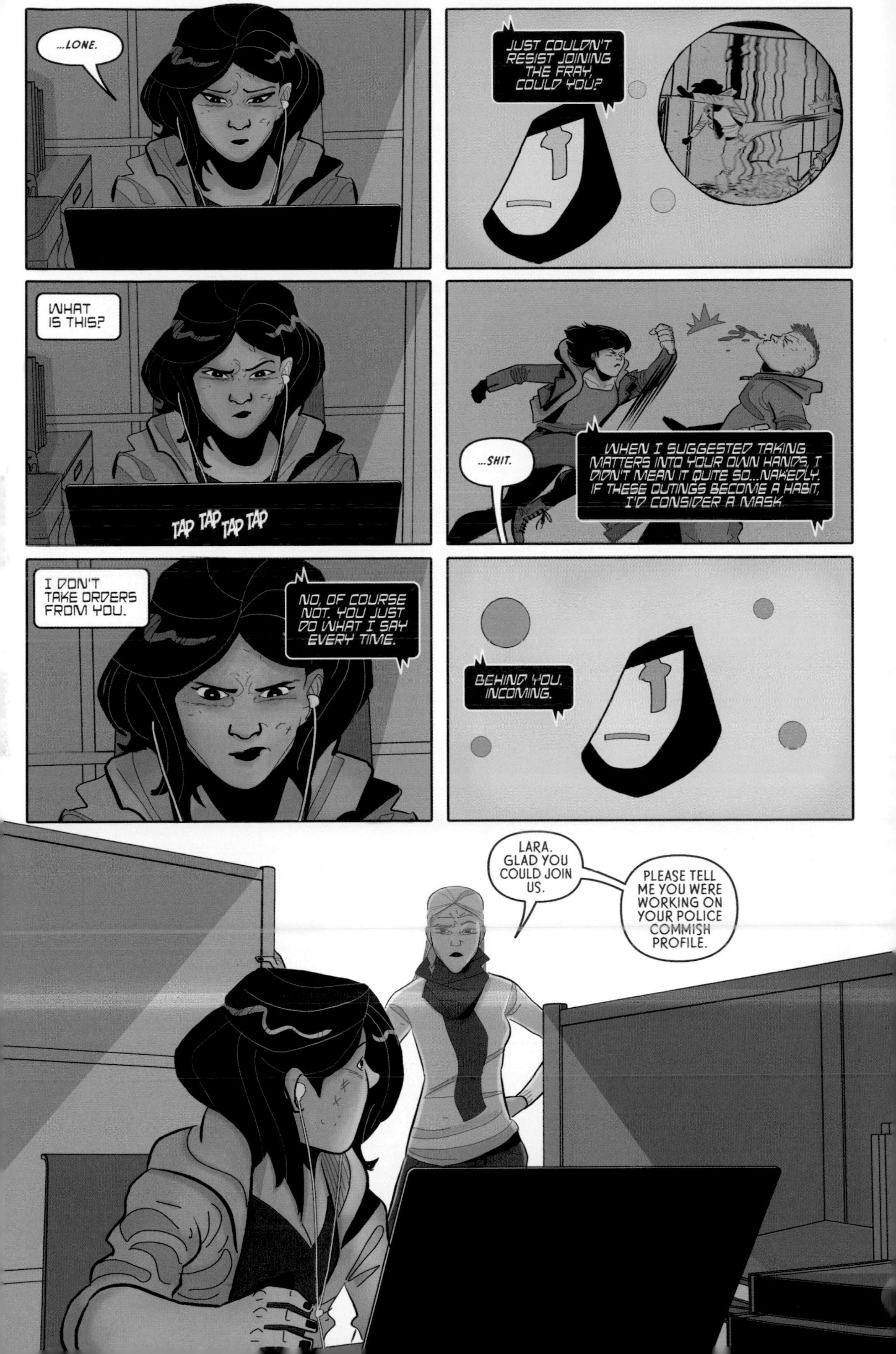
...LONE.
JUST COULDN'T RESIST JOINING THE FRAY, COULD YOU?
WHAT IS THIS?
TAP TAP TAP TAP
...SHIT.
WHEN I SUGGESTED TAKING MATTERS INTO YOUR OWN HANDS, I DIDN'T MEAN IT QUITE SO...NAKEDLY. IF THESE OUTINGS BECOME A HABIT, I'D CONSIDER A MASK.
I DON'T TAKE ORDERS FROM YOU.
NO, OF COURSE NOT. YOU JUST DO WHAT I SAY EVERY TIME.
BEHIND YOU. INCOMING.
LARA. GLAD YOU COULD JOIN US.
PLEASE TELL ME YOU WERE WORKING ON YOUR POLICE COMMISH PROFILE.

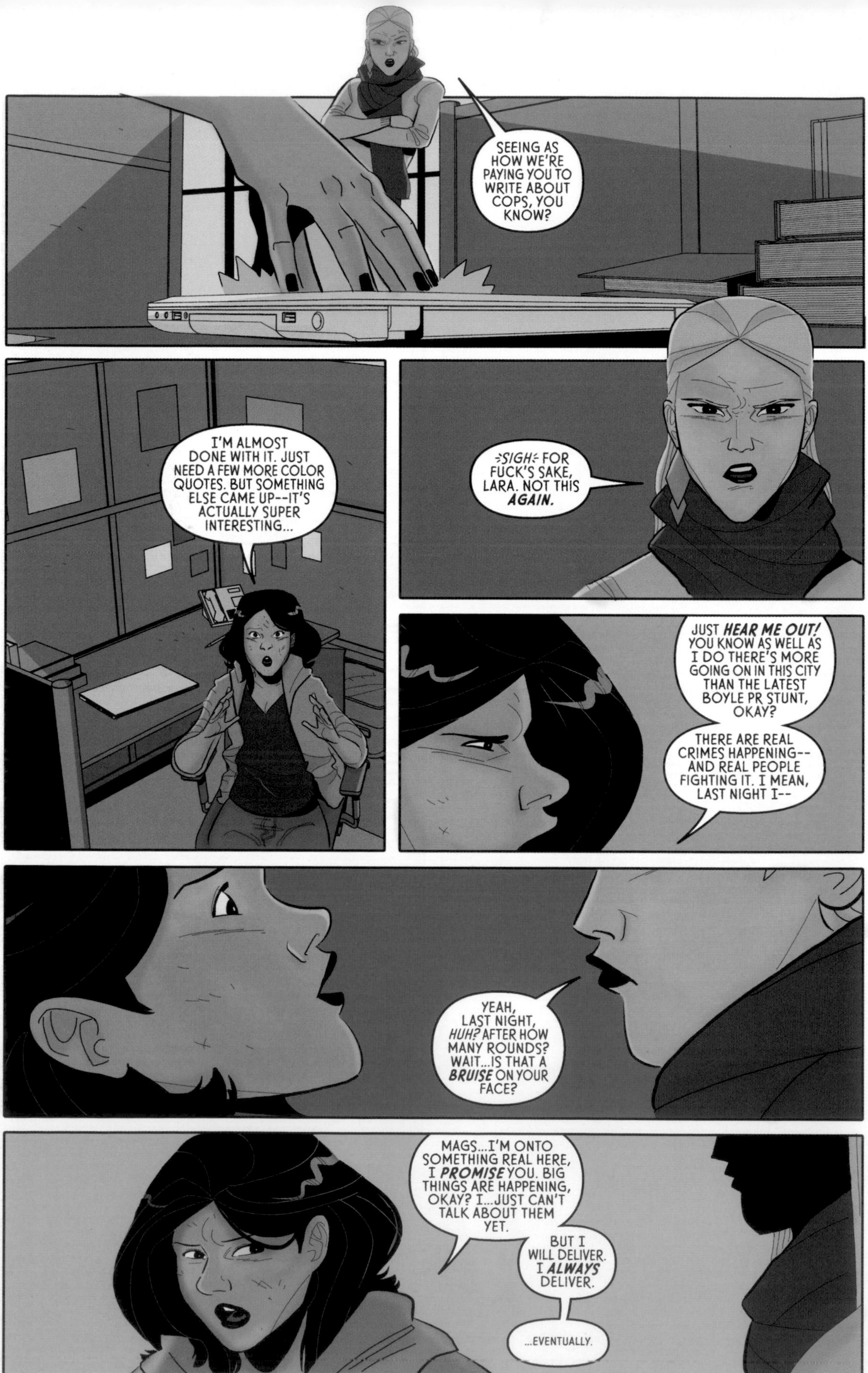
SEEING AS HOW WE'RE PAYING YOU TO WRITE ABOUT COPS, YOU KNOW?
*SIGH* FOR FUCK'S SAKE, LARA. NOT THIS ***AGAIN.***
I'M ALMOST DONE WITH IT. JUST NEED A FEW MORE COLOR QUOTES. BUT SOMETHING ELSE CAME UP--IT'S ACTUALLY SUPER INTERESTING...
JUST ***HEAR ME OUT!*** YOU KNOW AS WELL AS I DO THERE'S MORE GOING ON IN THIS CITY THAN THE LATEST BOYLE PR STUNT, OKAY?
THERE ARE REAL CRIMES HAPPENING--AND REAL PEOPLE FIGHTING IT. I MEAN, LAST NIGHT I--
YEAH, LAST NIGHT, *HUH?* AFTER HOW MANY ROUNDS? WAIT...IS THAT A ***BRUISE*** ON YOUR FACE?
MAGS...I'M ONTO SOMETHING REAL HERE, I ***PROMISE*** YOU. BIG THINGS ARE HAPPENING, OKAY? I...JUST CAN'T TALK ABOUT THEM YET.
BUT I WILL DELIVER. I ***ALWAYS*** DELIVER.
...EVENTUALLY.

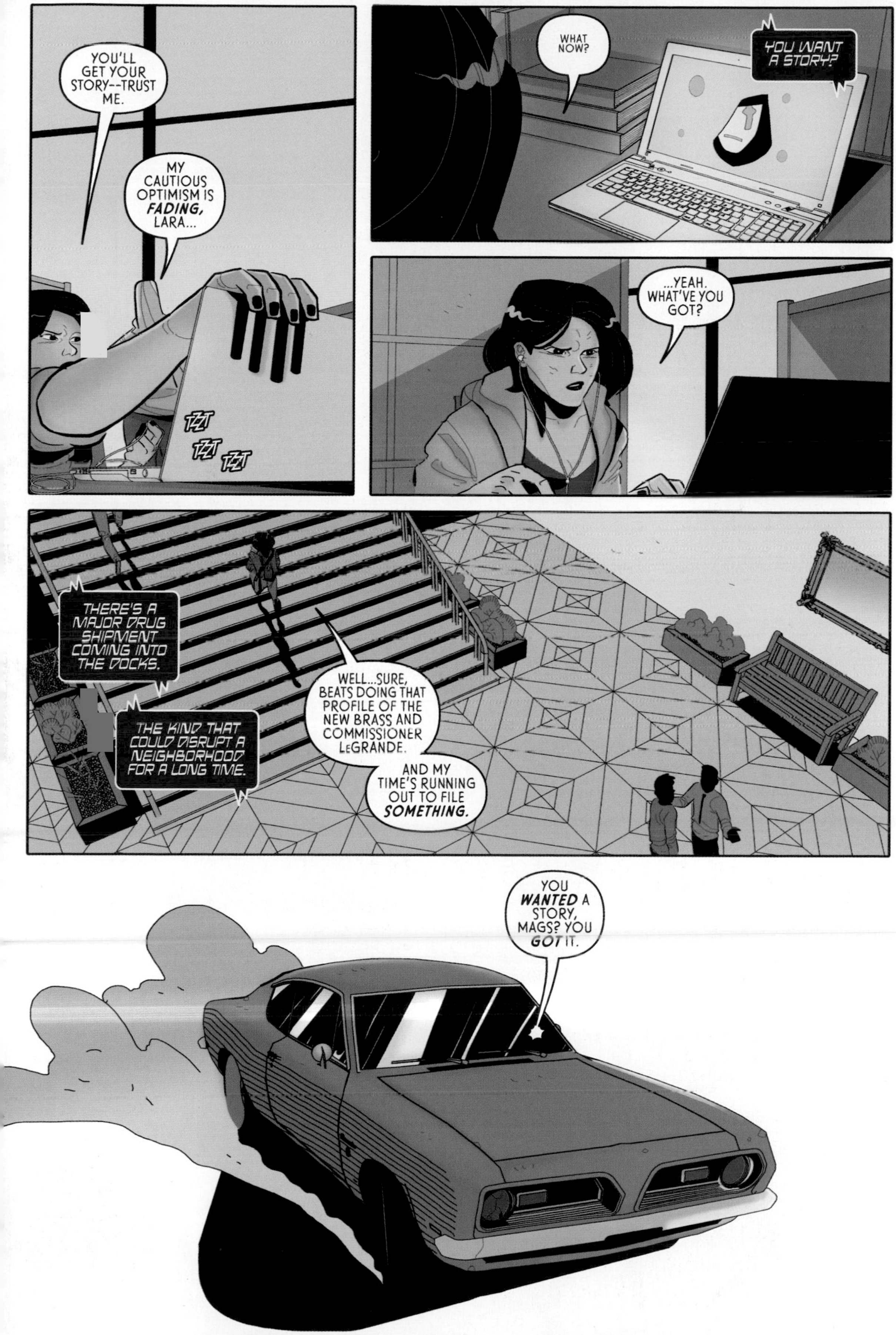
YOU'LL GET YOUR STORY--TRUST ME.
MY CAUTIOUS OPTIMISM IS *FADING,* LARA...
TZZT
TZZT
TZZT
WHAT NOW?
YOU WANT A STORY?
...YEAH. WHAT'VE YOU GOT?
THERE'S A MAJOR DRUG SHIPMENT COMING INTO THE DOCKS.
THE KIND THAT COULD DISRUPT A NEIGHBORHOOD FOR A LONG TIME.
WELL...SURE, BEATS DOING THAT PROFILE OF THE NEW BRASS AND COMMISSIONER LeGRANDE.
AND MY TIME'S RUNNING OUT TO FILE *SOMETHING.*
YOU *WANTED* A STORY, MAGS? YOU *GOT* IT.

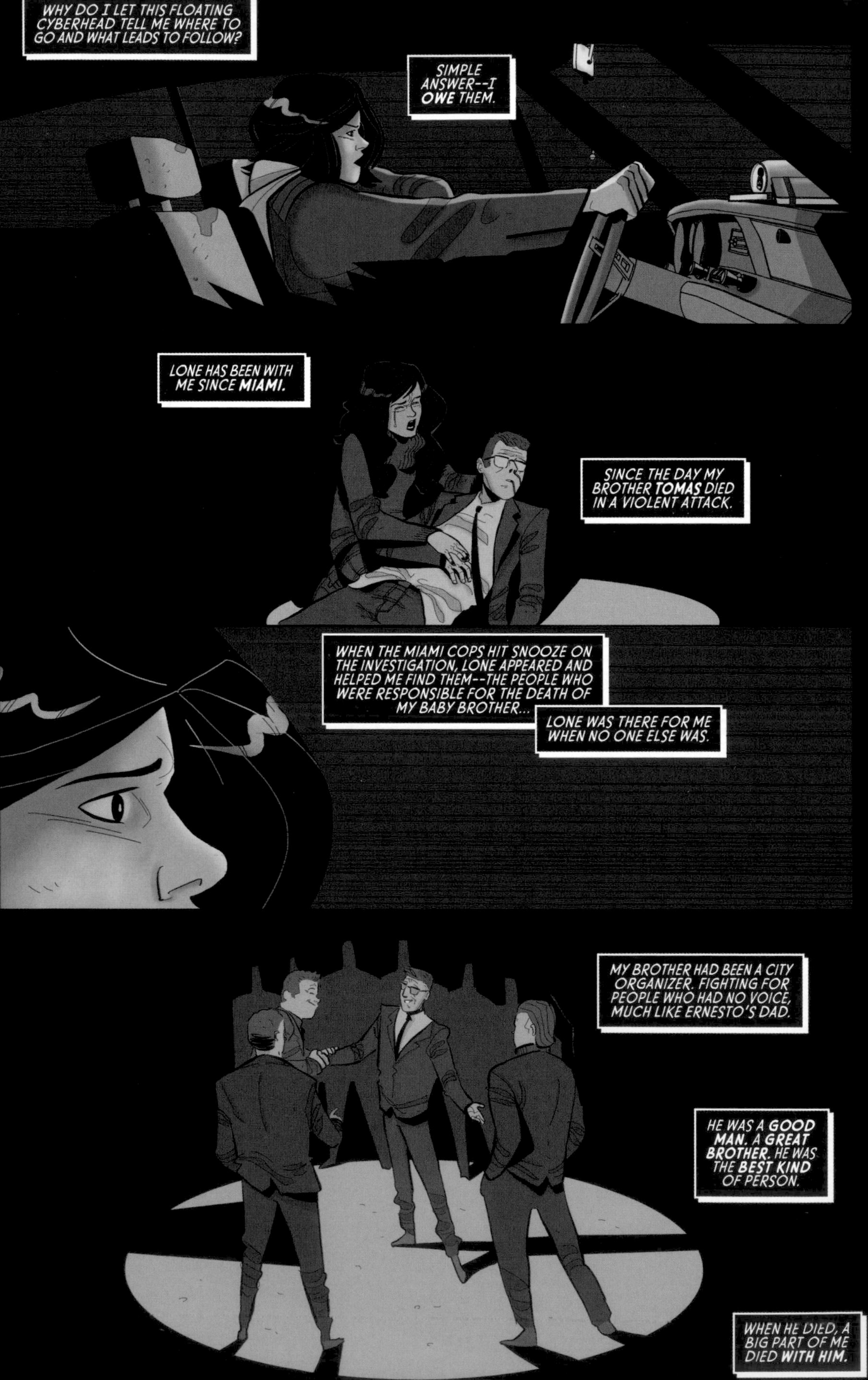
WHY DO I LET THIS FLOATING CYBERHEAD TELL ME WHERE TO GO AND WHAT LEADS TO FOLLOW?
SIMPLE ANSWER--I **OWE** THEM.
LONE HAS BEEN WITH ME SINCE **MIAMI.**
SINCE THE DAY MY BROTHER **TOMAS** DIED IN A VIOLENT ATTACK.
WHEN THE MIAMI COPS HIT SNOOZE ON THE INVESTIGATION, LONE APPEARED AND HELPED ME FIND THEM--THE PEOPLE WHO WERE RESPONSIBLE FOR THE DEATH OF MY BABY BROTHER...
LONE WAS THERE FOR ME WHEN NO ONE ELSE WAS.
MY BROTHER HAD BEEN A CITY ORGANIZER. FIGHTING FOR PEOPLE WHO HAD NO VOICE, MUCH LIKE ERNESTO'S DAD.
HE WAS A **GOOD MAN.** A **GREAT BROTHER.** HE WAS THE **BEST KIND** OF PERSON.
WHEN HE DIED, A BIG PART OF ME DIED **WITH HIM.**

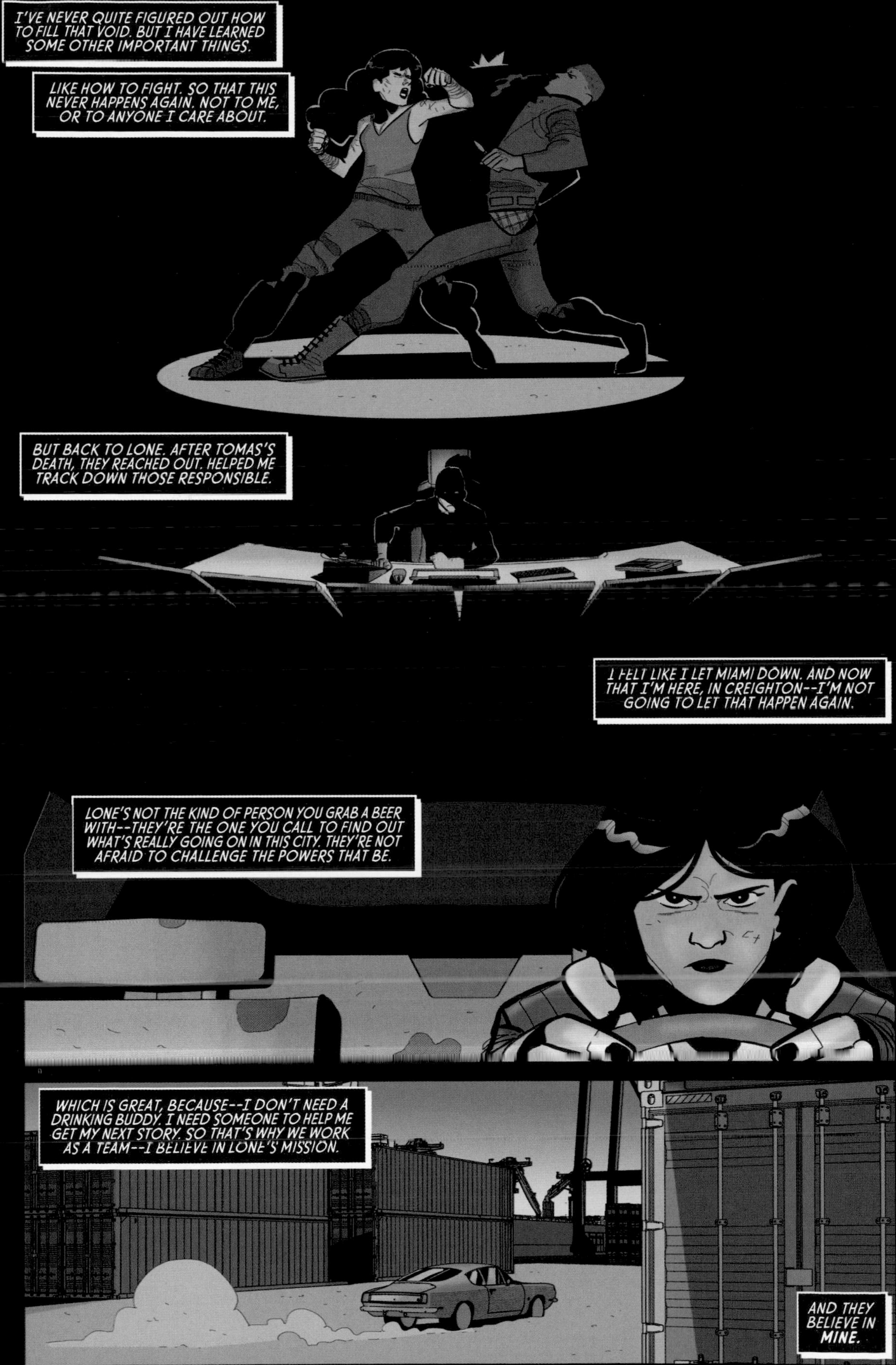
I'VE NEVER QUITE FIGURED OUT HOW TO FILL THAT VOID. BUT I HAVE LEARNED SOME OTHER IMPORTANT THINGS.
LIKE HOW TO FIGHT. SO THAT THIS NEVER HAPPENS AGAIN. NOT TO ME, OR TO ANYONE I CARE ABOUT.
BUT BACK TO LONE. AFTER TOMAS'S DEATH, THEY REACHED OUT. HELPED ME TRACK DOWN THOSE RESPONSIBLE.
I FELT LIKE I LET MIAMI DOWN. AND NOW THAT I'M HERE, IN CREIGHTON--I'M NOT GOING TO LET THAT HAPPEN AGAIN.
LONE'S NOT THE KIND OF PERSON YOU GRAB A BEER WITH--THEY'RE THE ONE YOU CALL TO FIND OUT WHAT'S REALLY GOING ON IN THIS CITY. THEY'RE NOT AFRAID TO CHALLENGE THE POWERS THAT BE.
WHICH IS GREAT, BECAUSE--I DON'T NEED A DRINKING BUDDY. I NEED SOMEONE TO HELP ME GET MY NEXT STORY. SO THAT'S WHY WE WORK AS A TEAM--I BELIEVE IN LONE'S MISSION.
AND THEY BELIEVE IN MINE.

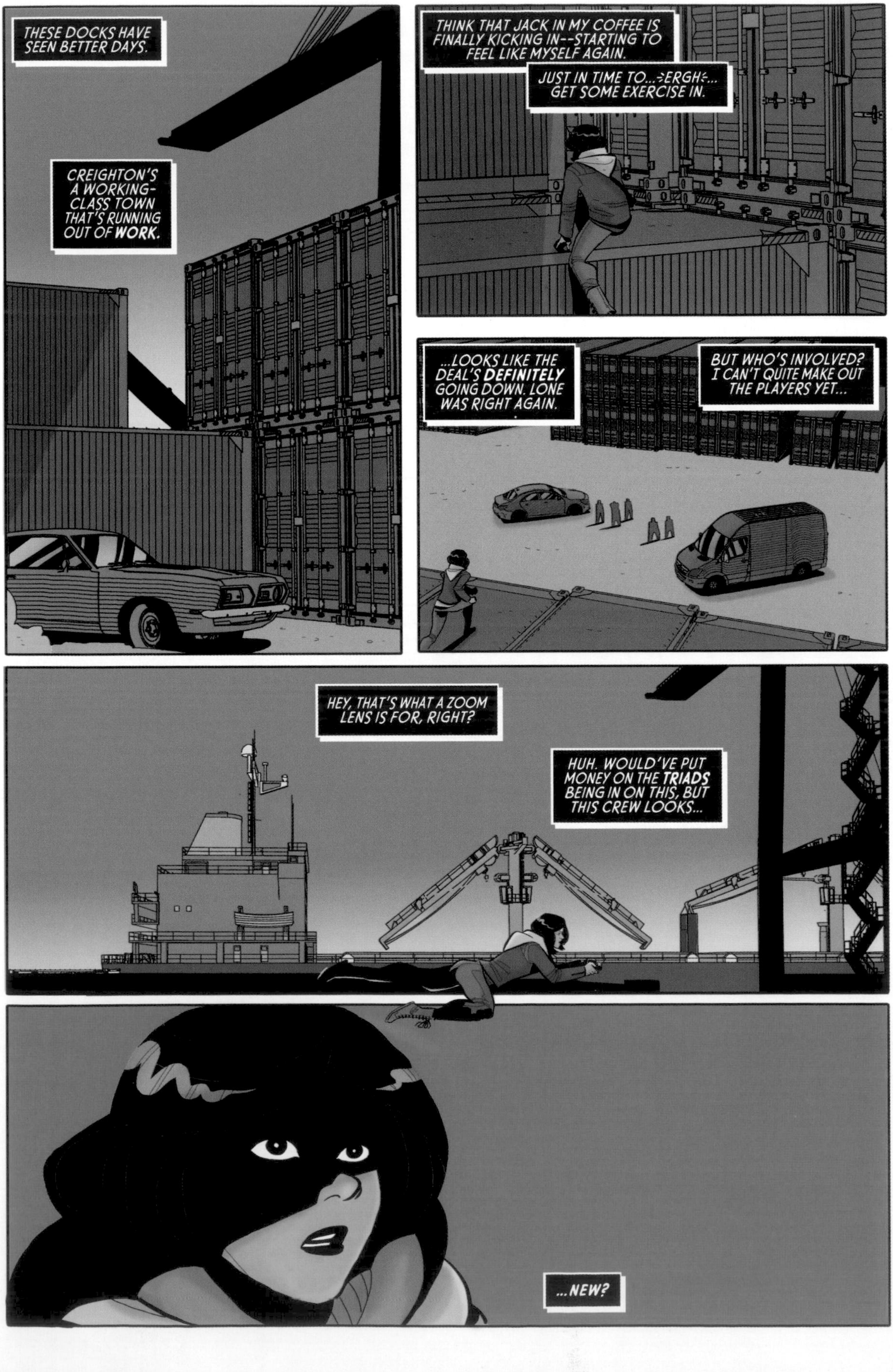
THESE DOCKS HAVE SEEN BETTER DAYS.
CREIGHTON'S A WORKING-CLASS TOWN THAT'S RUNNING OUT OF **WORK.**
THINK THAT JACK IN MY COFFEE IS FINALLY KICKING IN--STARTING TO FEEL LIKE MYSELF AGAIN.
JUST IN TIME TO...>ERGH<... GET SOME EXERCISE IN.
...LOOKS LIKE THE DEAL'S **DEFINITELY** GOING DOWN. LONE WAS RIGHT AGAIN.
BUT WHO'S INVOLVED? I CAN'T QUITE MAKE OUT THE PLAYERS YET...
HEY, THAT'S WHAT A ZOOM LENS IS FOR, RIGHT?
HUH. WOULD'VE PUT MONEY ON THE **TRIADS** BEING IN ON THIS, BUT THIS CREW LOOKS...
...NEW?

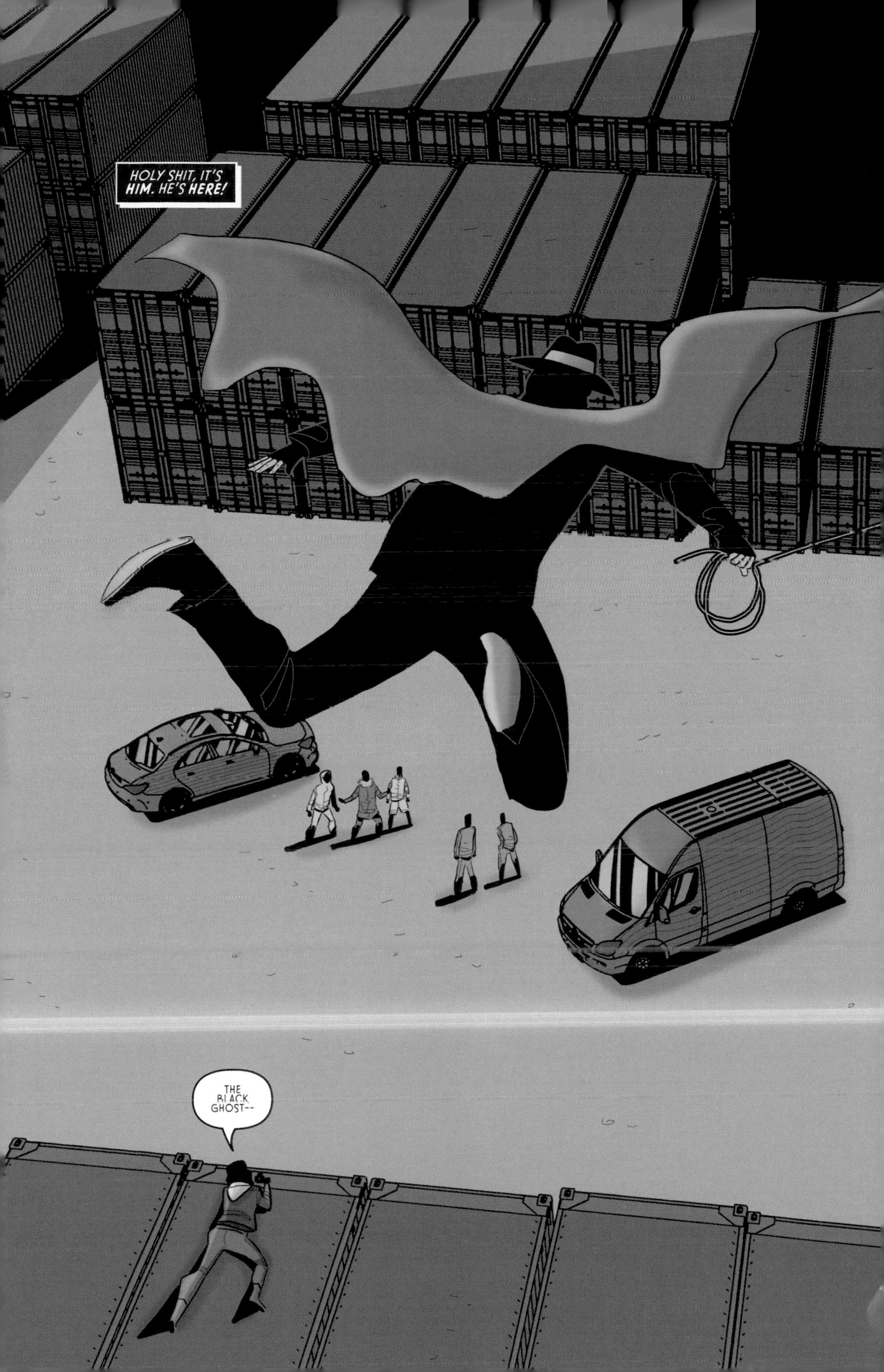
HOLY SHIT, IT'S HIM. HE'S HERE!
THE BLACK GHOST--

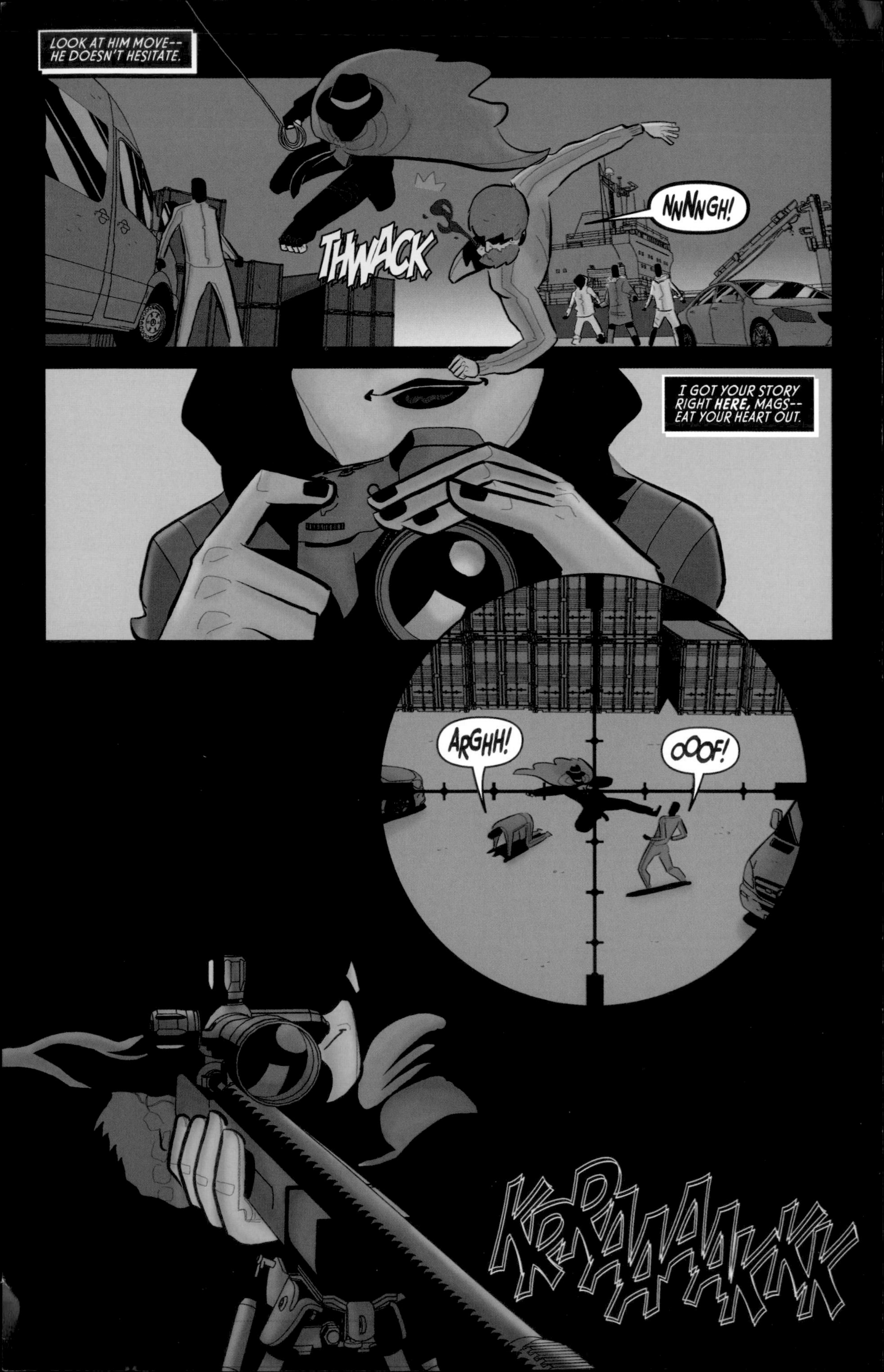
LOOK AT HIM MOVE--
HE DOESN'T HESITATE.
THWACK
NNNNGH!
I GOT YOUR STORY
RIGHT HERE, MAGS--
EAT YOUR HEART OUT.
ARGHH!
OOOF!

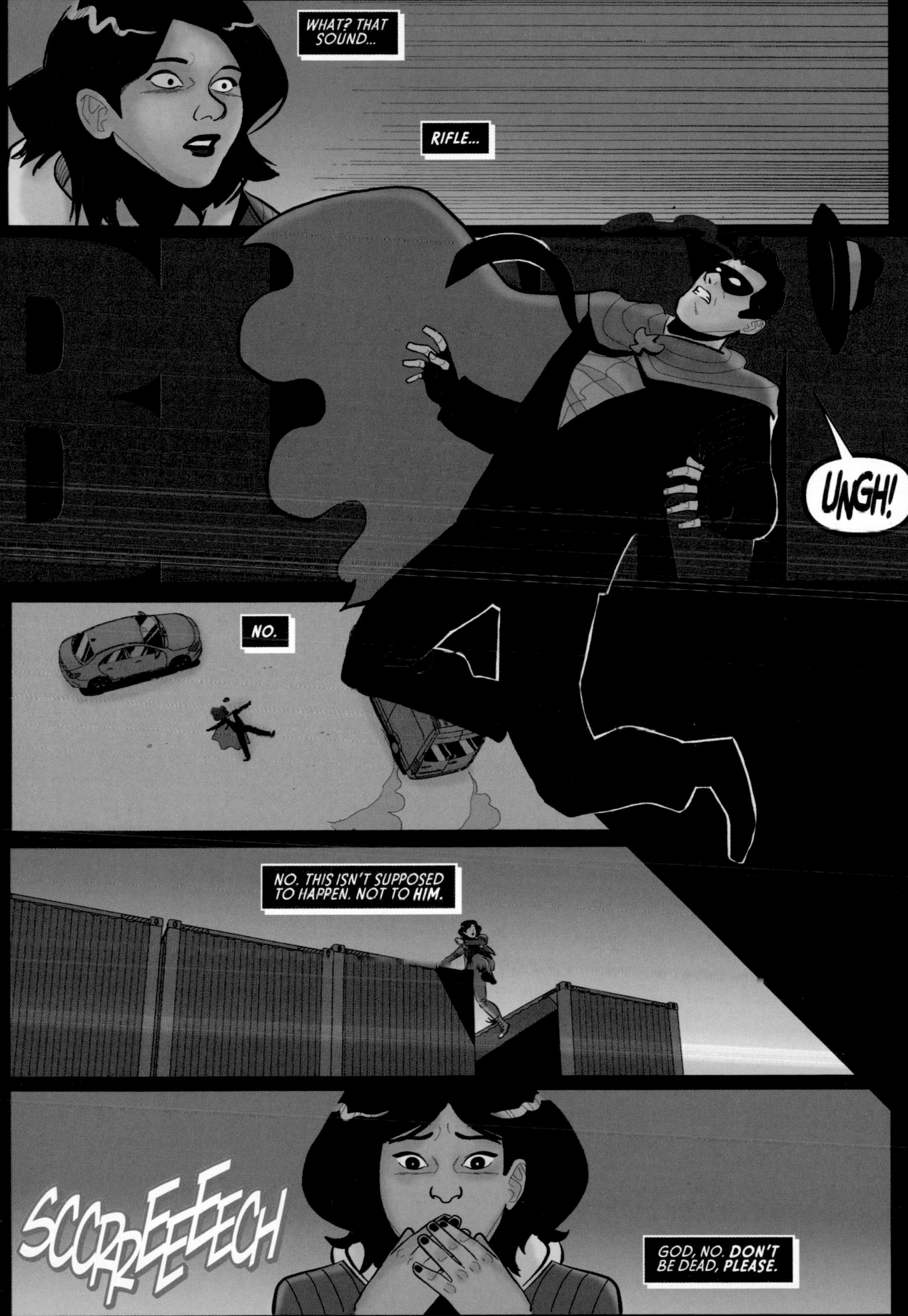
WHAT? THAT SOUND...
RIFLE...
UNGH!
NO.
NO. THIS ISN'T SUPPOSED TO HAPPEN. NOT TO **HIM**.
SCCRREEEEECH
GOD, NO. **DON'T** BE DEAD, **PLEASE**.

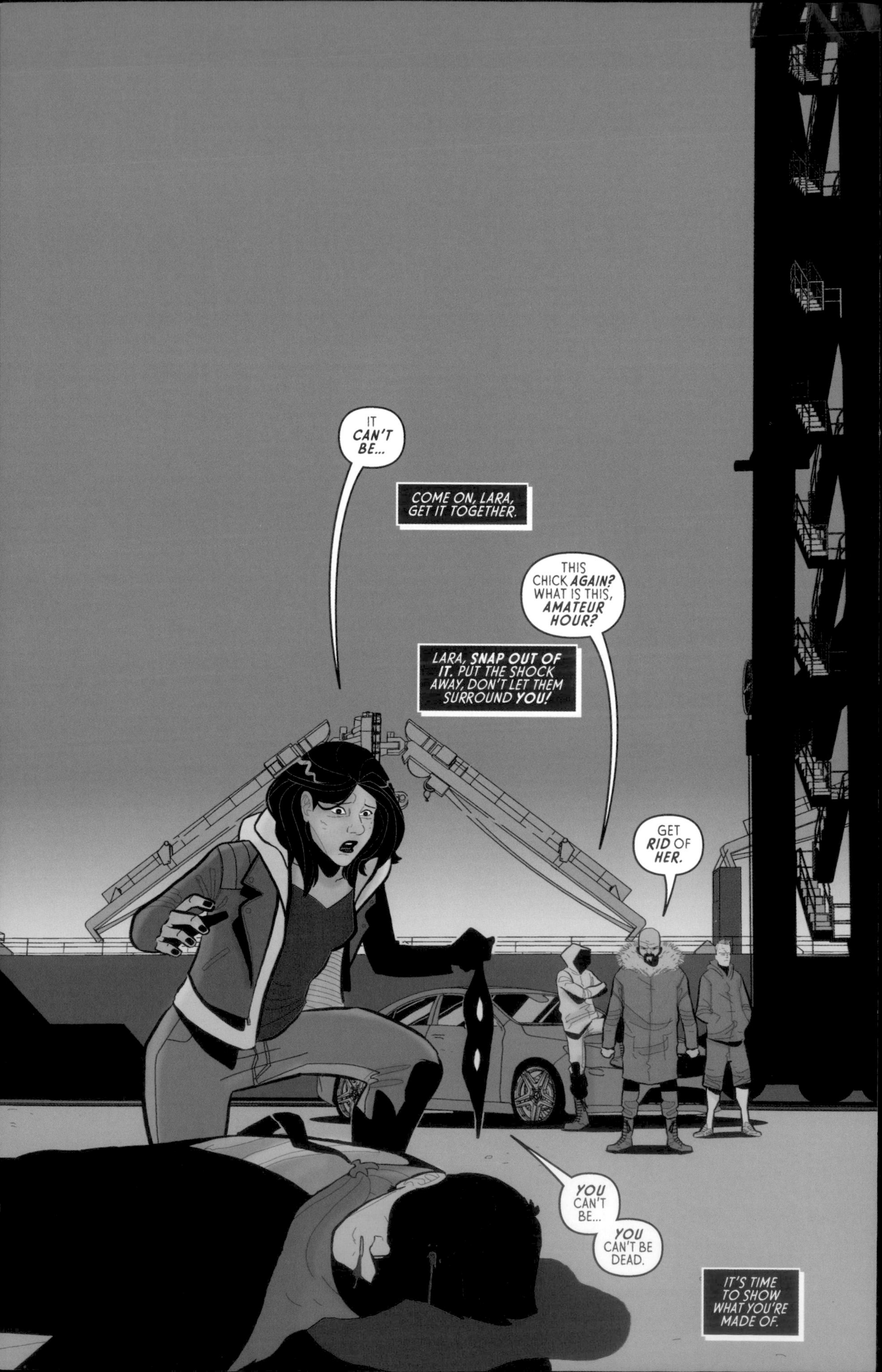
IT CAN'T BE...
COME ON, LARA, GET IT TOGETHER.
THIS CHICK AGAIN? WHAT IS THIS, AMATEUR HOUR?
LARA, SNAP OUT OF IT. PUT THE SHOCK AWAY, DON'T LET THEM SURROUND YOU!
GET RID OF HER.
YOU CAN'T BE...
YOU CAN'T BE DEAD.
IT'S TIME TO SHOW WHAT YOU'RE MADE OF.

# CHAPTER 2
## DO EVIL IN RETURN
COVER BY FRANCESCO FRANCAVILLA

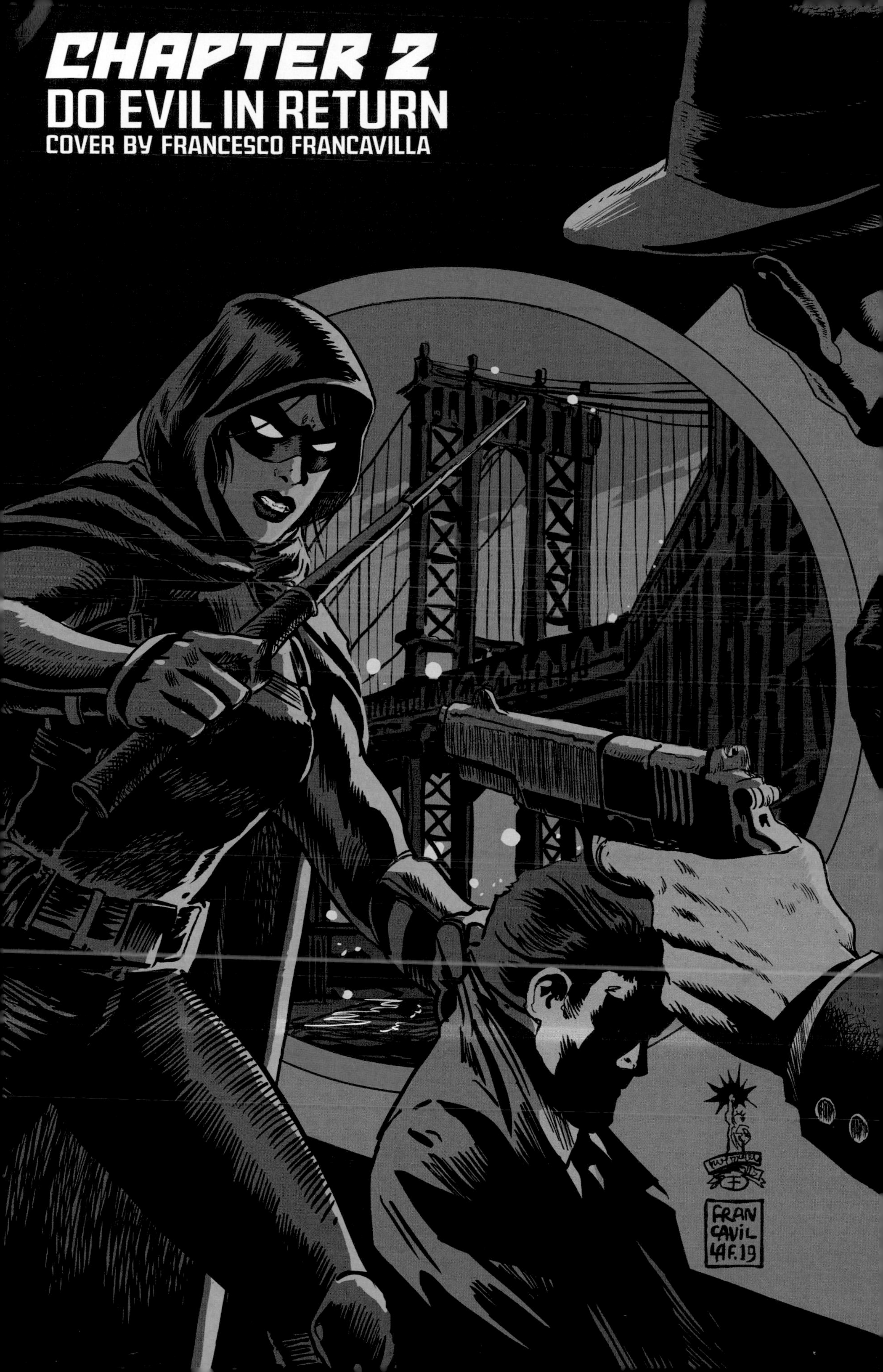
FRAN CAVIL LA F.19

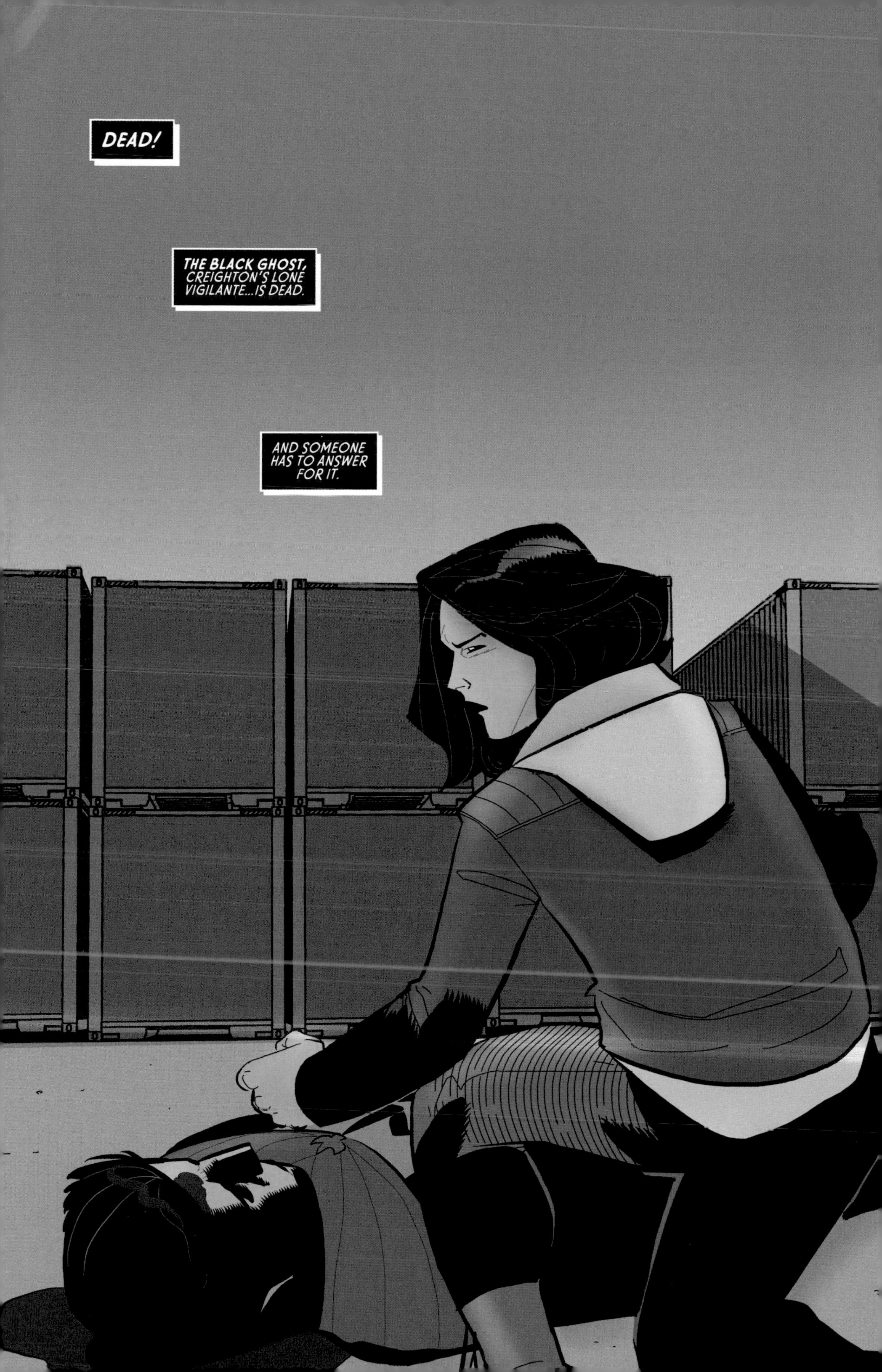
DEAD!
THE BLACK GHOST, CREIGHTON'S LONE VIGILANTE...IS DEAD.
AND SOMEONE HAS TO ANSWER FOR IT.

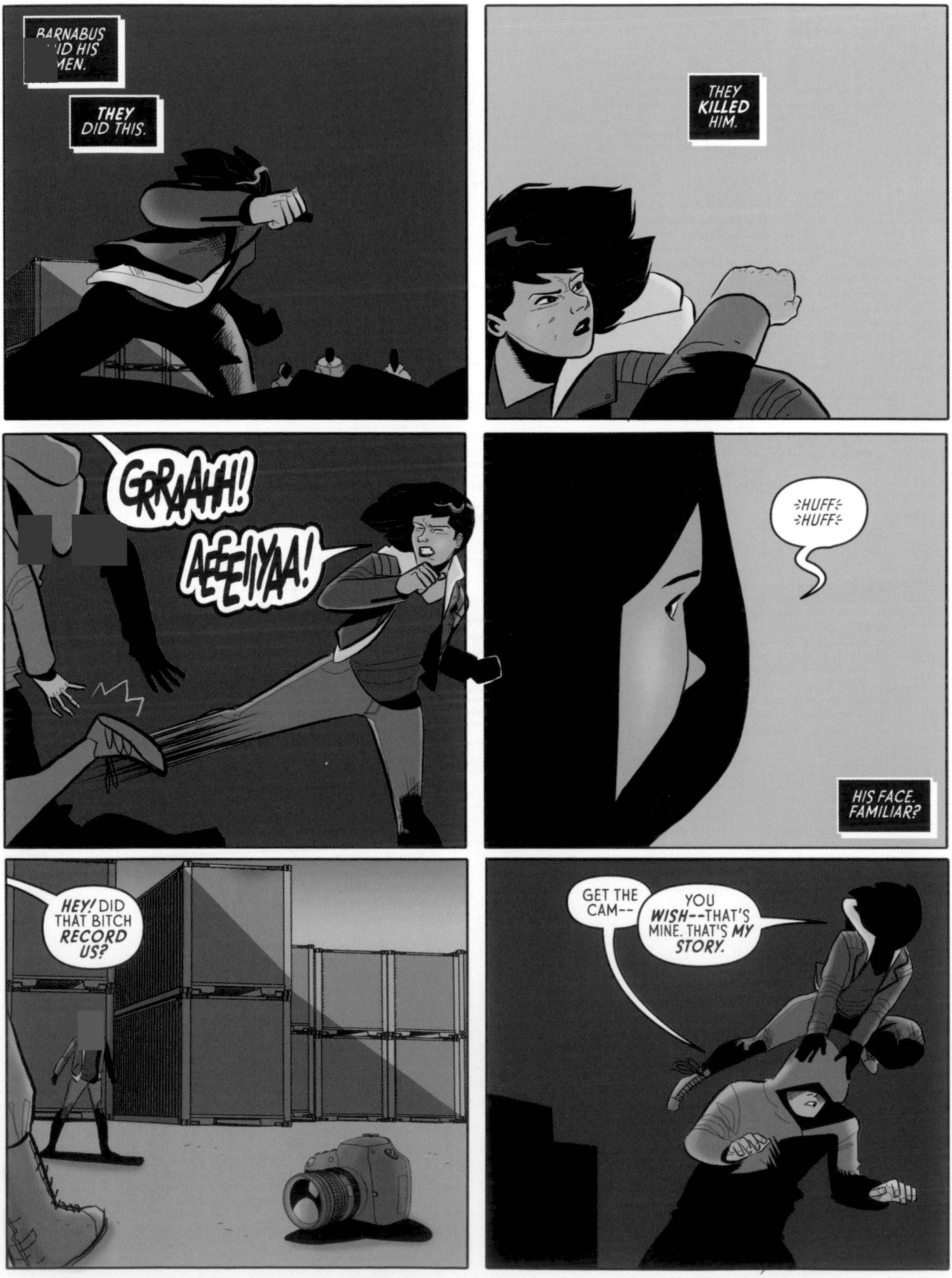

BARNABUS [redacted]ND HIS MEN.
THEY DID THIS.
THEY KILLED HIM.
GRRAAHH!
AEEEIIYAA!
HUFF HUFF
HIS FACE. FAMILIAR?
HEY! DID THAT BITCH RECORD US?
GET THE CAM--
YOU WISH--THAT'S MINE. THAT'S MY STORY.

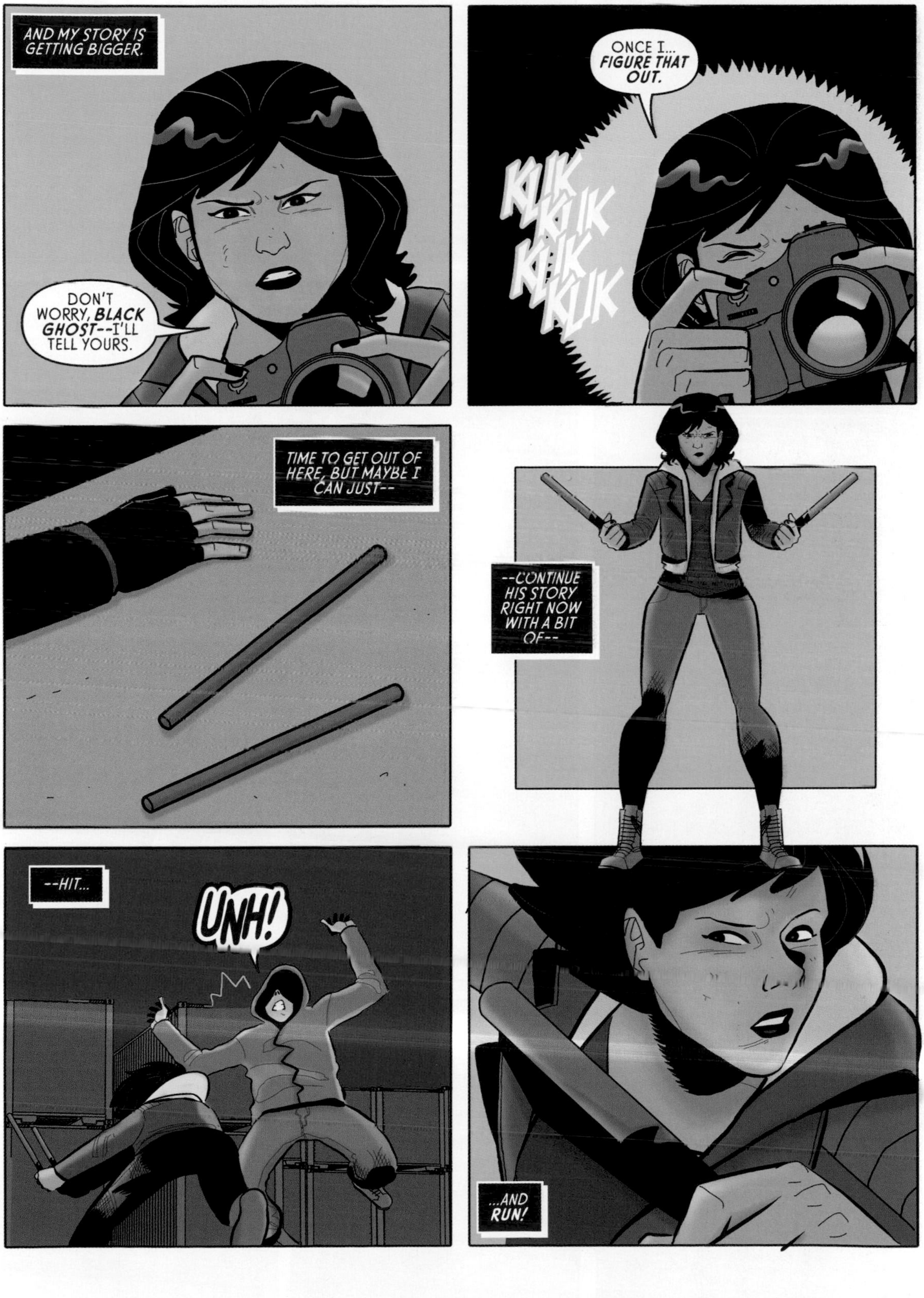
AND MY STORY IS GETTING BIGGER.
DON'T WORRY, **BLACK GHOST**--I'LL TELL YOURS.
ONCE I... **FIGURE THAT OUT.**
KLIK KLIK KLIK KLIK
TIME TO GET OUT OF HERE, BUT MAYBE I CAN JUST--
--CONTINUE HIS STORY RIGHT NOW WITH A BIT OF--
--HIT...
UNH!
...AND **RUN!**

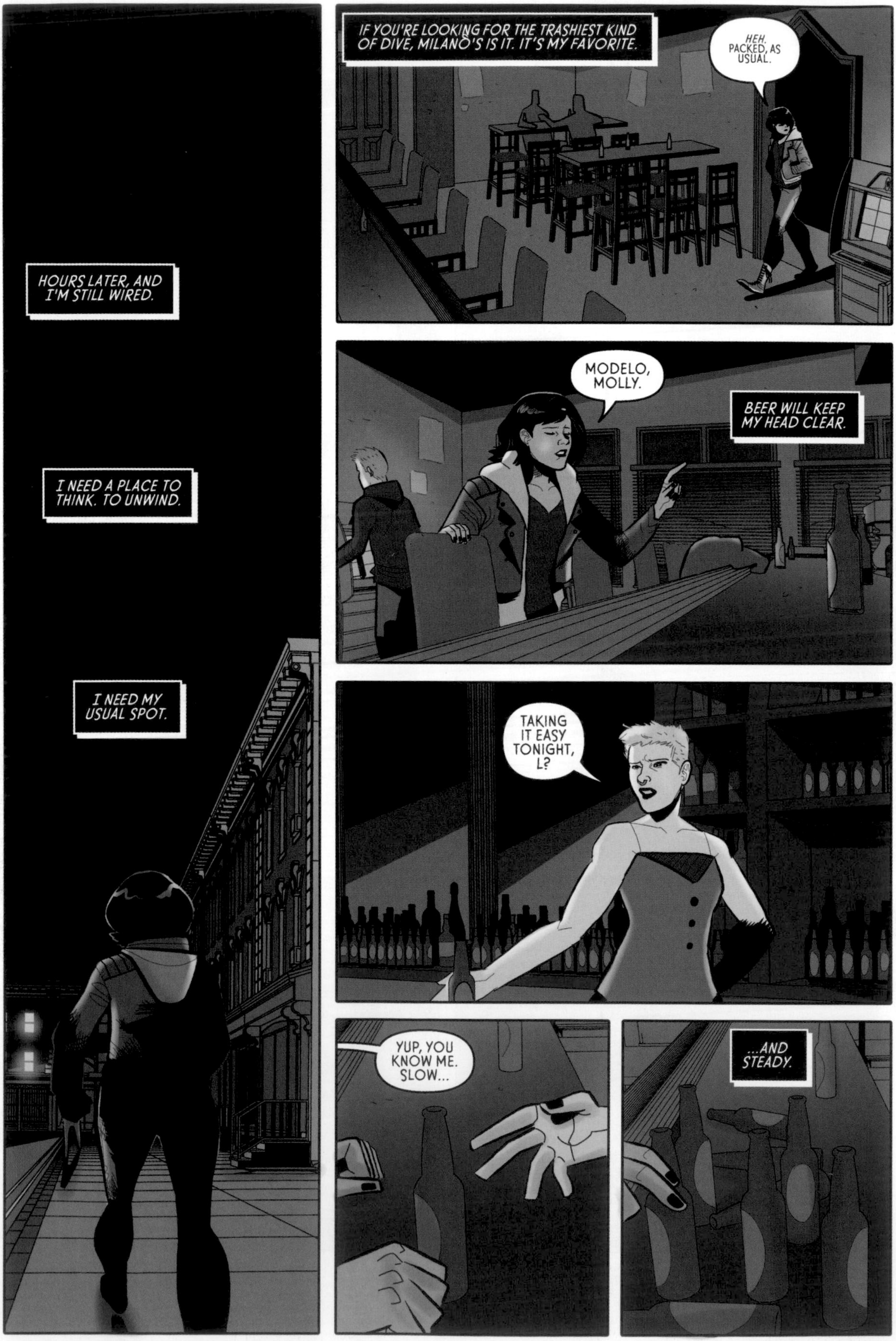
HOURS LATER, AND I'M STILL WIRED.
I NEED A PLACE TO THINK. TO UNWIND.
I NEED MY USUAL SPOT.
IF YOU'RE LOOKING FOR THE TRASHIEST KIND OF DIVE, MILANO'S IS IT. IT'S MY FAVORITE.
HEH. PACKED, AS USUAL.
MODELO, MOLLY.
BEER WILL KEEP MY HEAD CLEAR.
TAKING IT EASY TONIGHT, L?
YUP, YOU KNOW ME. SLOW...
...AND STEADY.

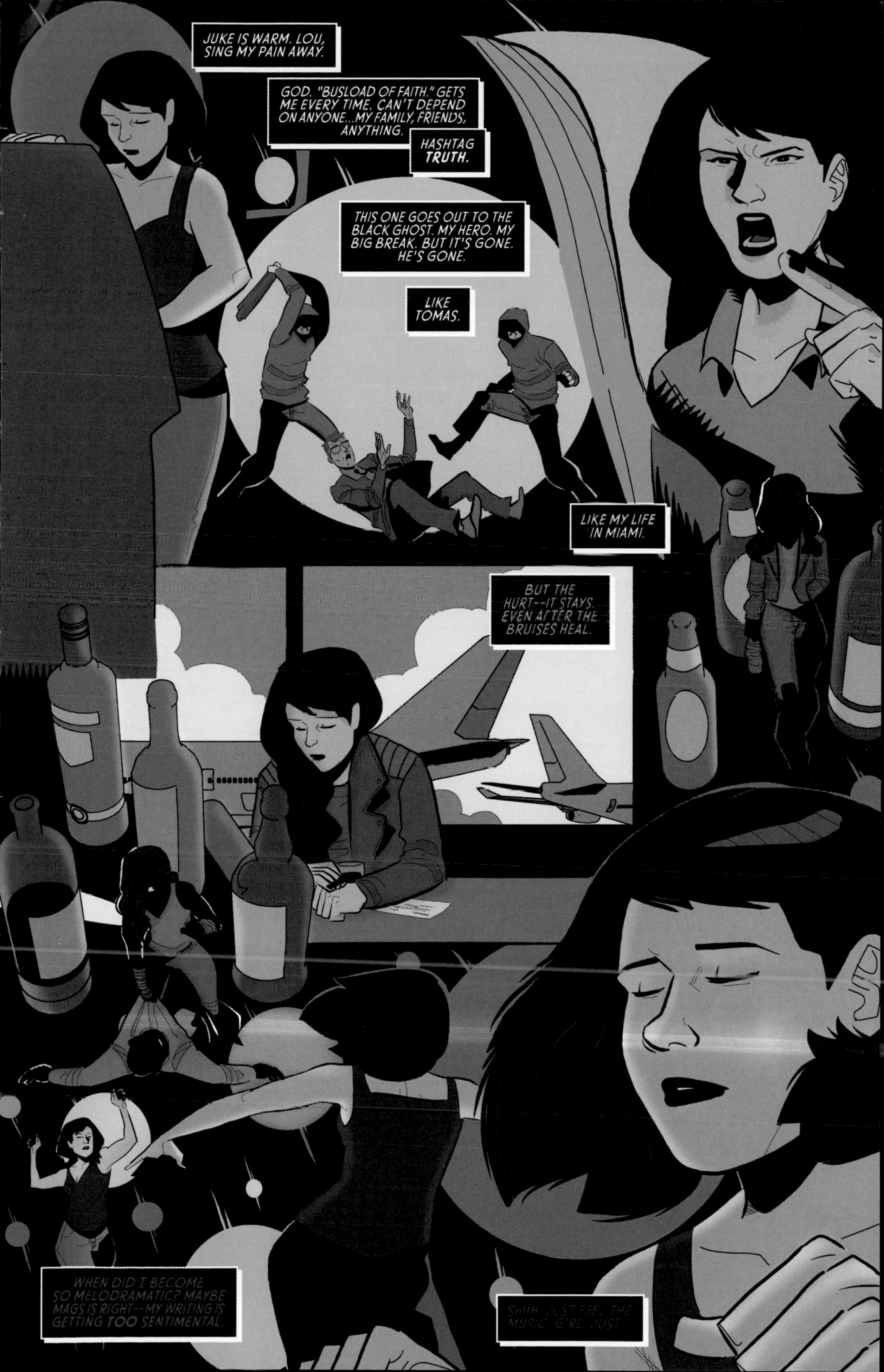
JUKE IS WARM. LOU, SING MY PAIN AWAY.
GOD. "BUSLOAD OF FAITH." GETS ME EVERY TIME. CAN'T DEPEND ON ANYONE...MY FAMILY, FRIENDS, ANYTHING.
HASHTAG TRUTH.
THIS ONE GOES OUT TO THE BLACK GHOST. MY HERO. MY BIG BREAK. BUT IT'S GONE. HE'S GONE.
LIKE TOMAS.
LIKE MY LIFE IN MIAMI.
BUT THE HURT--IT STAYS. EVEN AFTER THE BRUISES HEAL.
WHEN DID I BECOME SO MELODRAMATIC? MAYBE MAGS IS RIGHT--MY WRITING IS GETTING TOO SENTIMENTAL.
SHHH. JUST FEEL THE MUSIC, GIRL. JUST

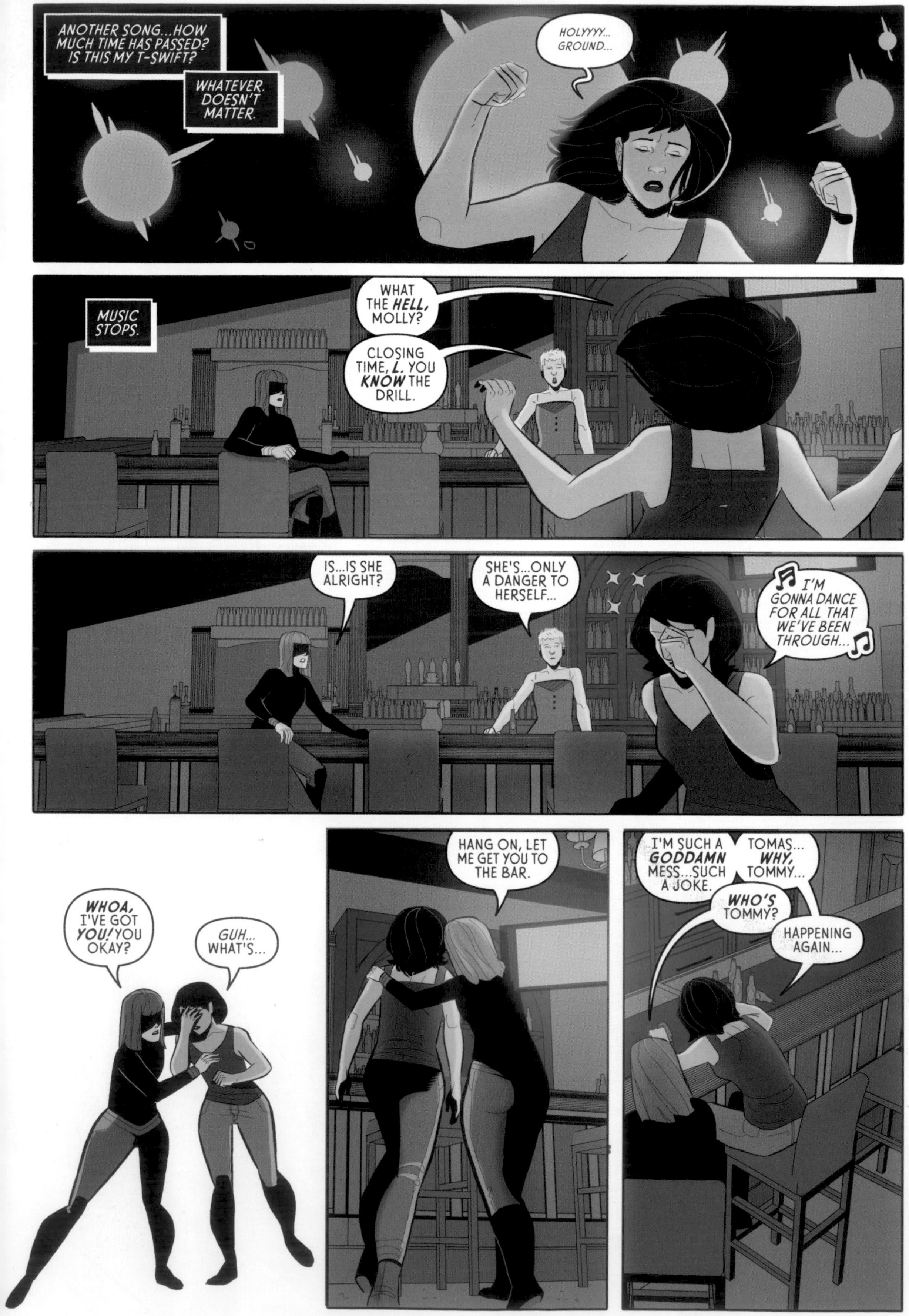
ANOTHER SONG...HOW MUCH TIME HAS PASSED? IS THIS MY T-SWIFT?
WHATEVER. DOESN'T MATTER.
HOLYYYY... GROUND...
MUSIC STOPS.
WHAT THE HELL, MOLLY?
CLOSING TIME, L. YOU KNOW THE DRILL.
IS...IS SHE ALRIGHT?
SHE'S...ONLY A DANGER TO HERSELF...
I'M GONNA DANCE FOR ALL THAT WE'VE BEEN THROUGH...
WHOA, I'VE GOT YOU! YOU OKAY?
GUH... WHAT'S...
HANG ON, LET ME GET YOU TO THE BAR.
I'M SUCH A GODDAMN MESS...SUCH A JOKE.
TOMAS... WHY, TOMMY...
WHO'S TOMMY?
HAPPENING AGAIN...

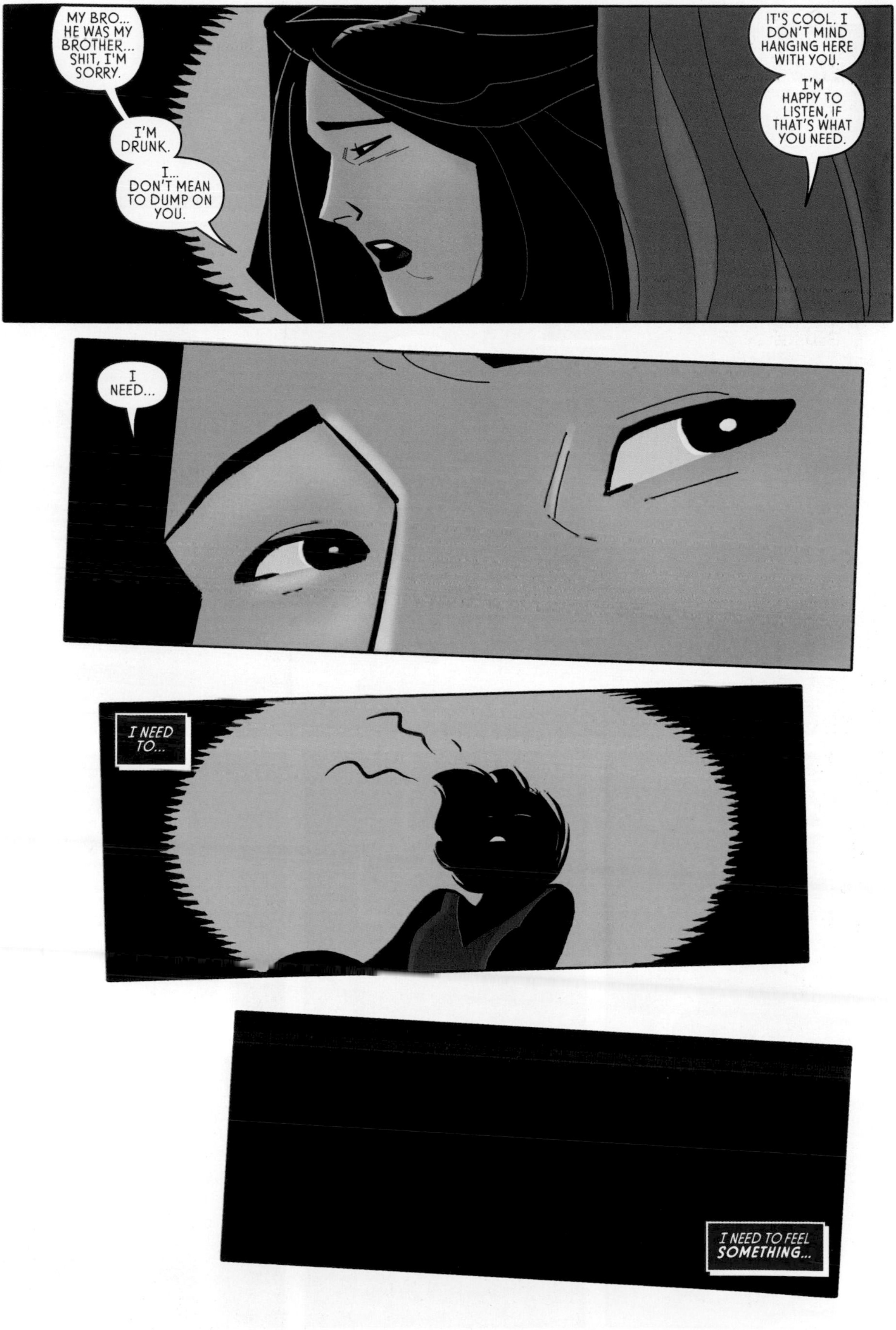
MY BRO... HE WAS MY BROTHER... SHIT, I'M SORRY.
I'M DRUNK.
I... DON'T MEAN TO DUMP ON YOU.
IT'S COOL. I DON'T MIND HANGING HERE WITH YOU.
I'M HAPPY TO LISTEN, IF THAT'S WHAT YOU NEED.
I NEED...
I NEED TO...
I NEED TO FEEL SOMETHING...

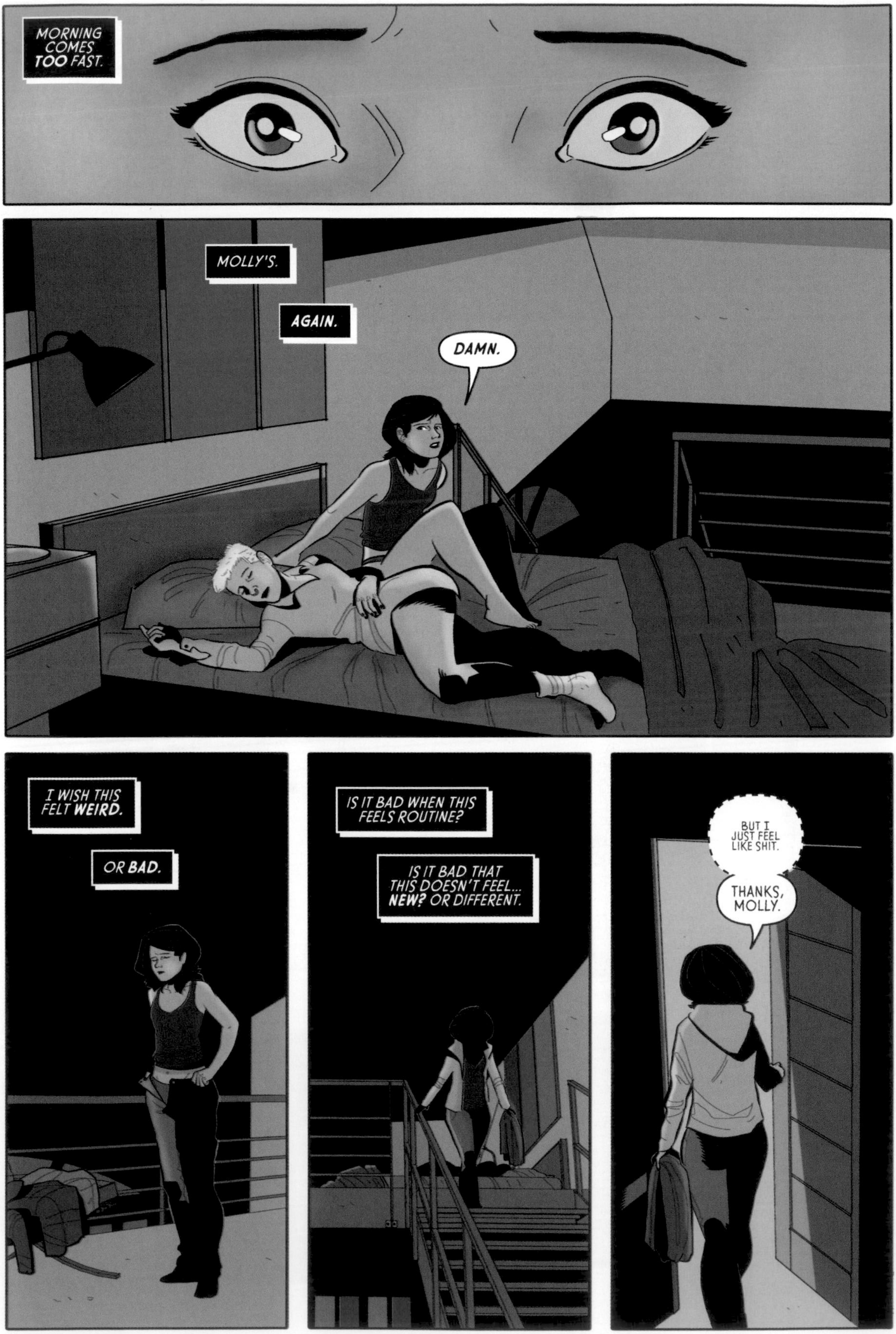
MORNING COMES TOO FAST.
MOLLY'S.
AGAIN.
DAMN.
I WISH THIS FELT WEIRD.
OR BAD.
IS IT BAD WHEN THIS FEELS ROUTINE?
IS IT BAD THAT THIS DOESN'T FEEL... NEW? OR DIFFERENT.
BUT I JUST FEEL LIKE SHIT.
THANKS, MOLLY.

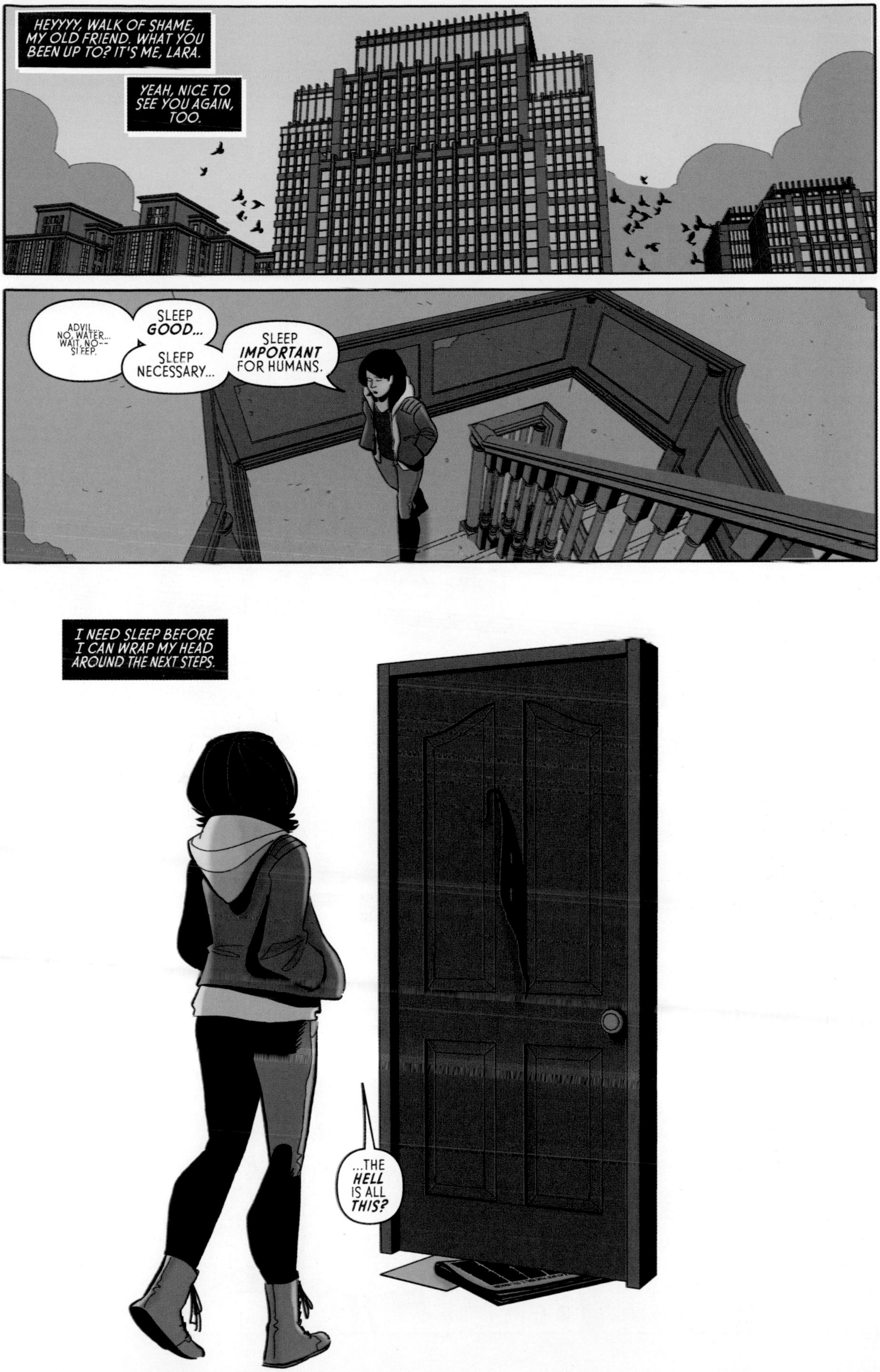
HEYYYY, WALK OF SHAME, MY OLD FRIEND. WHAT YOU BEEN UP TO? IT'S ME, LARA.
YEAH, NICE TO SEE YOU AGAIN, TOO.
ADVIL... NO, WATER... WAIT, NO-- SLEEP.
SLEEP GOOD...
SLEEP NECESSARY...
SLEEP IMPORTANT FOR HUMANS.
I NEED SLEEP BEFORE I CAN WRAP MY HEAD AROUND THE NEXT STEPS.
...THE HELL IS ALL THIS?

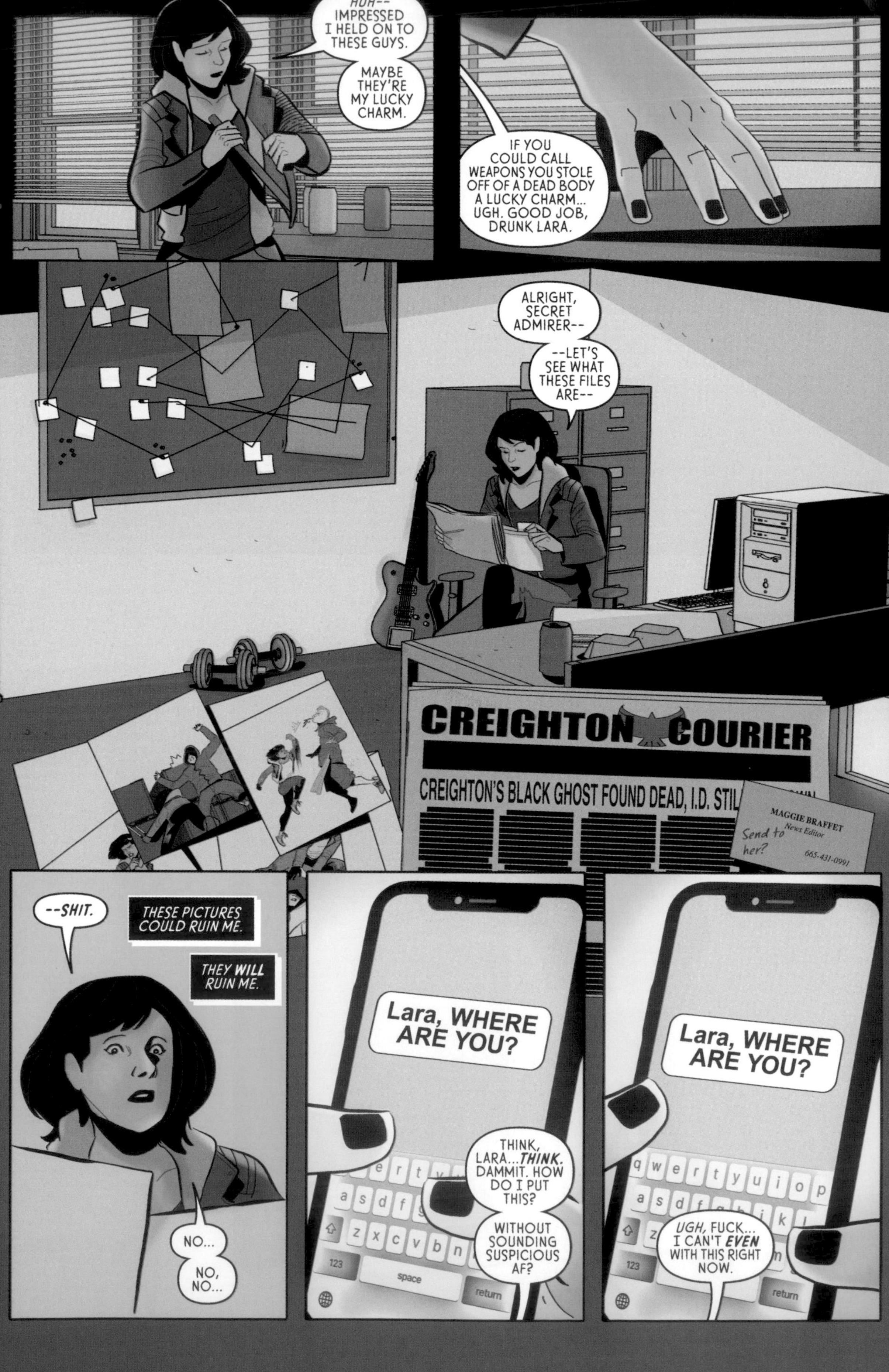
HUH-- IMPRESSED I HELD ON TO THESE GUYS.
MAYBE THEY'RE MY LUCKY CHARM.
IF YOU COULD CALL WEAPONS YOU STOLE OFF OF A DEAD BODY A LUCKY CHARM... UGH. GOOD JOB, DRUNK LARA.
ALRIGHT, SECRET ADMIRER--
--LET'S SEE WHAT THESE FILES ARE--
CREIGHTON COURIER
CREIGHTON'S BLACK GHOST FOUND DEAD, I.D. STIL
MAGGIE BRAFFET
News Editor
665-431-0991
Send to her?
--SHIT.
THESE PICTURES COULD RUIN ME.
THEY WILL RUIN ME.
NO...
NO, NO...
Lara, WHERE ARE YOU?
THINK, LARA...THINK. DAMMIT. HOW DO I PUT THIS?
WITHOUT SOUNDING SUSPICIOUS AF?
Lara, WHERE ARE YOU?
UGH, FUCK... I CAN'T EVEN WITH THIS RIGHT NOW.

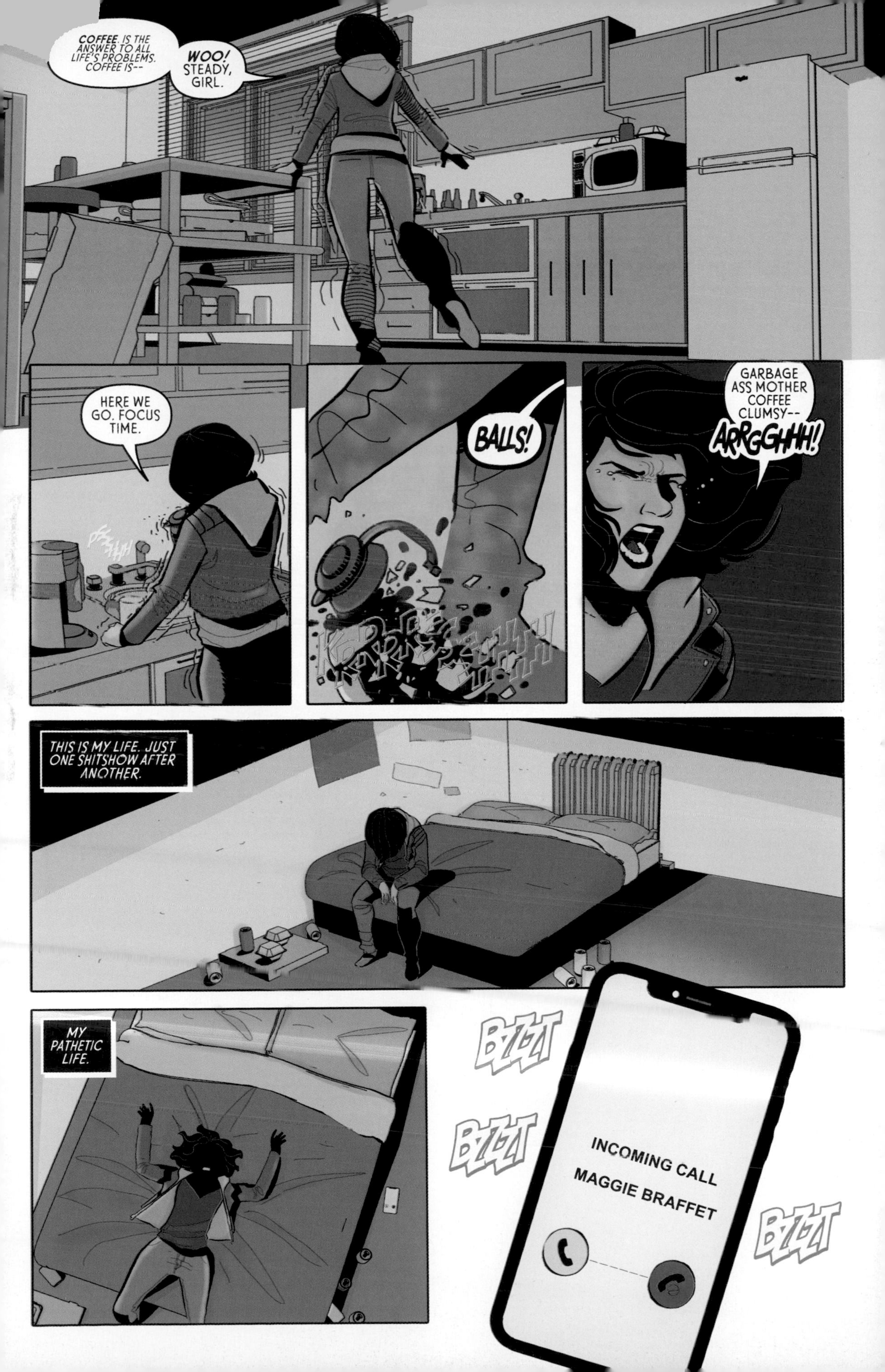
COFFEE. IS THE ANSWER TO ALL LIFE'S PROBLEMS. COFFEE IS--
WOO! STEADY, GIRL.
HERE WE GO. FOCUS TIME.
PSSSHHH
BALLS!
GARBAGE ASS MOTHER COFFEE CLUMSY-- ARRGGHHH!
THIS IS MY LIFE. JUST ONE SHITSHOW AFTER ANOTHER.
MY PATHETIC LIFE.
BZZZT
BZZZT
INCOMING CALL
MAGGIE BRAFFET
BZZZT

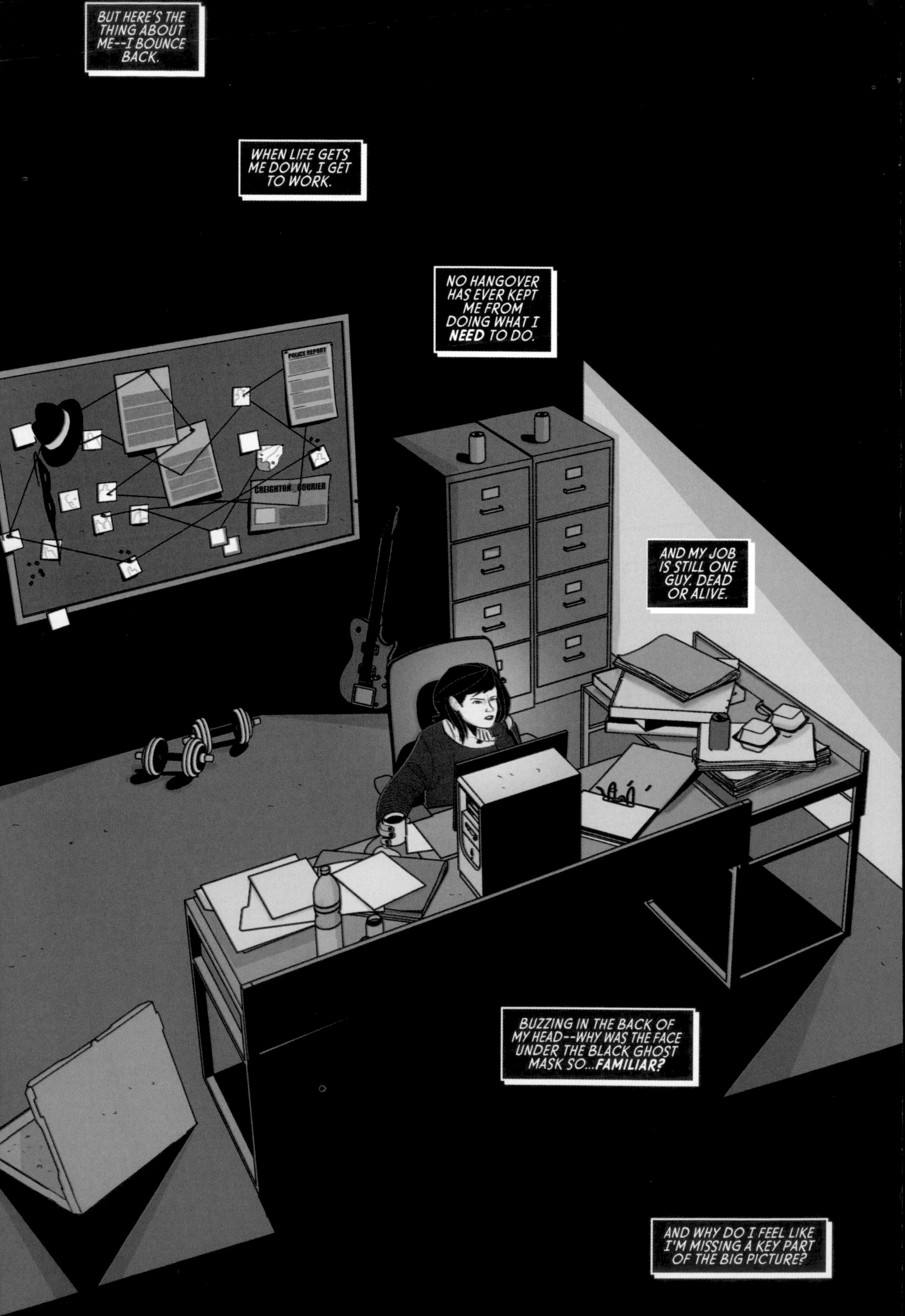
BUT HERE'S THE THING ABOUT ME--I BOUNCE BACK.
WHEN LIFE GETS ME DOWN, I GET TO WORK.
NO HANGOVER HAS EVER KEPT ME FROM DOING WHAT I **NEED** TO DO.
POLICE REPORT
CREIGHTON COURIER
AND MY JOB IS STILL ONE GUY. DEAD OR ALIVE.
BUZZING IN THE BACK OF MY HEAD--WHY WAS THE FACE UNDER THE BLACK GHOST MASK SO...**FAMILIAR?**
AND WHY DO I FEEL LIKE I'M MISSING A KEY PART OF THE BIG PICTURE?

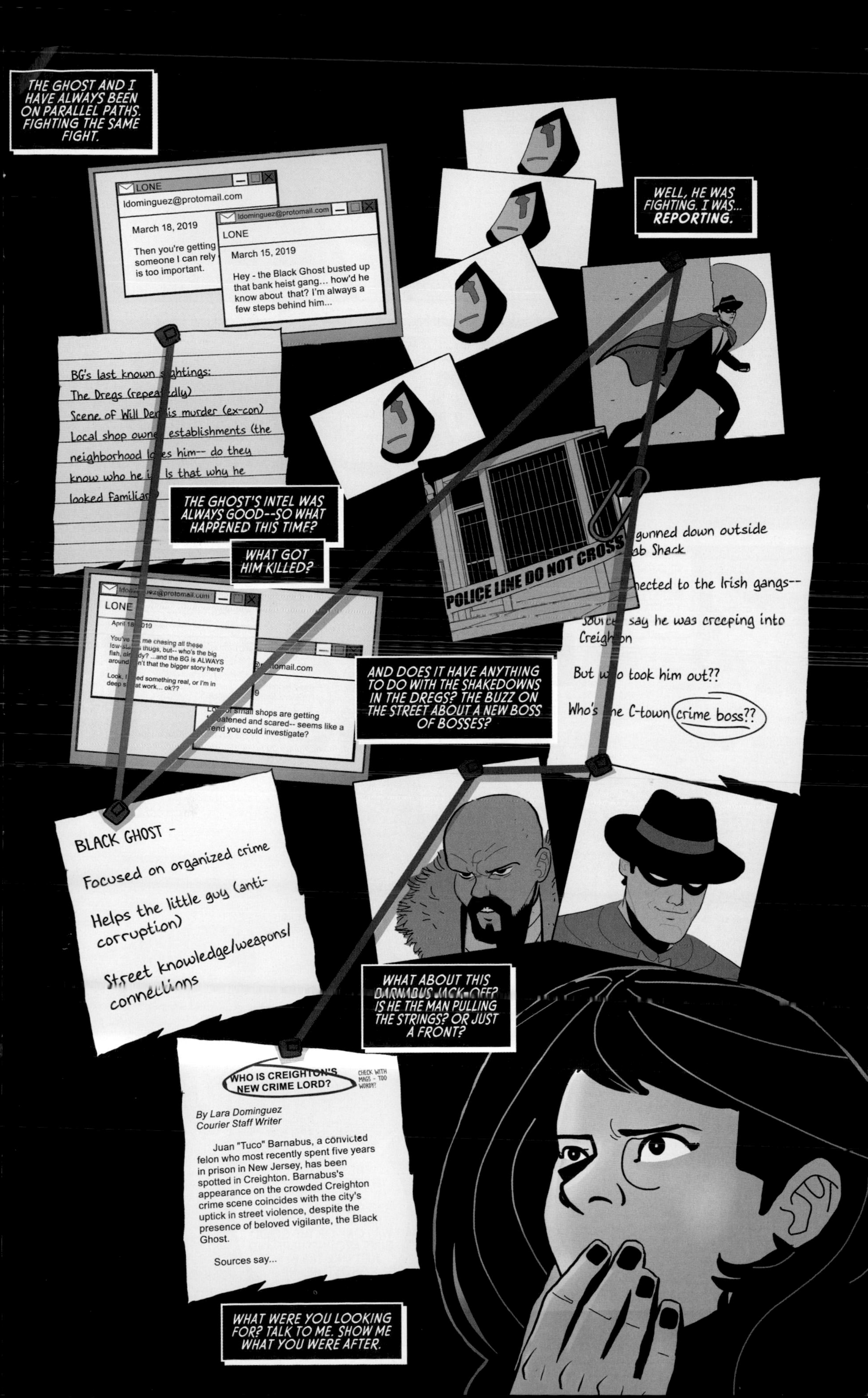
THE GHOST AND I HAVE ALWAYS BEEN ON PARALLEL PATHS. FIGHTING THE SAME FIGHT.
LONE
ldominguez@protomail.com
March 18, 2019
Then you're getting someone I can rely is too important.
ldominguez@protomail.com
LONE
March 15, 2019
Hey - the Black Ghost busted up that bank heist gang... how'd he know about that? I'm always a few steps behind him...
WELL, HE WAS FIGHTING. I WAS... REPORTING.
BG's last known sightings:
The Dregs (repeatedly)
Scene of Will Dennis murder (ex-con)
Local shop owner establishments (the neighborhood loves him-- do they know who he is? Is that why he looked familiar?)
THE GHOST'S INTEL WAS ALWAYS GOOD--SO WHAT HAPPENED THIS TIME?
WHAT GOT HIM KILLED?
POLICE LINE DO NOT CROSS
gunned down outside ab Shack
nected to the Irish gangs--
Sources say he was creeping into Creighton
But who took him out??
Who's the C-town crime boss??
LONE
April 18, 2019
You've me chasing all these low-level thugs, but-- who's the big fish, already? ...and the BG is ALWAYS around. Isn't that the bigger story here?
Look, I need something real, or I'm in deep at work... ok??
otomail.com
Lots of small shops are getting threatened and scared-- seems like a trend you could investigate?
AND DOES IT HAVE ANYTHING TO DO WITH THE SHAKEDOWNS IN THE DREGS? THE BUZZ ON THE STREET ABOUT A NEW BOSS OF BOSSES?
BLACK GHOST -
Focused on organized crime
Helps the little guy (anti-corruption)
Street knowledge/weapons/ connections
WHAT ABOUT THIS BARNABUS JACK-OFF? IS HE THE MAN PULLING THE STRINGS? OR JUST A FRONT?
WHO IS CREIGHTON'S NEW CRIME LORD?
CHECK WITH MAGS - TOO WORDY?
By Lara Dominguez
Courier Staff Writer
Juan "Tuco" Barnabus, a convicted felon who most recently spent five years in prison in New Jersey, has been spotted in Creighton. Barnabus's appearance on the crowded Creighton crime scene coincides with the city's uptick in street violence, despite the presence of beloved vigilante, the Black Ghost.
Sources say...
WHAT WERE YOU LOOKING FOR? TALK TO ME. SHOW ME WHAT YOU WERE AFTER.

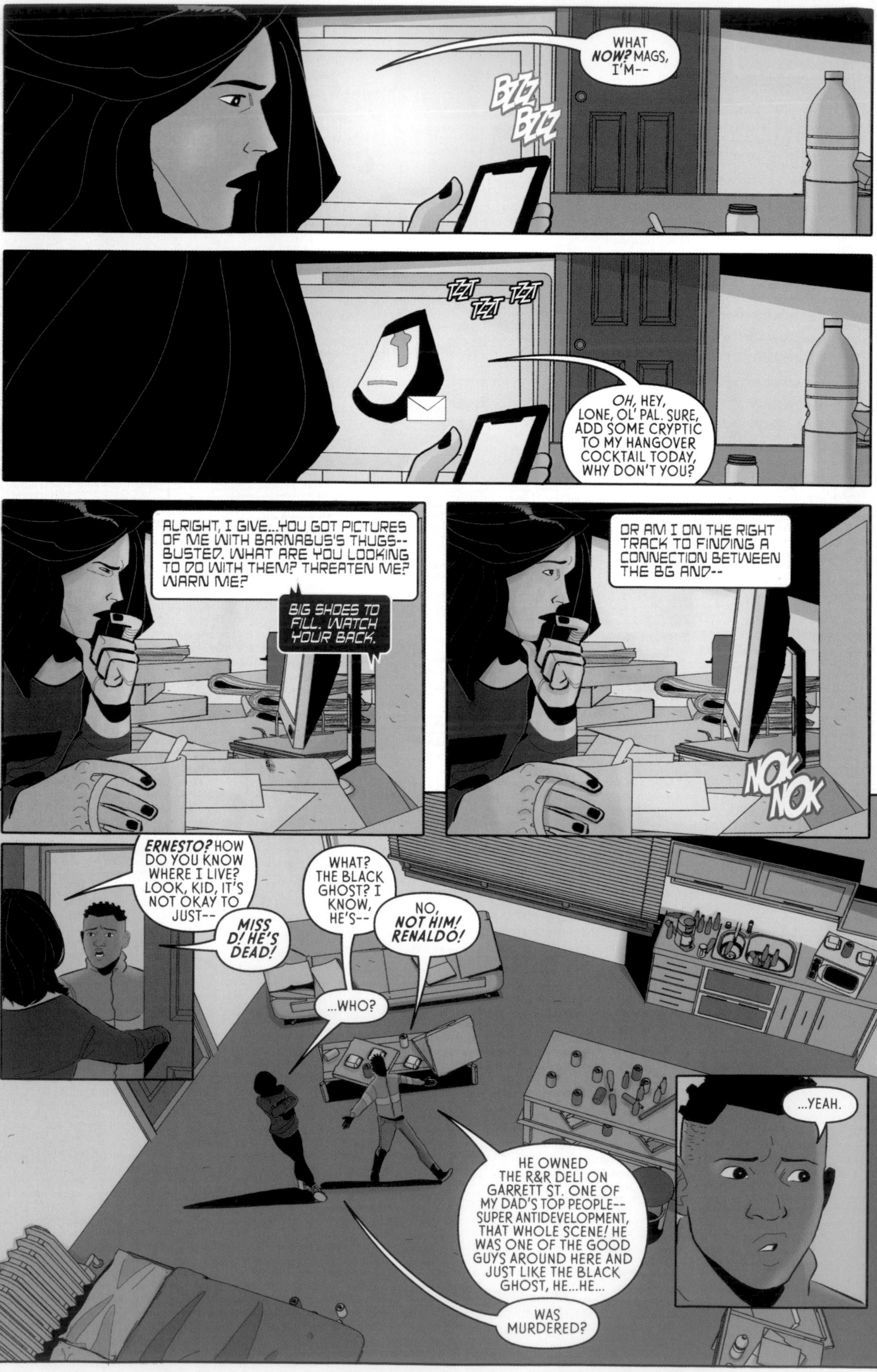
WHAT NOW? MAGS, I'M--
BZZZ BZZZ
TZZT TZZT TZZT
OH, HEY, LONE, OL' PAL. SURE, ADD SOME CRYPTIC TO MY HANGOVER COCKTAIL TODAY, WHY DON'T YOU?
ALRIGHT, I GIVE...YOU GOT PICTURES OF ME WITH BARNABUS'S THUGS-- BUSTED. WHAT ARE YOU LOOKING TO DO WITH THEM? THREATEN ME? WARN ME?
BIG SHOES TO FILL. WATCH YOUR BACK.
OR AM I ON THE RIGHT TRACK TO FINDING A CONNECTION BETWEEN THE BG AND--
NOK NOK
ERNESTO? HOW DO YOU KNOW WHERE I LIVE? LOOK, KID, IT'S NOT OKAY TO JUST--
MISS D! HE'S DEAD!
WHAT? THE BLACK GHOST? I KNOW, HE'S--
NO, NOT HIM! RENALDO!
...WHO?
HE OWNED THE R&R DELI ON GARRETT ST. ONE OF MY DAD'S TOP PEOPLE-- SUPER ANTIDEVELOPMENT, THAT WHOLE SCENE! HE WAS ONE OF THE GOOD GUYS AROUND HERE AND JUST LIKE THE BLACK GHOST, HE...HE...
WAS MURDERED?
...YEAH.

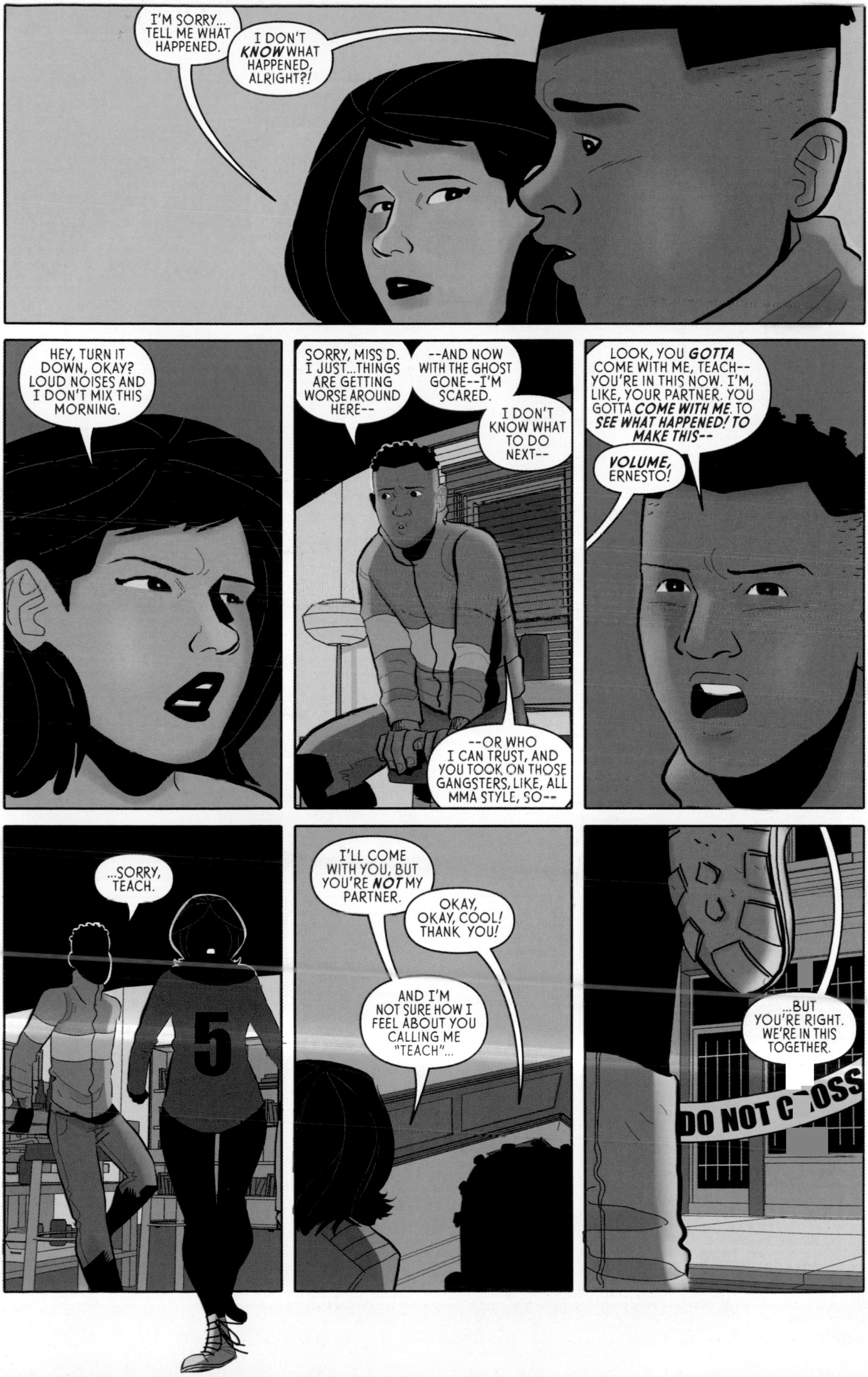
I'M SORRY... TELL ME WHAT HAPPENED.
I DON'T **KNOW** WHAT HAPPENED, ALRIGHT?!
HEY, TURN IT DOWN, OKAY? LOUD NOISES AND I DON'T MIX THIS MORNING.
SORRY, MISS D. I JUST...THINGS ARE GETTING WORSE AROUND HERE--
--AND NOW WITH THE GHOST GONE--I'M SCARED.
I DON'T KNOW WHAT TO DO NEXT--
--OR WHO I CAN TRUST, AND YOU TOOK ON THOSE GANGSTERS, LIKE, ALL MMA STYLE, SO--
LOOK, YOU **GOTTA** COME WITH ME, TEACH-- YOU'RE IN THIS NOW. I'M, LIKE, YOUR PARTNER. YOU GOTTA **COME WITH ME**. TO **SEE WHAT HAPPENED! TO MAKE THIS--**
**VOLUME,** ERNESTO!
...SORRY, TEACH.
5
I'LL COME WITH YOU, BUT YOU'RE **NOT** MY PARTNER.
OKAY, OKAY, COOL! THANK YOU!
AND I'M NOT SURE HOW I FEEL ABOUT YOU CALLING ME "TEACH"...
...BUT YOU'RE RIGHT. WE'RE IN THIS TOGETHER.
DO NOT C OSS

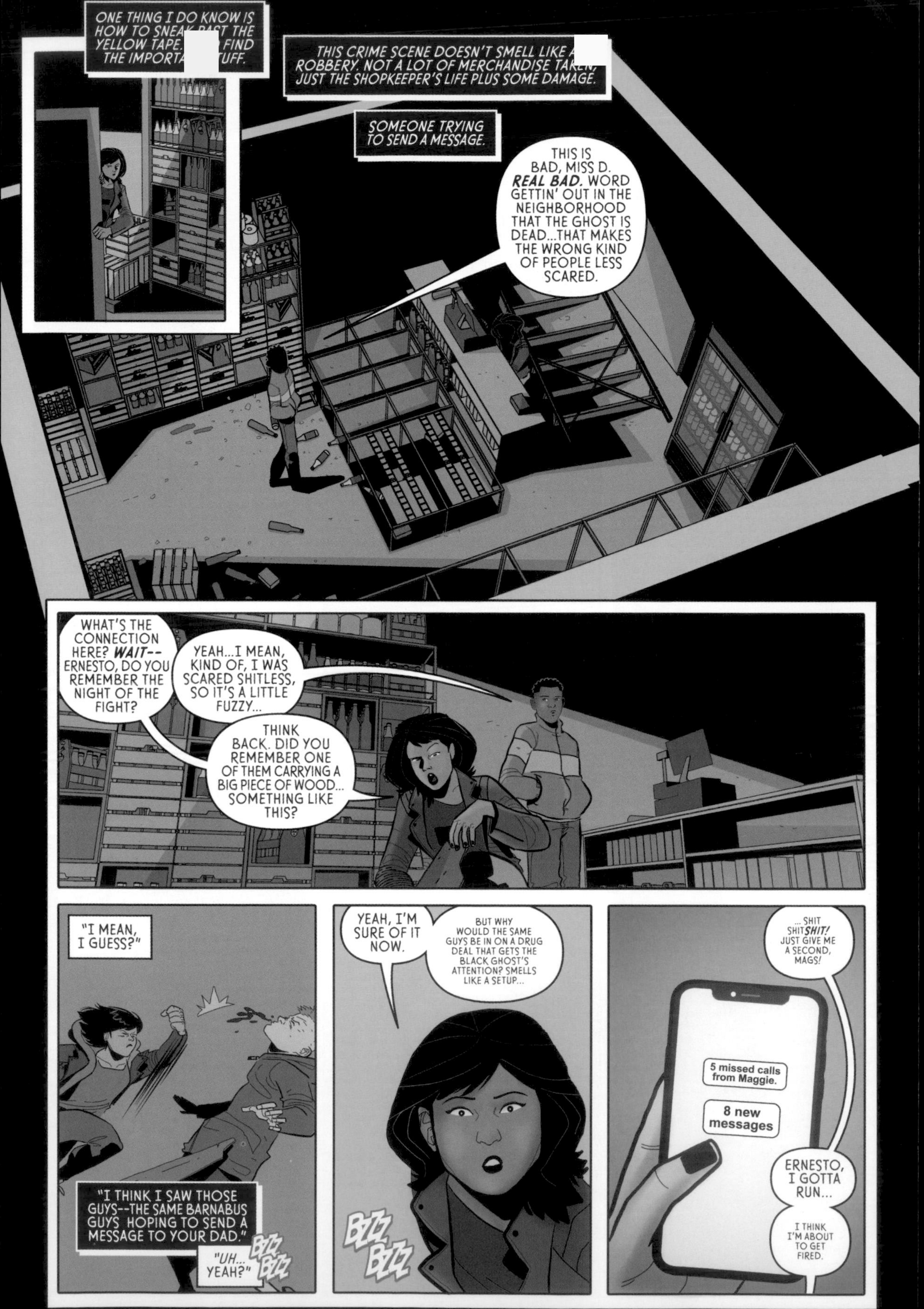

ONE THING I DO KNOW IS HOW TO SNEAK PAST THE YELLOW TAPE. FIND THE IMPORTA UFF.
THIS CRIME SCENE DOESN'T SMELL LIKE A ROBBERY. NOT A LOT OF MERCHANDISE TAKEN, JUST THE SHOPKEEPER'S LIFE PLUS SOME DAMAGE.
SOMEONE TRYING TO SEND A MESSAGE.
THIS IS BAD, MISS D. **REAL BAD.** WORD GETTIN' OUT IN THE NEIGHBORHOOD THAT THE GHOST IS DEAD...THAT MAKES THE WRONG KIND OF PEOPLE LESS SCARED.
WHAT'S THE CONNECTION HERE? ***WAIT--*** ERNESTO, DO YOU REMEMBER THE NIGHT OF THE FIGHT?
YEAH...I MEAN, KIND OF, I WAS SCARED SHITLESS, SO IT'S A LITTLE FUZZY...
THINK BACK. DID YOU REMEMBER ONE OF THEM CARRYING A BIG PIECE OF WOOD... SOMETHING LIKE THIS?
"I MEAN, I GUESS?"
"I THINK I SAW THOSE GUYS--THE SAME BARNABUS GUYS HOPING TO SEND A MESSAGE TO YOUR DAD."
"UH... YEAH?"
BZZZ BZZZ
YEAH, I'M SURE OF IT NOW.
BUT WHY WOULD THE SAME GUYS BE IN ON A DRUG DEAL THAT GETS THE BLACK GHOST'S ATTENTION? SMELLS LIKE A SETUP...
BZZZ BZZZ
... SHIT SHIT ***SHIT!*** JUST GIVE ME A SECOND, MAGS!
5 missed calls from Maggie.
8 new messages
ERNESTO, I GOTTA RUN...
I THINK I'M ABOUT TO GET FIRED.

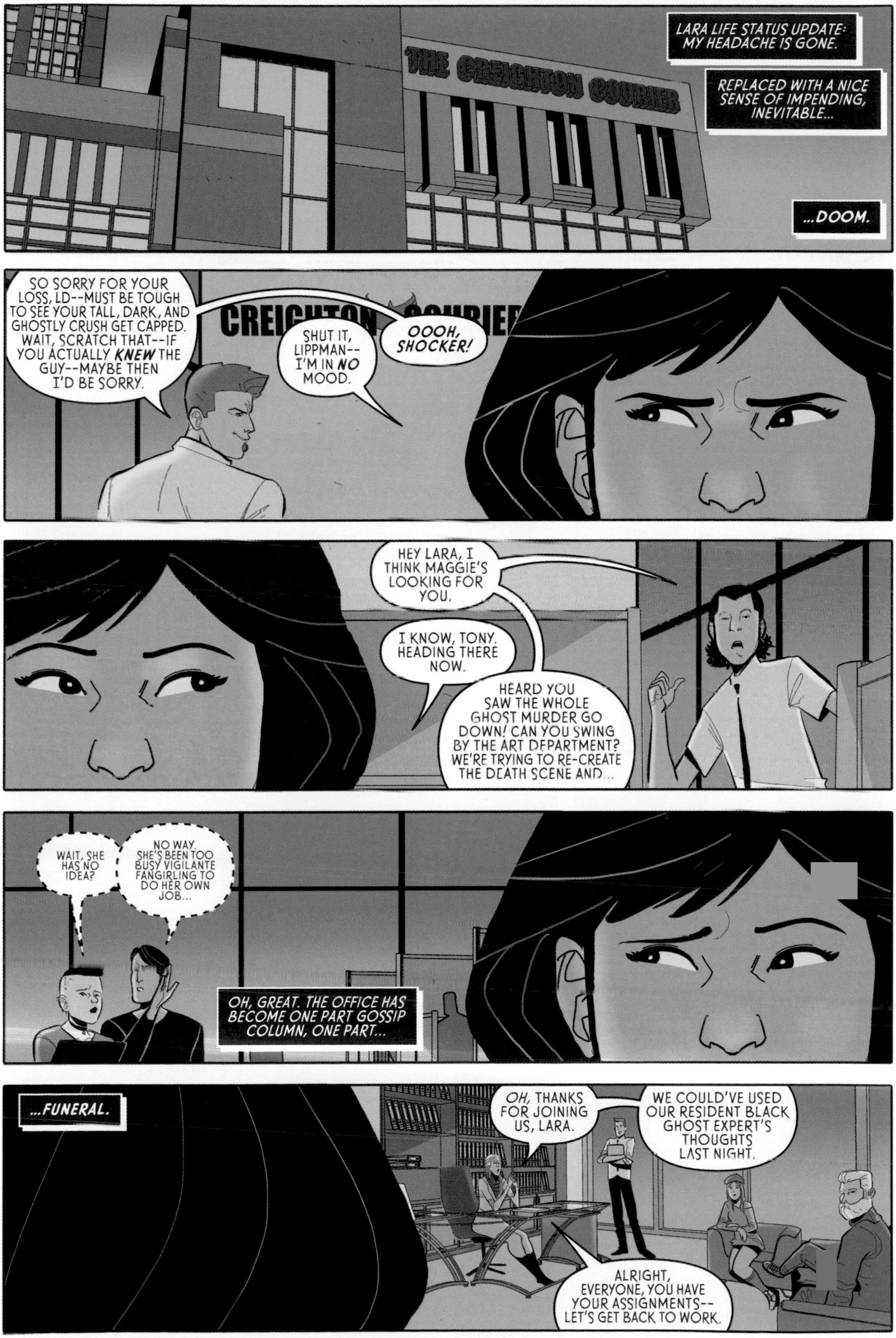
LARA LIFE STATUS UPDATE: MY HEADACHE IS GONE.
REPLACED WITH A NICE SENSE OF IMPENDING, INEVITABLE...
...DOOM.
THE CREIGHTON COURIER
SO SORRY FOR YOUR LOSS, LD--MUST BE TOUGH TO SEE YOUR TALL, DARK, AND GHOSTLY CRUSH GET CAPPED. WAIT, SCRATCH THAT--IF YOU ACTUALLY *KNEW* THE GUY--MAYBE THEN I'D BE SORRY.
OOOH, SHOCKER!
SHUT IT, LIPPMAN--I'M IN *NO* MOOD.
HEY LARA, I THINK MAGGIE'S LOOKING FOR YOU.
I KNOW, TONY. HEADING THERE NOW.
HEARD YOU SAW THE WHOLE GHOST MURDER GO DOWN! CAN YOU SWING BY THE ART DEPARTMENT? WE'RE TRYING TO RE-CREATE THE DEATH SCENE AND...
WAIT, SHE HAS NO IDEA?
NO WAY. SHE'S BEEN TOO BUSY VIGILANTE FANGIRLING TO DO HER OWN JOB...
OH, GREAT. THE OFFICE HAS BECOME ONE PART GOSSIP COLUMN, ONE PART...
...FUNERAL.
*OH,* THANKS FOR JOINING US, LARA.
WE COULD'VE USED OUR RESIDENT BLACK GHOST EXPERT'S THOUGHTS LAST NIGHT.
ALRIGHT, EVERYONE, YOU HAVE YOUR ASSIGNMENTS--LET'S GET BACK TO WORK.

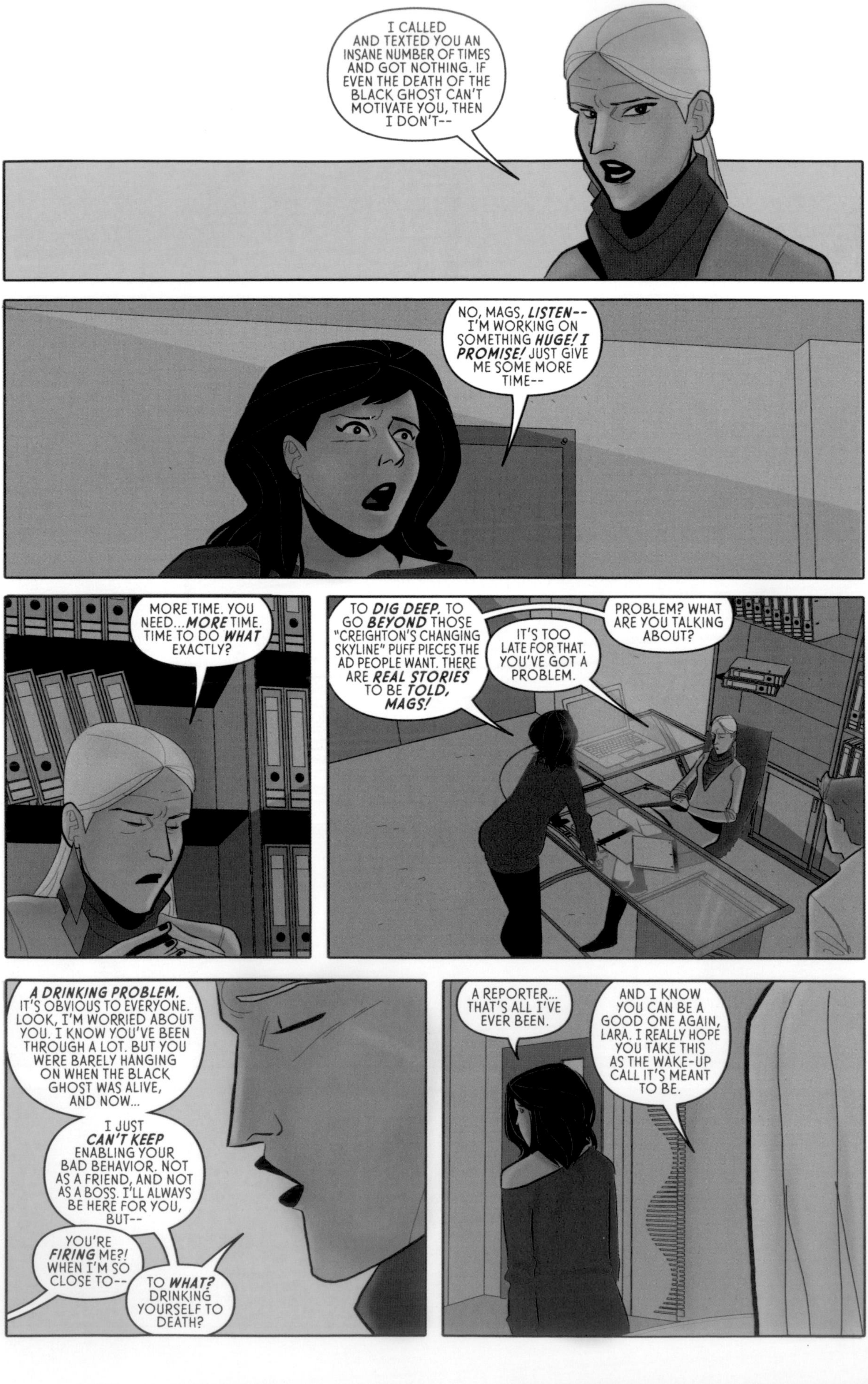
I CALLED AND TEXTED YOU AN INSANE NUMBER OF TIMES AND GOT NOTHING. IF EVEN THE DEATH OF THE BLACK GHOST CAN'T MOTIVATE YOU, THEN I DON'T--
NO, MAGS, ***LISTEN--*** I'M WORKING ON SOMETHING ***HUGE! I PROMISE!*** JUST GIVE ME SOME MORE TIME--
MORE TIME. YOU NEED... ***MORE*** TIME. TIME TO DO ***WHAT*** EXACTLY?
TO ***DIG DEEP.*** TO GO ***BEYOND*** THOSE "CREIGHTON'S CHANGING SKYLINE" PUFF PIECES THE AD PEOPLE WANT. THERE ARE ***REAL STORIES*** TO BE ***TOLD, MAGS!***
IT'S TOO LATE FOR THAT. YOU'VE GOT A PROBLEM.
PROBLEM? WHAT ARE YOU TALKING ABOUT?
***A DRINKING PROBLEM.*** IT'S OBVIOUS TO EVERYONE. LOOK, I'M WORRIED ABOUT YOU. I KNOW YOU'VE BEEN THROUGH A LOT. BUT YOU WERE BARELY HANGING ON WHEN THE BLACK GHOST WAS ALIVE, AND NOW...
I JUST ***CAN'T KEEP*** ENABLING YOUR BAD BEHAVIOR. NOT AS A FRIEND, AND NOT AS A BOSS. I'LL ALWAYS BE HERE FOR YOU, BUT--
YOU'RE ***FIRING*** ME?! WHEN I'M SO CLOSE TO--
TO ***WHAT?*** DRINKING YOURSELF TO DEATH?
A REPORTER... THAT'S ALL I'VE EVER BEEN.
AND I KNOW YOU CAN BE A GOOD ONE AGAIN, LARA. I REALLY HOPE YOU TAKE THIS AS THE WAKE-UP CALL IT'S MEANT TO BE.

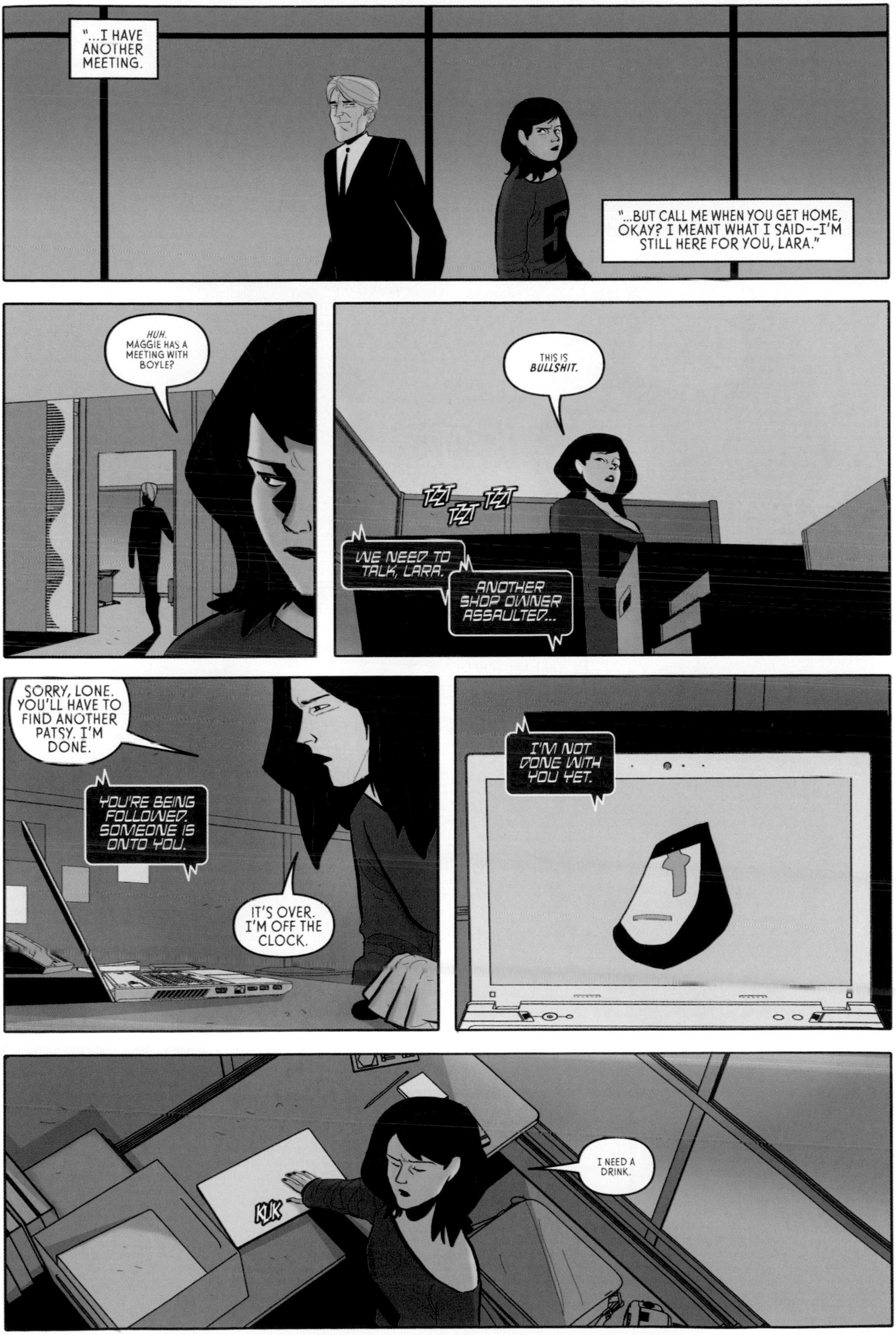
"...I HAVE ANOTHER MEETING.
"...BUT CALL ME WHEN YOU GET HOME, OKAY? I MEANT WHAT I SAID--I'M STILL HERE FOR YOU, LARA."
HUH. MAGGIE HAS A MEETING WITH BOYLE?
THIS IS BULLSHIT.
TZZT TZZT TZZT
WE NEED TO TALK, LARA.
ANOTHER SHOP OWNER ASSAULTED...
SORRY, LONE. YOU'LL HAVE TO FIND ANOTHER PATSY. I'M DONE.
YOU'RE BEING FOLLOWED. SOMEONE IS ONTO YOU.
IT'S OVER. I'M OFF THE CLOCK.
I'M NOT DONE WITH YOU YET.
KLIK
I NEED A DRINK.

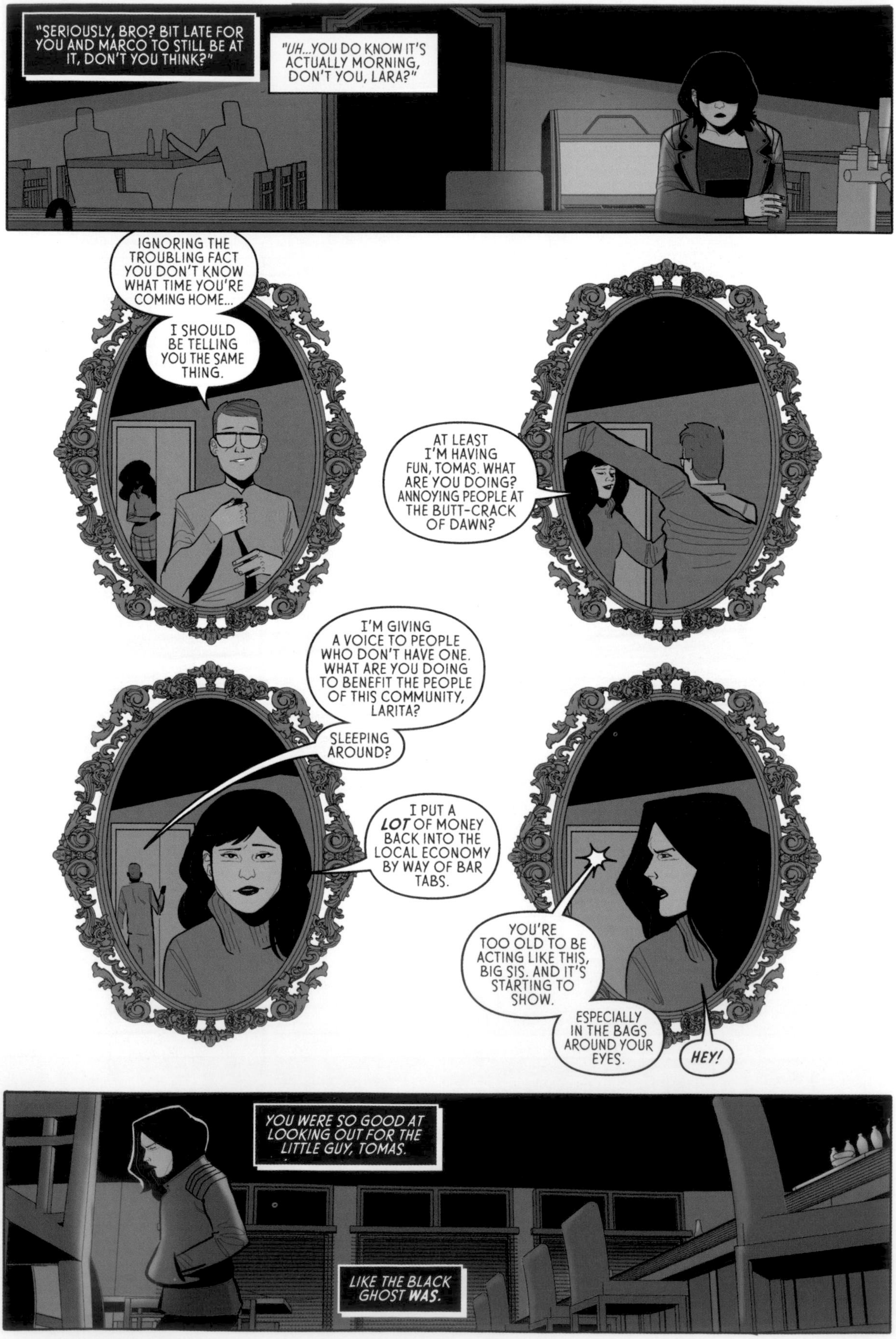
"SERIOUSLY, BRO? BIT LATE FOR YOU AND MARCO TO STILL BE AT IT, DON'T YOU THINK?"
"UH...YOU DO KNOW IT'S ACTUALLY MORNING, DON'T YOU, LARA?"
IGNORING THE TROUBLING FACT YOU DON'T KNOW WHAT TIME YOU'RE COMING HOME...
I SHOULD BE TELLING YOU THE SAME THING.
AT LEAST I'M HAVING FUN, TOMAS. WHAT ARE YOU DOING? ANNOYING PEOPLE AT THE BUTT-CRACK OF DAWN?
I'M GIVING A VOICE TO PEOPLE WHO DON'T HAVE ONE. WHAT ARE YOU DOING TO BENEFIT THE PEOPLE OF THIS COMMUNITY, LARITA?
SLEEPING AROUND?
I PUT A *LOT* OF MONEY BACK INTO THE LOCAL ECONOMY BY WAY OF BAR TABS.
YOU'RE TOO OLD TO BE ACTING LIKE THIS, BIG SIS. AND IT'S STARTING TO SHOW.
ESPECIALLY IN THE BAGS AROUND YOUR EYES.
*HEY!*
*YOU WERE SO GOOD AT LOOKING OUT FOR THE LITTLE GUY, TOMAS.*
*LIKE THE BLACK GHOST* ***WAS.***

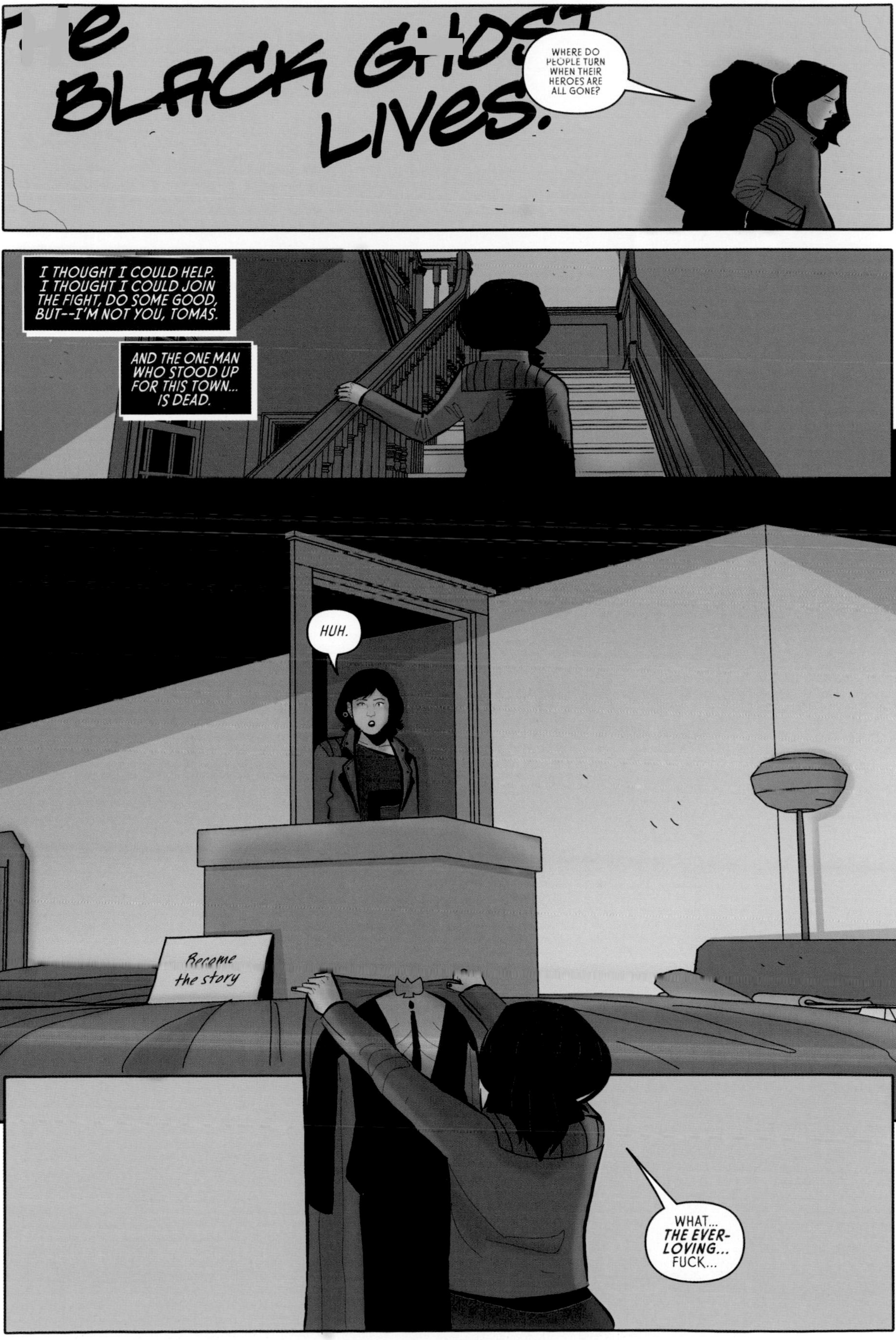
BLACK
LIVES.
WHERE DO PEOPLE TURN WHEN THEIR HEROES ARE ALL GONE?
I THOUGHT I COULD HELP. I THOUGHT I COULD JOIN THE FIGHT, DO SOME GOOD, BUT--I'M NOT YOU, TOMAS.
AND THE ONE MAN WHO STOOD UP FOR THIS TOWN... IS DEAD.
HUH.
Become the story
WHAT... THE EVER-LOVING... FUCK...

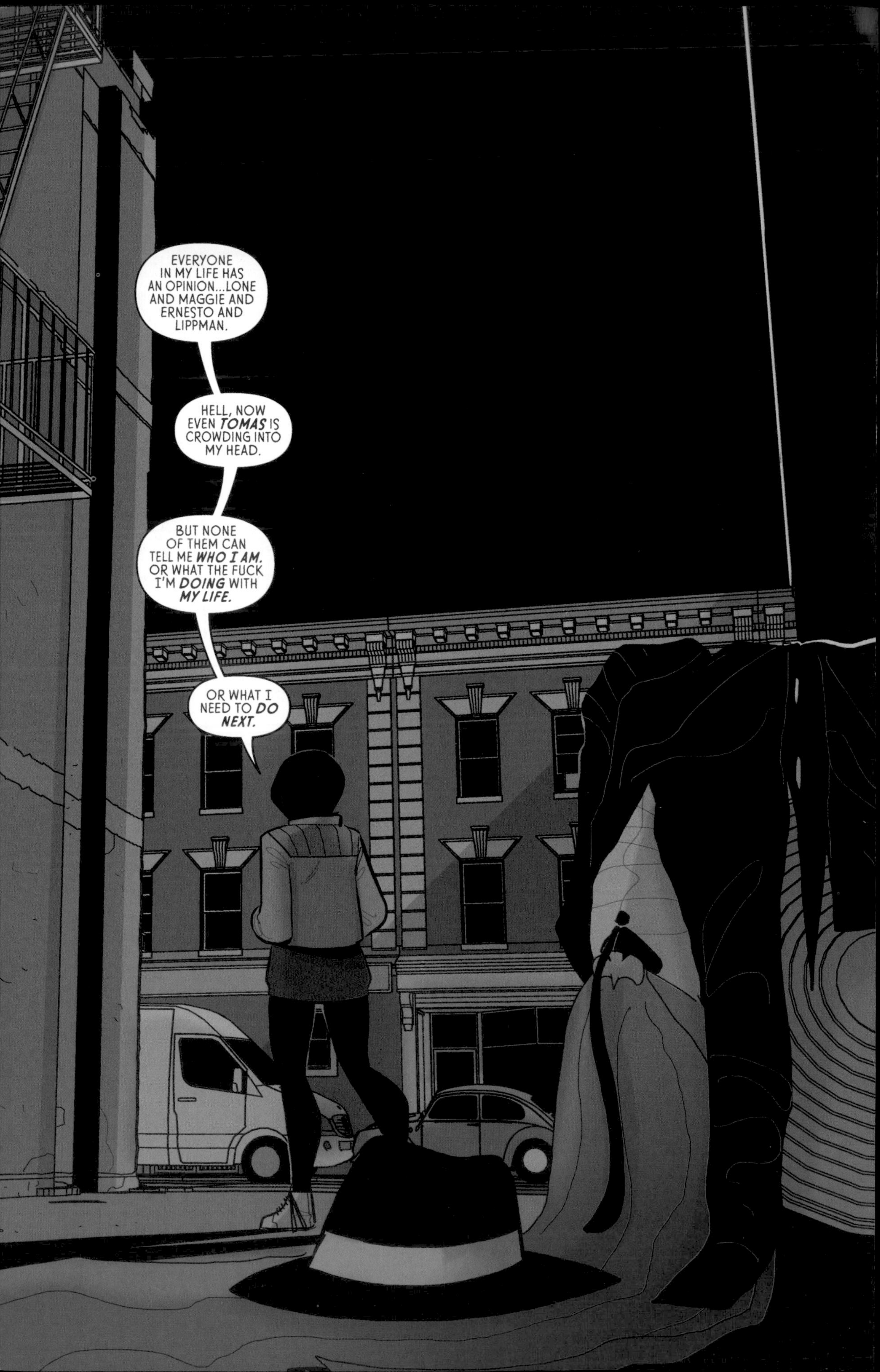
EVERYONE IN MY LIFE HAS AN OPINION...LONE AND MAGGIE AND ERNESTO AND LIPPMAN.
HELL, NOW EVEN *TOMAS* IS CROWDING INTO MY HEAD.
BUT NONE OF THEM CAN TELL ME *WHO I AM*, OR WHAT THE FUCK I'M *DOING* WITH *MY LIFE.*
OR WHAT I NEED TO *DO NEXT.*

# CHAPTER 3
## DO EVIL IN RETURN
COVER BY VERONICA FISH

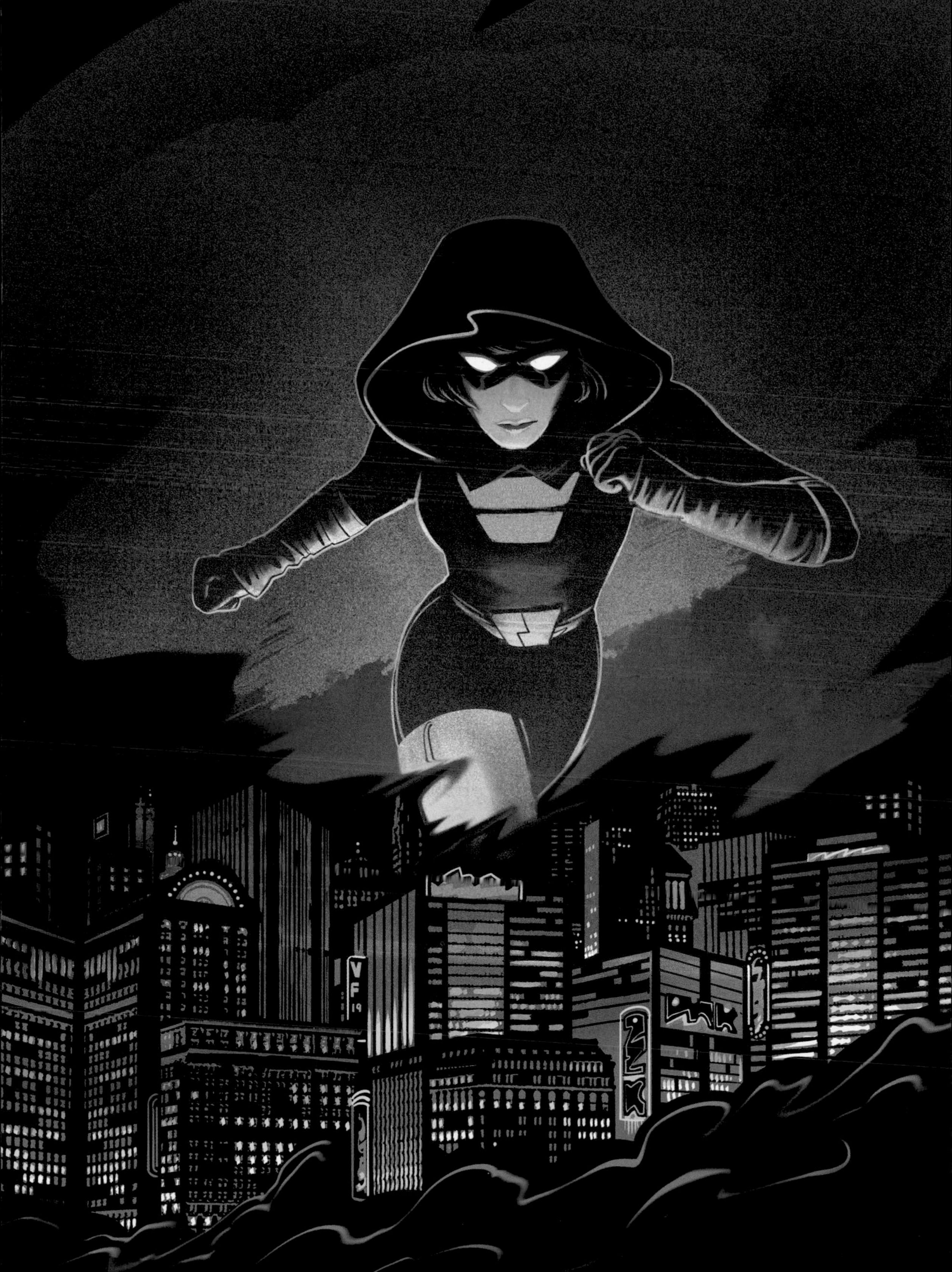

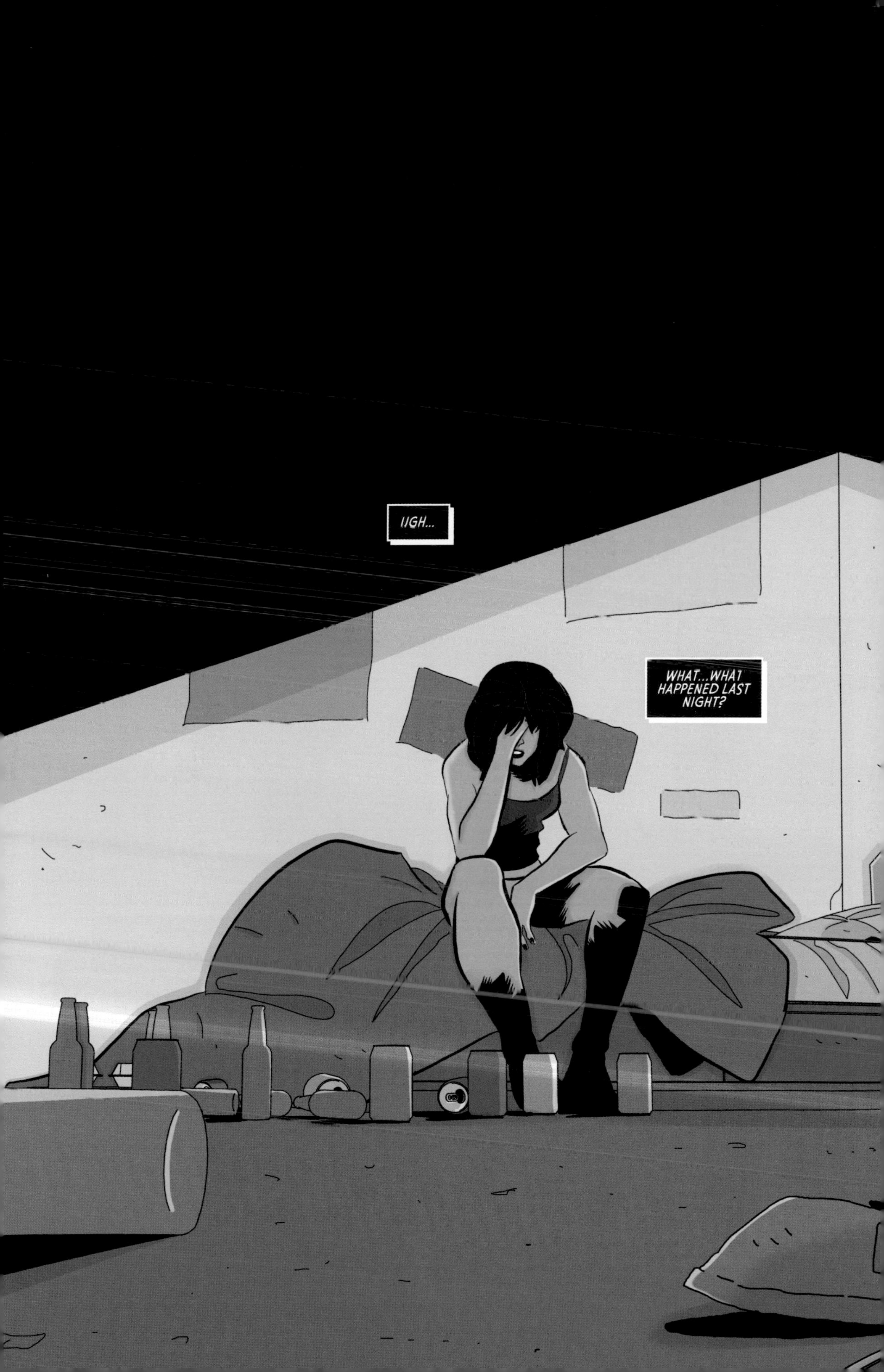
UGH...
WHAT...WHAT HAPPENED LAST NIGHT?

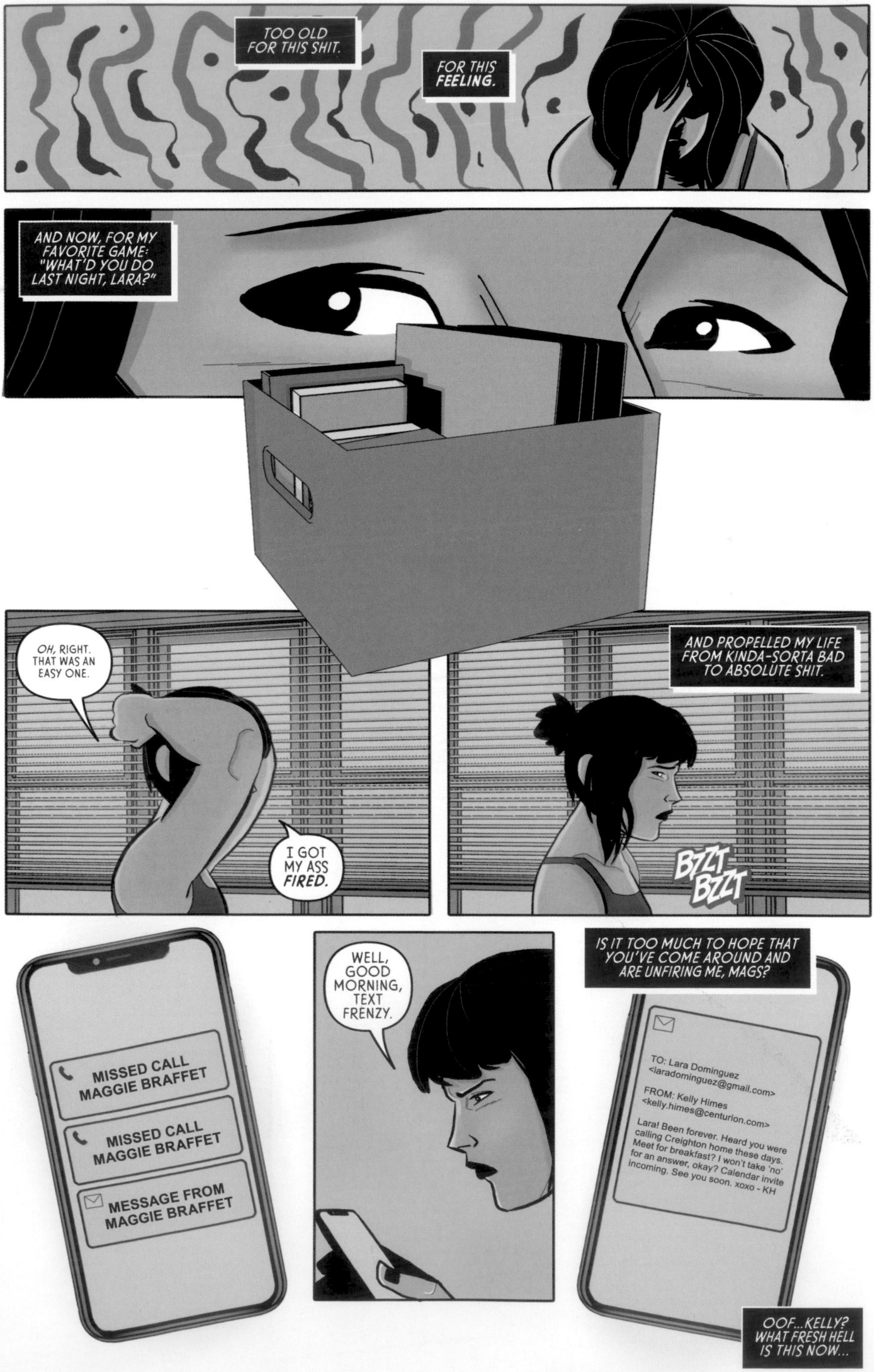
TOO OLD FOR THIS SHIT.
FOR THIS FEELING.
AND NOW, FOR MY FAVORITE GAME: "WHAT'D YOU DO LAST NIGHT, LARA?"
OH, RIGHT. THAT WAS AN EASY ONE.
I GOT MY ASS FIRED.
AND PROPELLED MY LIFE FROM KINDA-SORTA BAD TO ABSOLUTE SHIT.
BZZT BZZT
MISSED CALL MAGGIE BRAFFET
MISSED CALL MAGGIE BRAFFET
MESSAGE FROM MAGGIE BRAFFET
WELL, GOOD MORNING, TEXT FRENZY.
IS IT TOO MUCH TO HOPE THAT YOU'VE COME AROUND AND ARE UNFIRING ME, MAGS?
TO: Lara Dominguez <laradominguez@gmail.com>
FROM: Kelly Himes <kelly.himes@centurion.com>
Lara! Been forever. Heard you were calling Creighton home these days. Meet for breakfast? I won't take 'no' for an answer, okay? Calendar invite incoming. See you soon. xoxo - KH
OOF...KELLY? WHAT FRESH HELL IS THIS NOW...

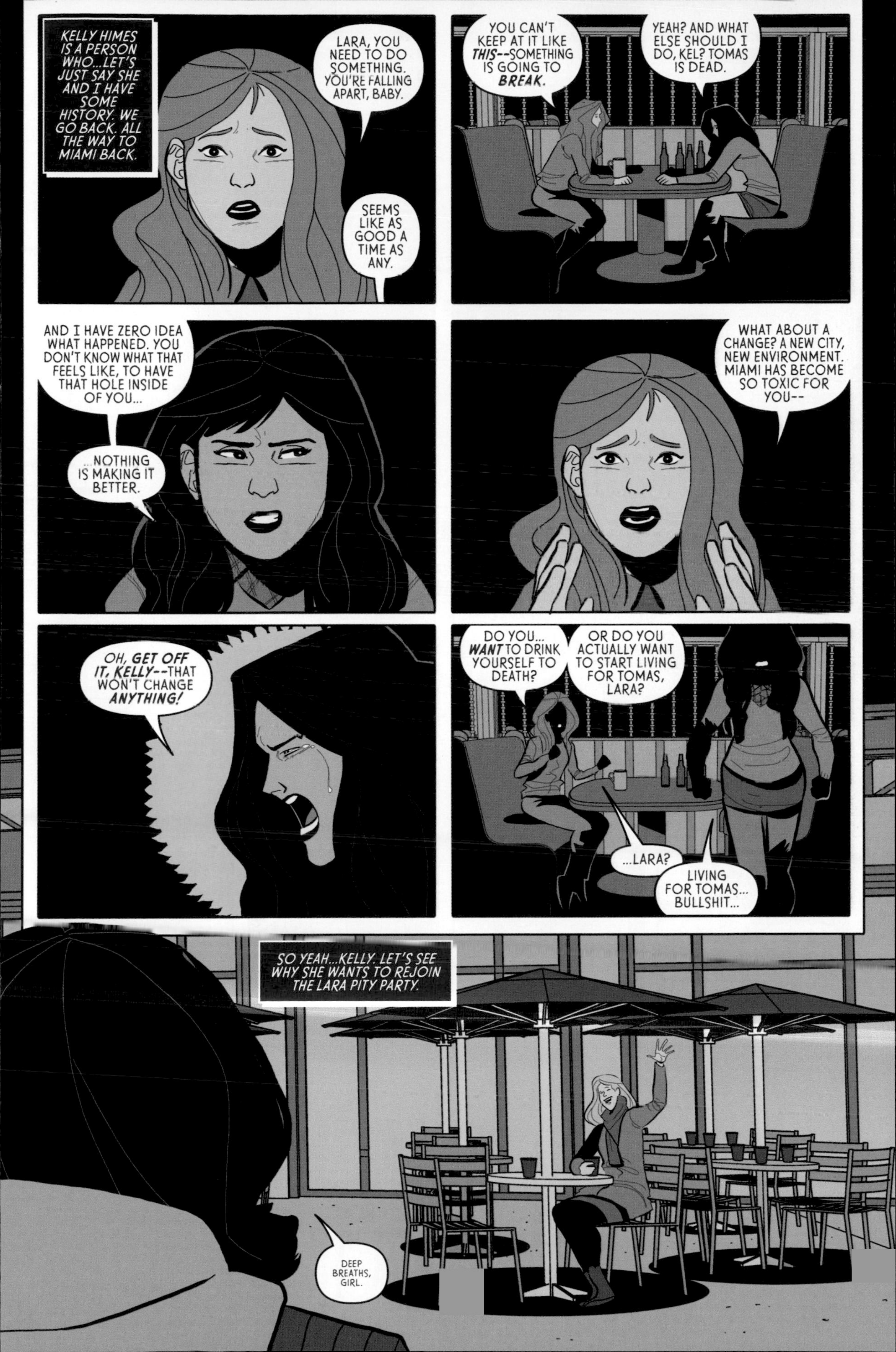

KELLY HIMES IS A PERSON WHO...LET'S JUST SAY SHE AND I HAVE SOME HISTORY. WE GO BACK. ALL THE WAY TO MIAMI BACK.
LARA, YOU NEED TO DO SOMETHING. YOU'RE FALLING APART, BABY.
SEEMS LIKE AS GOOD A TIME AS ANY.
YOU CAN'T KEEP AT IT LIKE **THIS**--SOMETHING IS GOING TO **BREAK.**
YEAH? AND WHAT ELSE SHOULD I DO, KEL? TOMAS IS DEAD.
AND I HAVE ZERO IDEA WHAT HAPPENED. YOU DON'T KNOW WHAT THAT FEELS LIKE, TO HAVE THAT HOLE INSIDE OF YOU...
...NOTHING IS MAKING IT BETTER.
WHAT ABOUT A CHANGE? A NEW CITY, NEW ENVIRONMENT. MIAMI HAS BECOME SO TOXIC FOR YOU--
OH, **GET OFF IT, KELLY**--THAT WON'T CHANGE **ANYTHING!**
DO YOU... **WANT** TO DRINK YOURSELF TO DEATH?
OR DO YOU ACTUALLY WANT TO START LIVING FOR TOMAS, LARA?
...LARA?
LIVING FOR TOMAS... BULLSHIT...
SO YEAH...KELLY. LET'S SEE WHY SHE WANTS TO REJOIN THE LARA PITY PARTY.
DEEP BREATHS, GIRL.

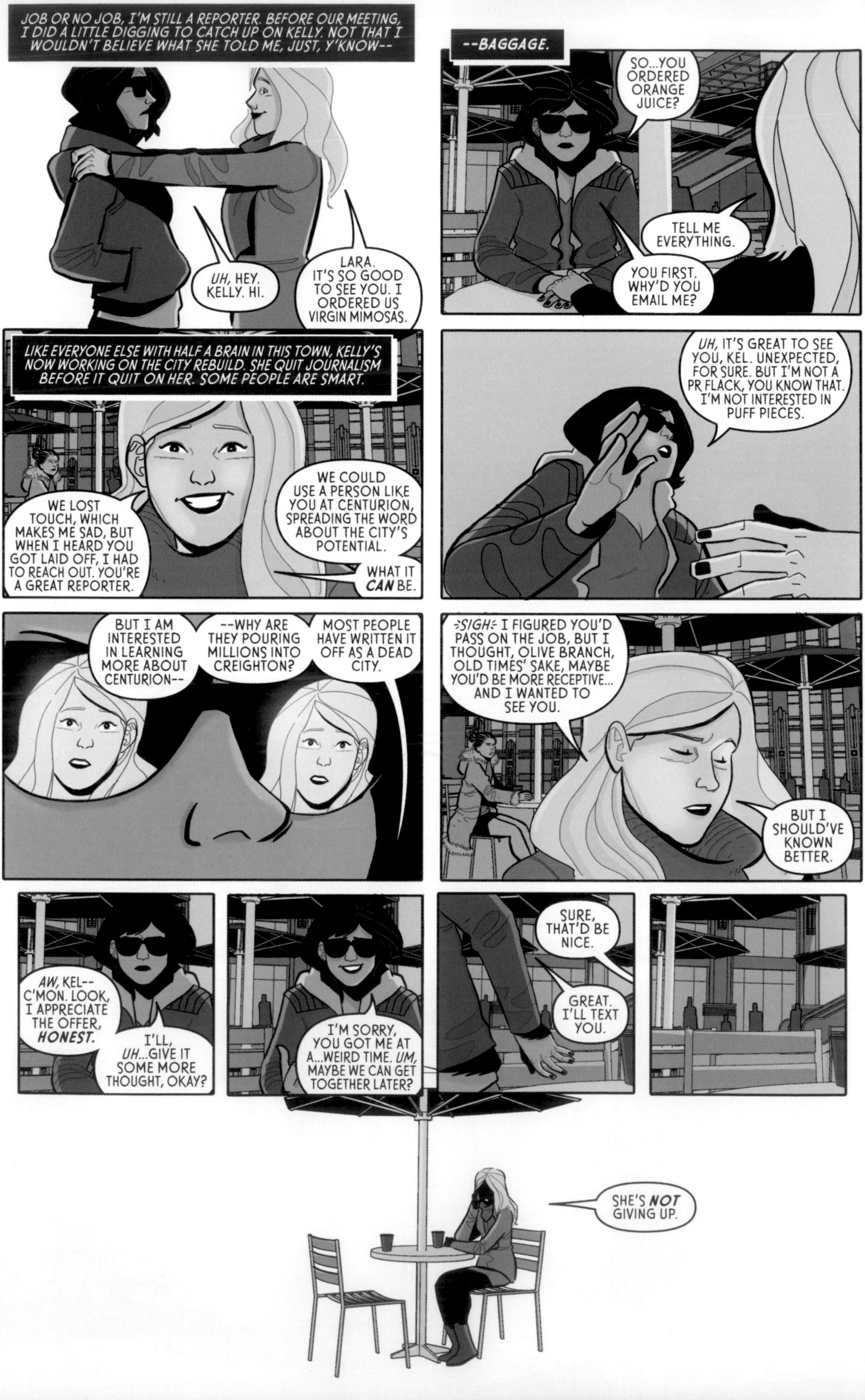
JOB OR NO JOB, I'M STILL A REPORTER. BEFORE OUR MEETING, I DID A LITTLE DIGGING TO CATCH UP ON KELLY. NOT THAT I WOULDN'T BELIEVE WHAT SHE TOLD ME, JUST, Y'KNOW--
LARA. IT'S SO GOOD TO SEE YOU. I ORDERED US VIRGIN MIMOSAS.
UH, HEY. KELLY. HI.
--BAGGAGE.
SO...YOU ORDERED ORANGE JUICE?
TELL ME EVERYTHING.
YOU FIRST. WHY'D YOU EMAIL ME?
LIKE EVERYONE ELSE WITH HALF A BRAIN IN THIS TOWN, KELLY'S NOW WORKING ON THE CITY REBUILD. SHE QUIT JOURNALISM BEFORE IT QUIT ON HER. SOME PEOPLE ARE SMART.
WE LOST TOUCH, WHICH MAKES ME SAD, BUT WHEN I HEARD YOU GOT LAID OFF, I HAD TO REACH OUT. YOU'RE A GREAT REPORTER.
WE COULD USE A PERSON LIKE YOU AT CENTURION, SPREADING THE WORD ABOUT THE CITY'S POTENTIAL.
WHAT IT CAN BE.
UH, IT'S GREAT TO SEE YOU, KEL. UNEXPECTED, FOR SURE. BUT I'M NOT A PR FLACK, YOU KNOW THAT. I'M NOT INTERESTED IN PUFF PIECES.
BUT I AM INTERESTED IN LEARNING MORE ABOUT CENTURION--
--WHY ARE THEY POURING MILLIONS INTO CREIGHTON?
MOST PEOPLE HAVE WRITTEN IT OFF AS A DEAD CITY.
≈SIGH≈ I FIGURED YOU'D PASS ON THE JOB, BUT I THOUGHT, OLIVE BRANCH, OLD TIMES' SAKE, MAYBE YOU'D BE MORE RECEPTIVE... AND I WANTED TO SEE YOU.
BUT I SHOULD'VE KNOWN BETTER.
AW, KEL-- C'MON. LOOK, I APPRECIATE THE OFFER, HONEST.
I'LL, UH...GIVE IT SOME MORE THOUGHT, OKAY?
I'M SORRY, YOU GOT ME AT A...WEIRD TIME. UM, MAYBE WE CAN GET TOGETHER LATER?
SURE, THAT'D BE NICE.
GREAT. I'LL TEXT YOU.
SHE'S NOT GIVING UP.

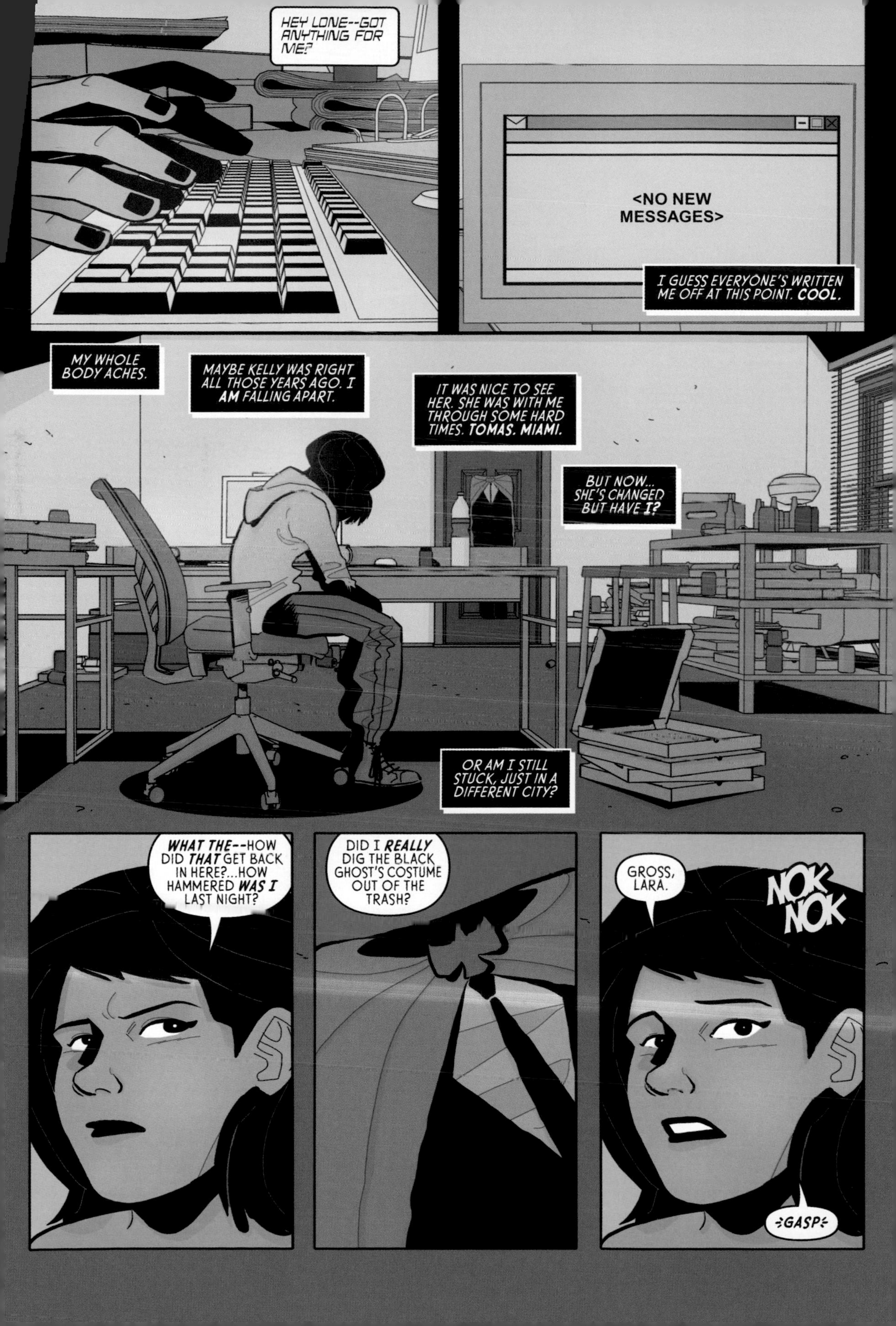
HEY LONE--GOT ANYTHING FOR ME?
<NO NEW MESSAGES>
I GUESS EVERYONE'S WRITTEN ME OFF AT THIS POINT. COOL.
MY WHOLE BODY ACHES.
MAYBE KELLY WAS RIGHT ALL THOSE YEARS AGO. I AM FALLING APART.
IT WAS NICE TO SEE HER. SHE WAS WITH ME THROUGH SOME HARD TIMES. TOMAS. MIAMI.
BUT NOW... SHE'S CHANGED BUT HAVE I?
OR AM I STILL STUCK, JUST IN A DIFFERENT CITY?
WHAT THE--HOW DID THAT GET BACK IN HERE?...HOW HAMMERED WAS I LAST NIGHT?
DID I REALLY DIG THE BLACK GHOST'S COSTUME OUT OF THE TRASH?
GROSS, LARA.
NOK NOK
GASP

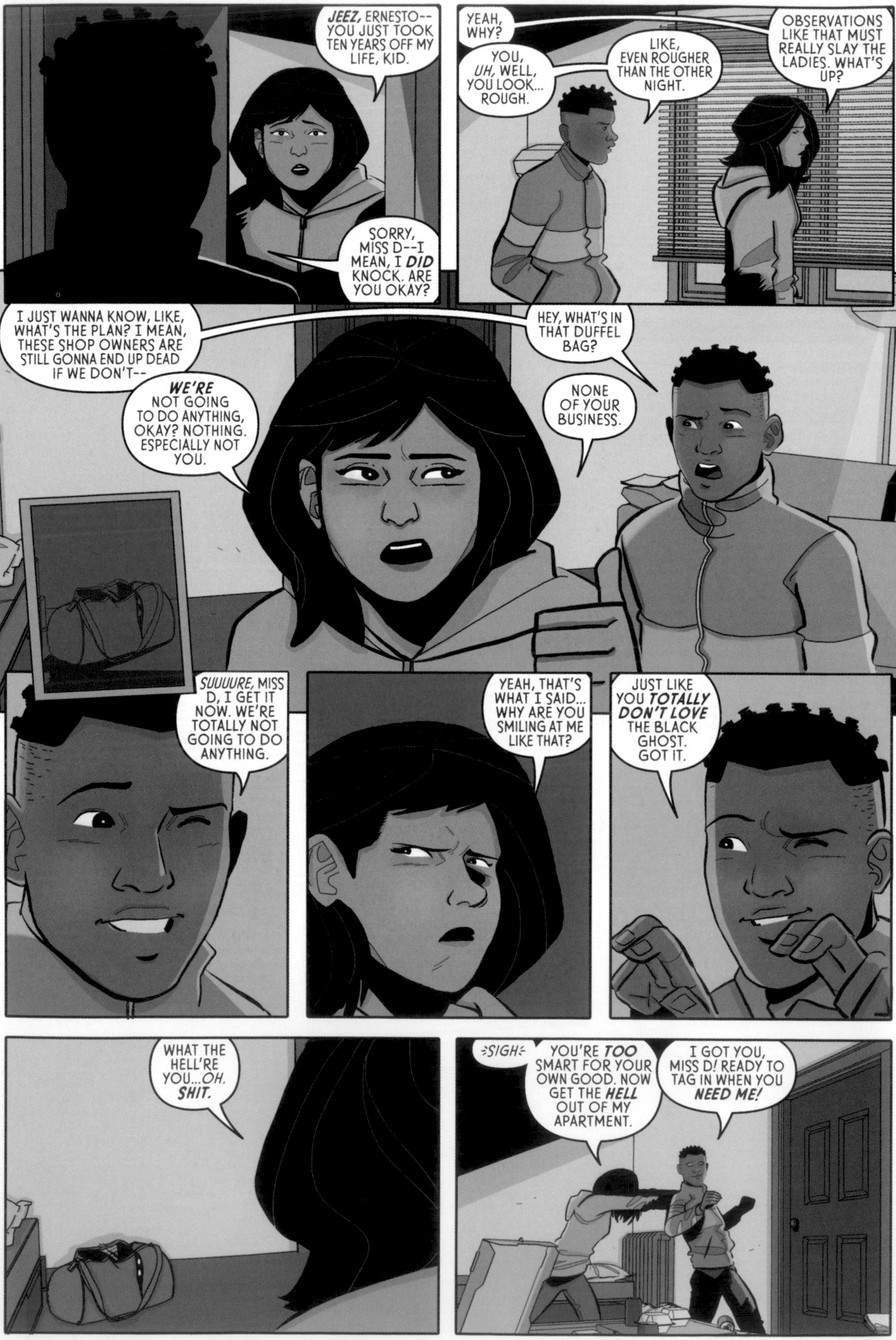

JEEZ, ERNESTO--YOU JUST TOOK TEN YEARS OFF MY LIFE, KID.
SORRY, MISS D--I MEAN, I DID KNOCK. ARE YOU OKAY?
YEAH, WHY?
YOU, UH, WELL, YOU LOOK... ROUGH.
LIKE, EVEN ROUGHER THAN THE OTHER NIGHT.
OBSERVATIONS LIKE THAT MUST REALLY SLAY THE LADIES. WHAT'S UP?
HEY, WHAT'S IN THAT DUFFEL BAG?
NONE OF YOUR BUSINESS.
I JUST WANNA KNOW, LIKE, WHAT'S THE PLAN? I MEAN, THESE SHOP OWNERS ARE STILL GONNA END UP DEAD IF WE DON'T--
WE'RE NOT GOING TO DO ANYTHING, OKAY? NOTHING. ESPECIALLY NOT YOU.
SUUUURE, MISS D, I GET IT NOW. WE'RE TOTALLY NOT GOING TO DO ANYTHING.
YEAH, THAT'S WHAT I SAID... WHY ARE YOU SMILING AT ME LIKE THAT?
JUST LIKE YOU TOTALLY DON'T LOVE THE BLACK GHOST. GOT IT.
WHAT THE HELL'RE YOU...OH. SHIT.
SIGH
YOU'RE TOO SMART FOR YOUR OWN GOOD. NOW GET THE HELL OUT OF MY APARTMENT.
I GOT YOU, MISS D! READY TO TAG IN WHEN YOU NEED ME!

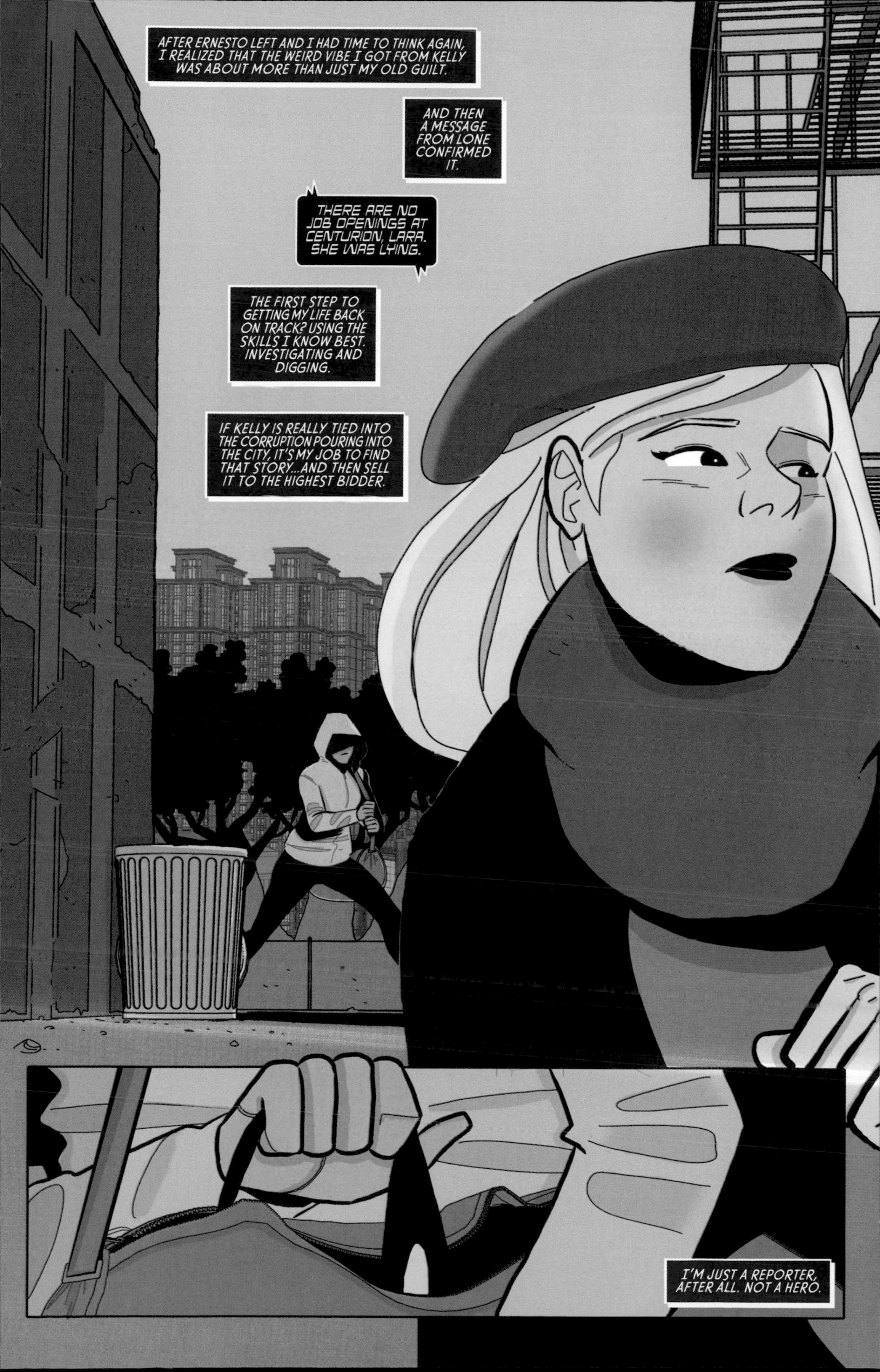
AFTER ERNESTO LEFT AND I HAD TIME TO THINK AGAIN, I REALIZED THAT THE WEIRD VIBE I GOT FROM KELLY WAS ABOUT MORE THAN JUST MY OLD GUILT.
AND THEN A MESSAGE FROM LONE CONFIRMED IT.
THERE ARE NO JOB OPENINGS AT CENTURION, LARA. SHE WAS LYING.
THE FIRST STEP TO GETTING MY LIFE BACK ON TRACK? USING THE SKILLS I KNOW BEST. INVESTIGATING AND DIGGING.
IF KELLY IS REALLY TIED INTO THE CORRUPTION POURING INTO THE CITY, IT'S MY JOB TO FIND THAT STORY...AND THEN SELL IT TO THE HIGHEST BIDDER.
I'M JUST A REPORTER, AFTER ALL. NOT A HERO.

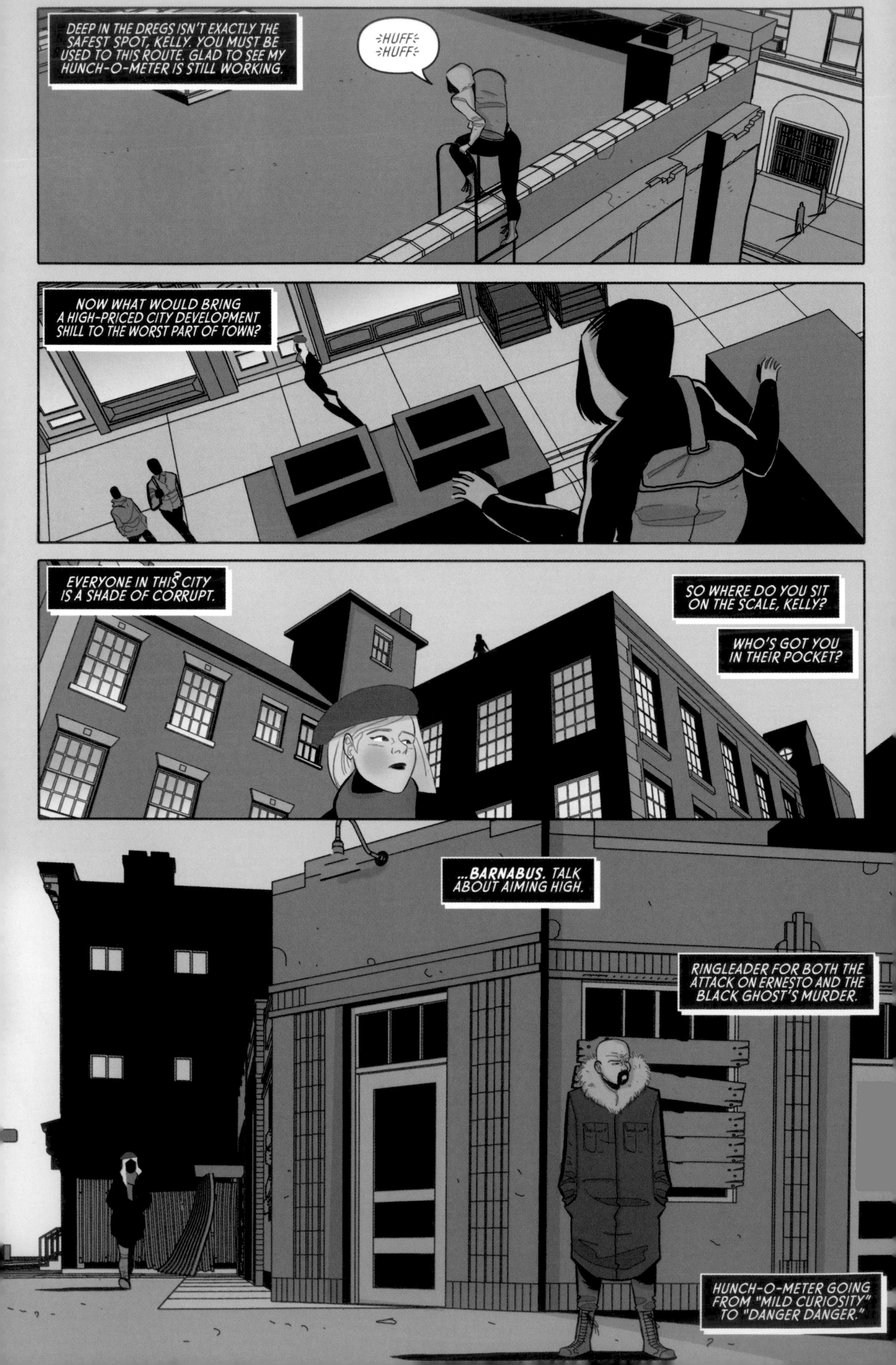
DEEP IN THE DREGS ISN'T EXACTLY THE SAFEST SPOT, KELLY. YOU MUST BE USED TO THIS ROUTE. GLAD TO SEE MY HUNCH-O-METER IS STILL WORKING.
HUFF HUFF
NOW WHAT WOULD BRING A HIGH-PRICED CITY DEVELOPMENT SHILL TO THE WORST PART OF TOWN?
EVERYONE IN THIS CITY IS A SHADE OF CORRUPT.
SO WHERE DO YOU SIT ON THE SCALE, KELLY?
WHO'S GOT YOU IN THEIR POCKET?
...BARNABUS. TALK ABOUT AIMING HIGH.
RINGLEADER FOR BOTH THE ATTACK ON ERNESTO AND THE BLACK GHOST'S MURDER.
HUNCH-O-METER GOING FROM "MILD CURIOSITY" TO "DANGER DANGER."

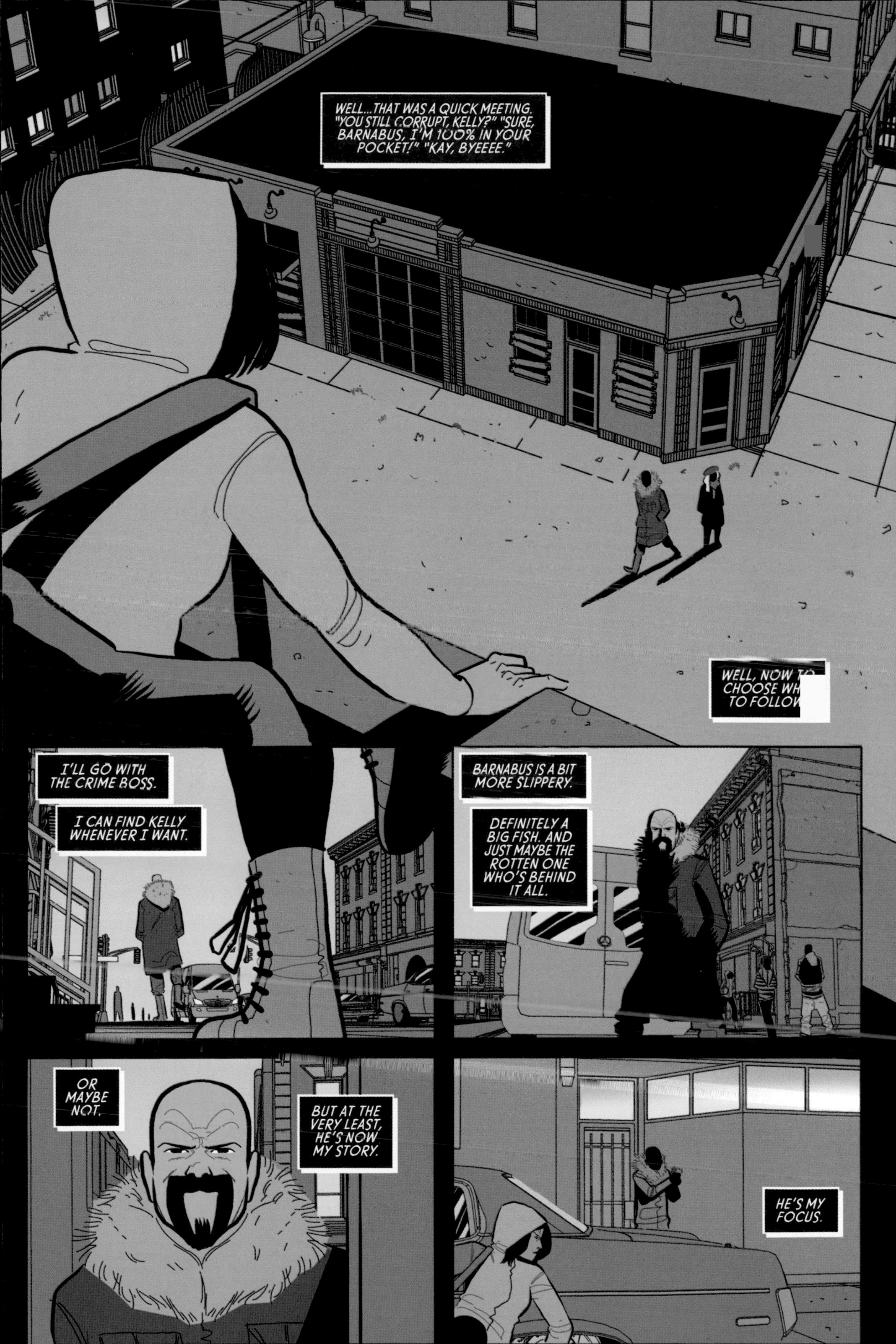
WELL...THAT WAS A QUICK MEETING. "YOU STILL CORRUPT, KELLY?" "SURE, BARNABUS, I'M 100% IN YOUR POCKET!" "KAY, BYEEEE."
WELL, NOW TO CHOOSE WH TO FOLLOW
I'LL GO WITH THE CRIME BOSS.
I CAN FIND KELLY WHENEVER I WANT.
BARNABUS IS A BIT MORE SLIPPERY.
DEFINITELY A BIG FISH. AND JUST MAYBE THE ROTTEN ONE WHO'S BEHIND IT ALL.
OR MAYBE NOT.
BUT AT THE VERY LEAST, HE'S NOW MY STORY.
HE'S MY FOCUS.

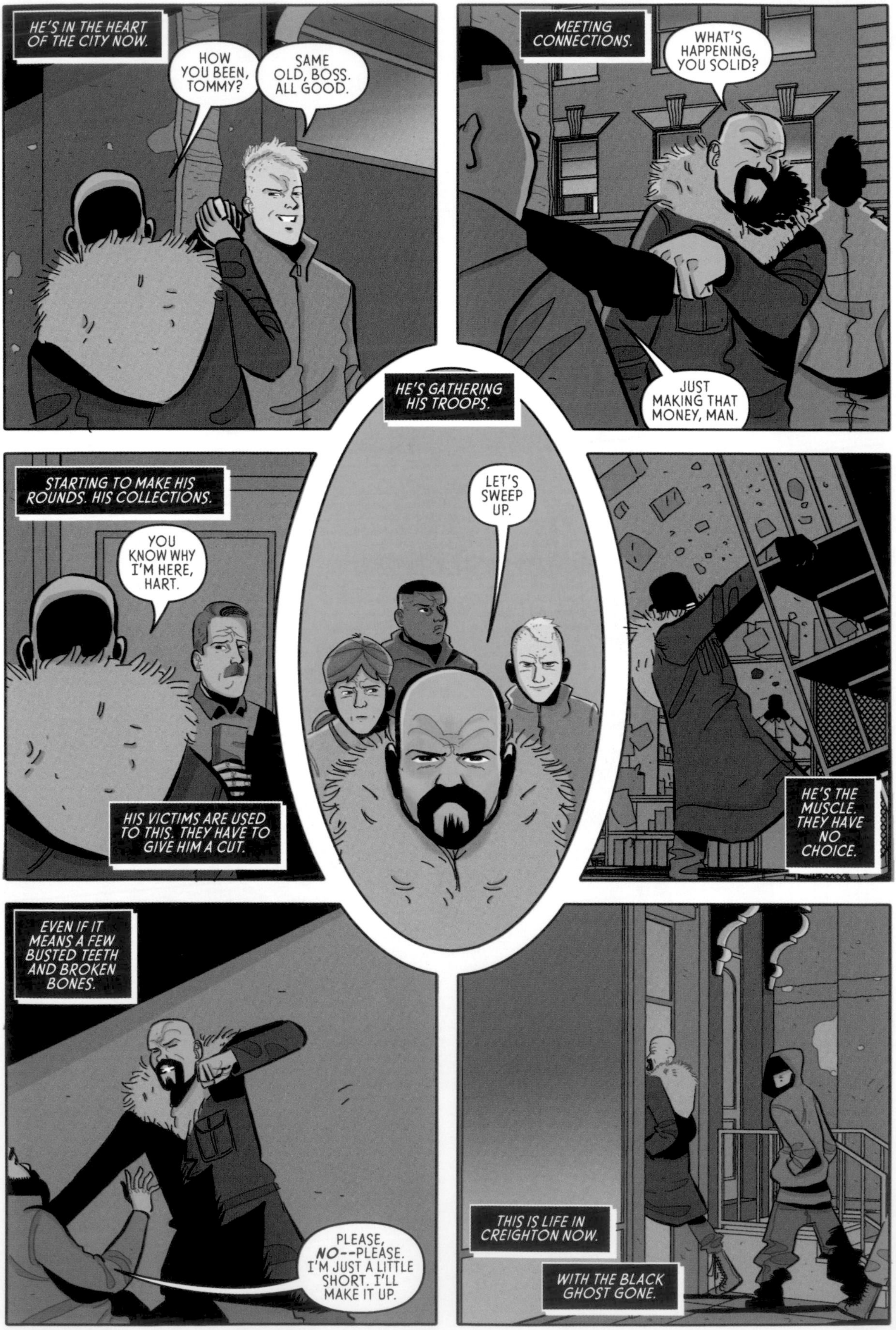
HE'S IN THE HEART OF THE CITY NOW.
HOW YOU BEEN, TOMMY?
SAME OLD, BOSS. ALL GOOD.
MEETING CONNECTIONS.
WHAT'S HAPPENING, YOU SOLID?
JUST MAKING THAT MONEY, MAN.
HE'S GATHERING HIS TROOPS.
LET'S SWEEP UP.
STARTING TO MAKE HIS ROUNDS. HIS COLLECTIONS.
YOU KNOW WHY I'M HERE, HART.
HIS VICTIMS ARE USED TO THIS. THEY HAVE TO GIVE HIM A CUT.
HE'S THE MUSCLE. THEY HAVE NO CHOICE.
EVEN IF IT MEANS A FEW BUSTED TEETH AND BROKEN BONES.
PLEASE, NO--PLEASE. I'M JUST A LITTLE SHORT. I'LL MAKE IT UP.
THIS IS LIFE IN CREIGHTON NOW.
WITH THE BLACK GHOST GONE.

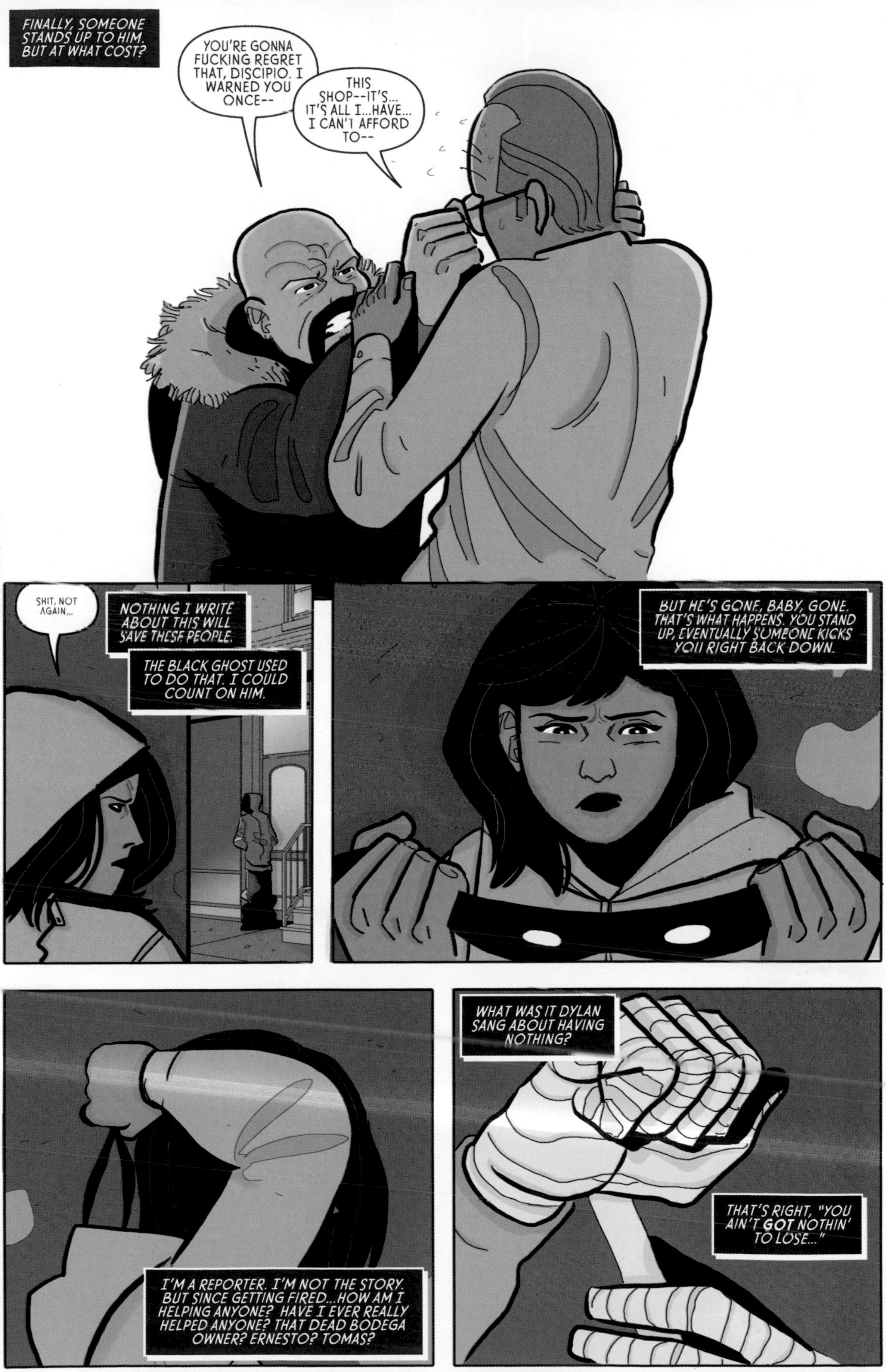
FINALLY, SOMEONE STANDS UP TO HIM. BUT AT WHAT COST?
YOU'RE GONNA FUCKING REGRET THAT, DISCIPIO. I WARNED YOU ONCE--
THIS SHOP--IT'S... IT'S ALL I...HAVE... I CAN'T AFFORD TO--
SHIT, NOT AGAIN...
NOTHING I WRITE ABOUT THIS WILL SAVE THESE PEOPLE.
THE BLACK GHOST USED TO DO THAT. I COULD COUNT ON HIM.
BUT HE'S GONE, BABY, GONE. THAT'S WHAT HAPPENS. YOU STAND UP, EVENTUALLY SOMEONE KICKS YOU RIGHT BACK DOWN.
I'M A REPORTER. I'M NOT THE STORY. BUT SINCE GETTING FIRED...HOW AM I HELPING ANYONE? HAVE I EVER REALLY HELPED ANYONE? THAT DEAD BODEGA OWNER? ERNESTO? TOMAS?
WHAT WAS IT DYLAN SANG ABOUT HAVING NOTHING?
THAT'S RIGHT, "YOU AIN'T GOT NOTHIN' TO LOSE..."

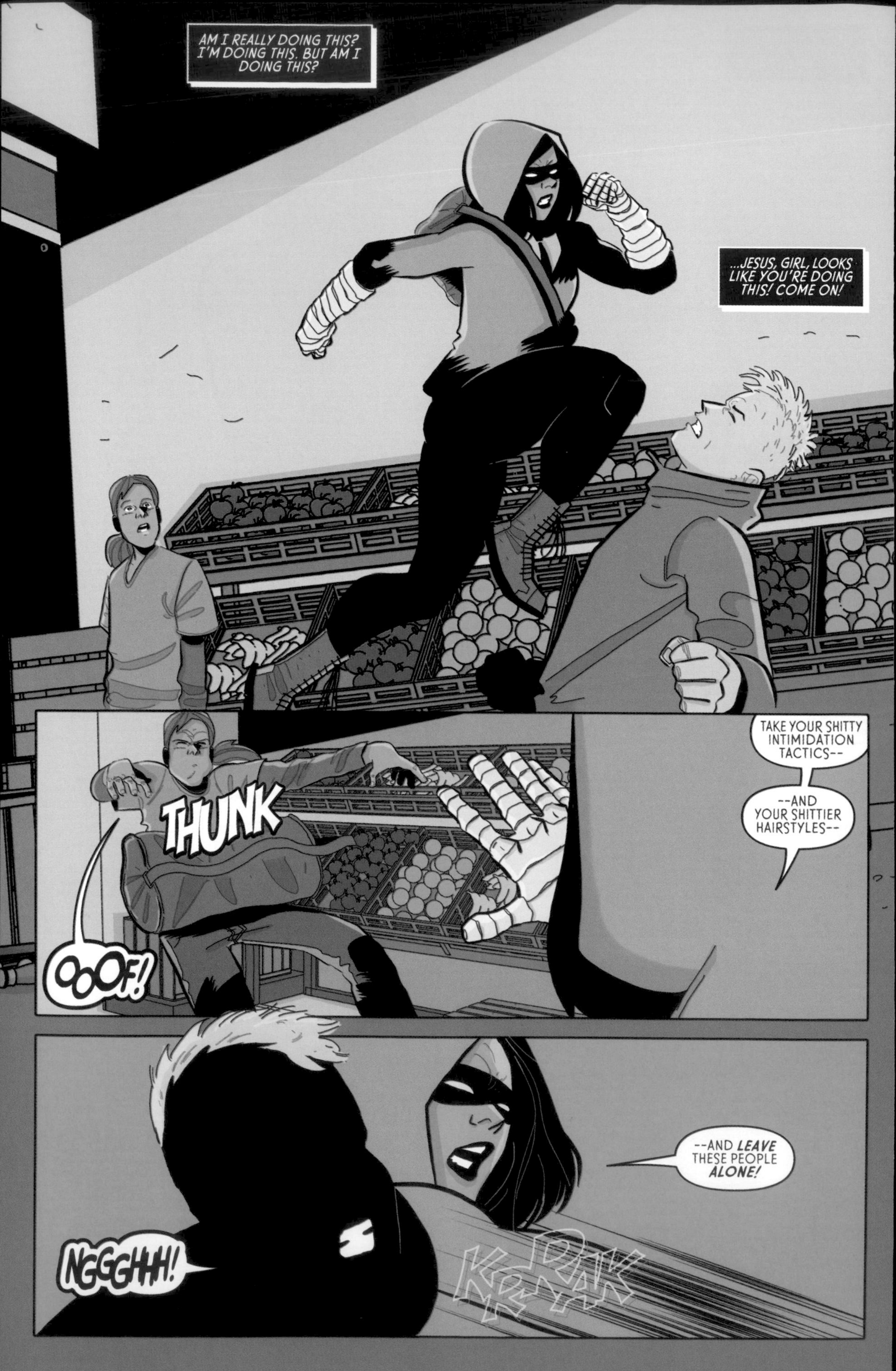
AM I REALLY DOING THIS? I'M DOING THIS. BUT AM I DOING THIS?
...JESUS, GIRL, LOOKS LIKE YOU'RE DOING THIS! COME ON!
TAKE YOUR SHITTY INTIMIDATION TACTICS--
--AND YOUR SHITTIER HAIRSTYLES--
THUNK
OOOF!
--AND *LEAVE* THESE PEOPLE *ALONE!*
NGGGHH!

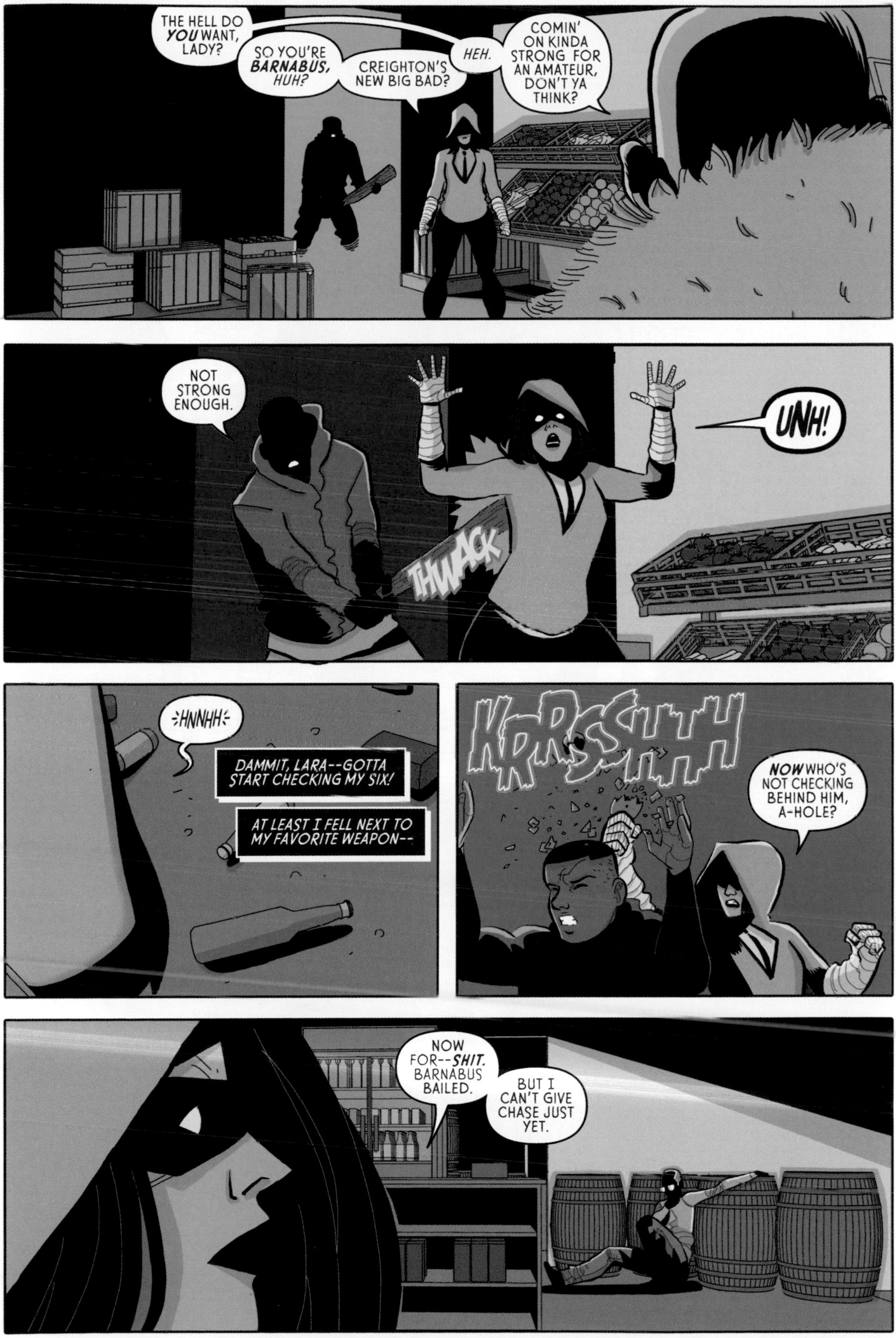
THE HELL DO *YOU* WANT, LADY?
SO YOU'RE *BARNABUS,* HUH?
CREIGHTON'S NEW BIG BAD?
HEH.
COMIN' ON KINDA STRONG FOR AN AMATEUR, DON'T YA THINK?
NOT STRONG ENOUGH.
UNH!
THWACK
HNNHH
DAMMIT, LARA--GOTTA START CHECKING MY SIX!
AT LEAST I FELL NEXT TO MY FAVORITE WEAPON--
KRRSSHHH
*NOW* WHO'S NOT CHECKING BEHIND HIM, A-HOLE?
NOW FOR--*SHIT.* BARNABUS BAILED.
BUT I CAN'T GIVE CHASE JUST YET.

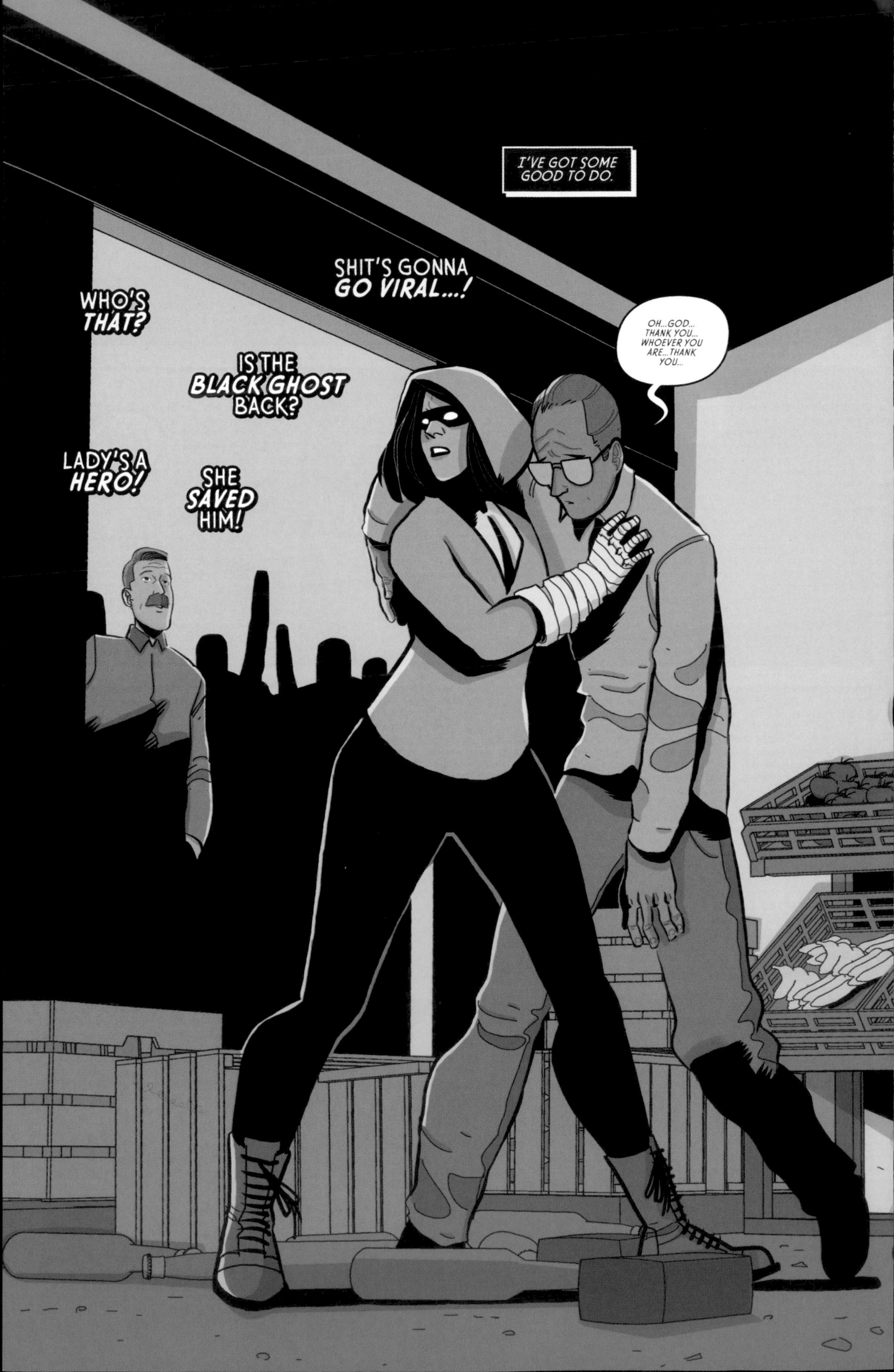
I'VE GOT SOME GOOD TO DO.
SHIT'S GONNA GO VIRAL...!
OH...GOD... THANK YOU... WHOEVER YOU ARE...THANK YOU...
WHO'S THAT?
IS THE BLACK GHOST BACK?
LADY'S A HERO!
SHE SAVED HIM!

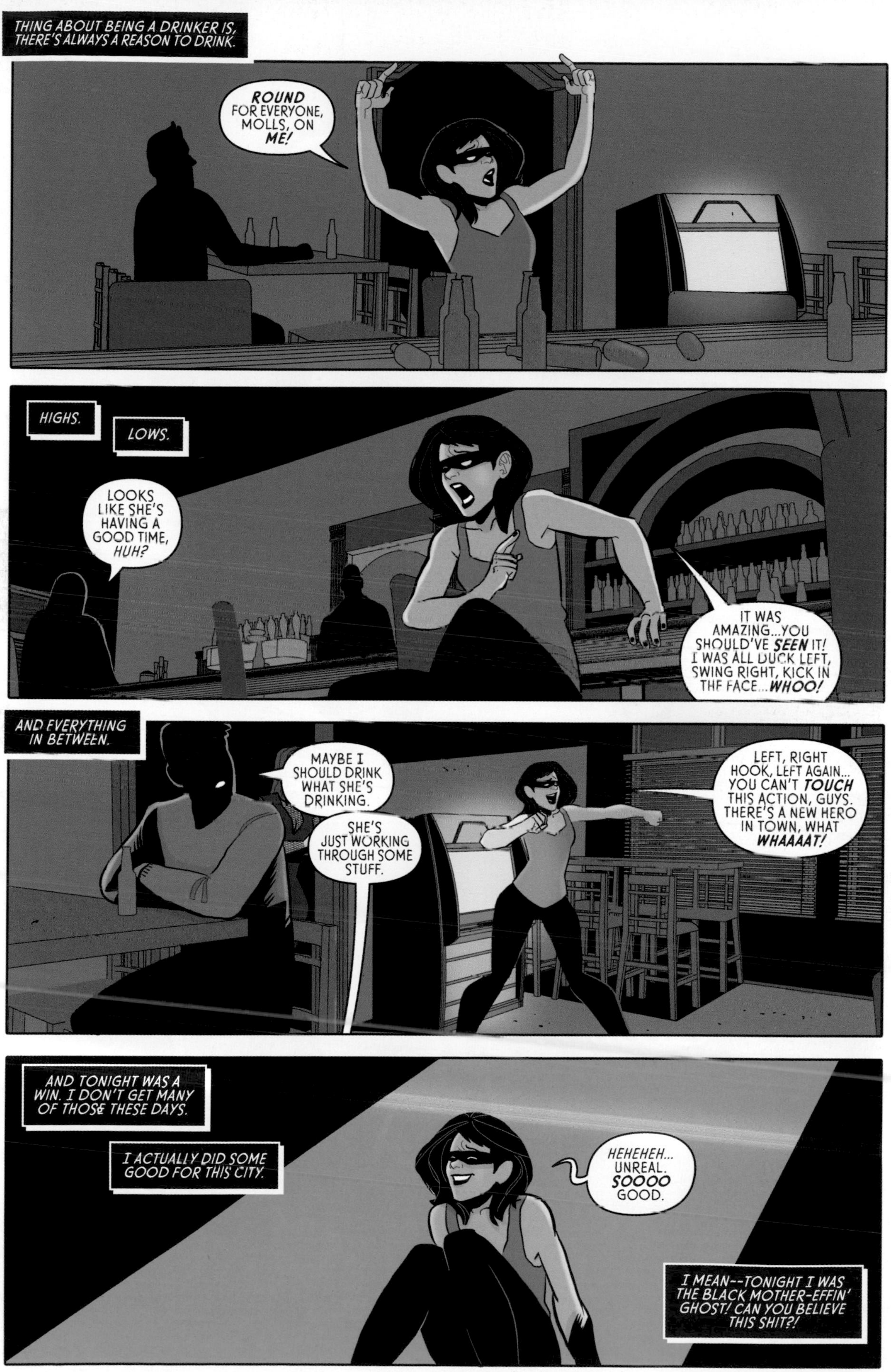
THING ABOUT BEING A DRINKER IS, THERE'S ALWAYS A REASON TO DRINK.
ROUND FOR EVERYONE, MOLLS, ON ME!
HIGHS.
LOWS.
LOOKS LIKE SHE'S HAVING A GOOD TIME, HUH?
IT WAS AMAZING...YOU SHOULD'VE SEEN IT! I WAS ALL DUCK LEFT, SWING RIGHT, KICK IN THE FACE...WHOO!
AND EVERYTHING IN BETWEEN.
MAYBE I SHOULD DRINK WHAT SHE'S DRINKING.
SHE'S JUST WORKING THROUGH SOME STUFF.
LEFT, RIGHT HOOK, LEFT AGAIN... YOU CAN'T TOUCH THIS ACTION, GUYS. THERE'S A NEW HERO IN TOWN, WHAT WHAAAAT!
AND TONIGHT WAS A WIN. I DON'T GET MANY OF THOSE THESE DAYS.
I ACTUALLY DID SOME GOOD FOR THIS CITY.
HEHEHEH... UNREAL. SOOOO GOOD.
I MEAN--TONIGHT I WAS THE BLACK MOTHER-EFFIN' GHOST! CAN YOU BELIEVE THIS SHIT?!

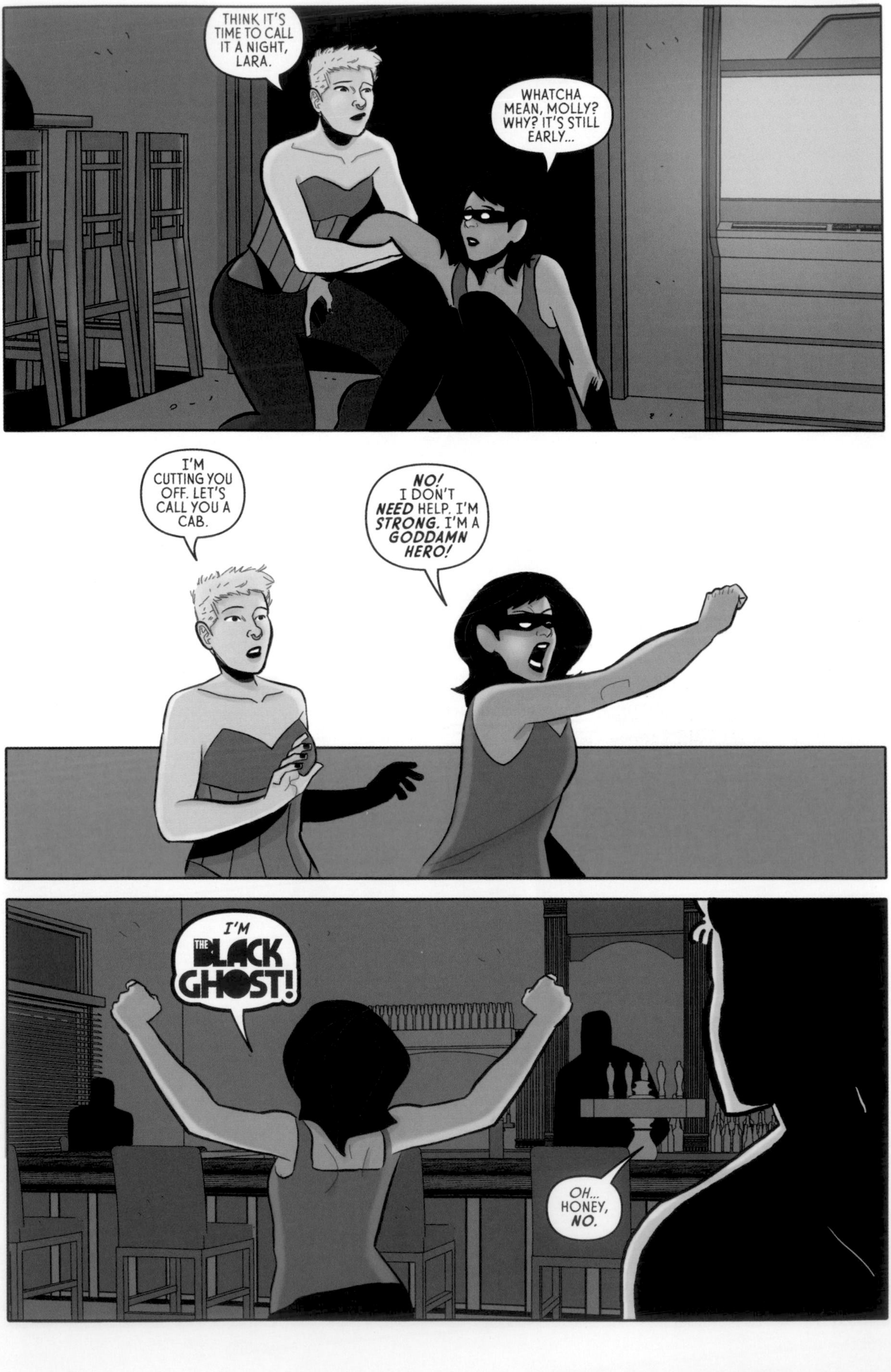
THINK IT'S TIME TO CALL IT A NIGHT, LARA.
WHATCHA MEAN, MOLLY? WHY? IT'S STILL EARLY...
I'M CUTTING YOU OFF. LET'S CALL YOU A CAB.
***NO!*** I DON'T ***NEED*** HELP. I'M ***STRONG***. I'M A ***GODDAMN HERO!***
I'M THE BLACK GHOST!
OH... HONEY, ***NO.***

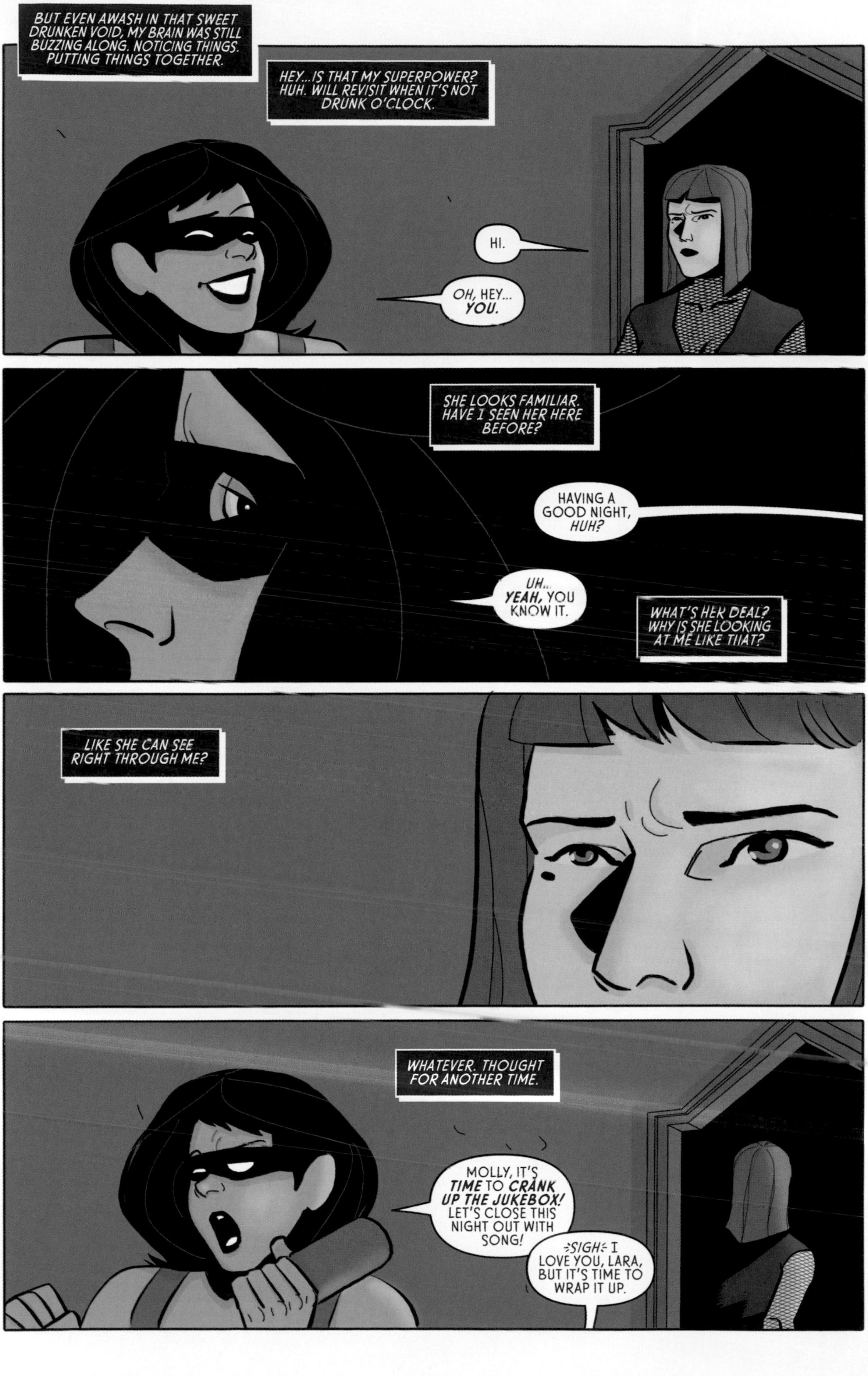
BUT EVEN AWASH IN THAT SWEET DRUNKEN VOID, MY BRAIN WAS STILL BUZZING ALONG. NOTICING THINGS. PUTTING THINGS TOGETHER.
HEY...IS THAT MY SUPERPOWER? HUH. WILL REVISIT WHEN IT'S NOT DRUNK O'CLOCK.
HI.
OH, HEY... YOU.
SHE LOOKS FAMILIAR. HAVE I SEEN HER HERE BEFORE?
HAVING A GOOD NIGHT, HUH?
UH... YEAH, YOU KNOW IT.
WHAT'S HER DEAL? WHY IS SHE LOOKING AT ME LIKE THAT?
LIKE SHE CAN SEE RIGHT THROUGH ME?
WHATEVER. THOUGHT FOR ANOTHER TIME.
MOLLY, IT'S TIME TO CRANK UP THE JUKEBOX! LET'S CLOSE THIS NIGHT OUT WITH SONG!
⇒SIGH⇐ I LOVE YOU, LARA, BUT IT'S TIME TO WRAP IT UP.

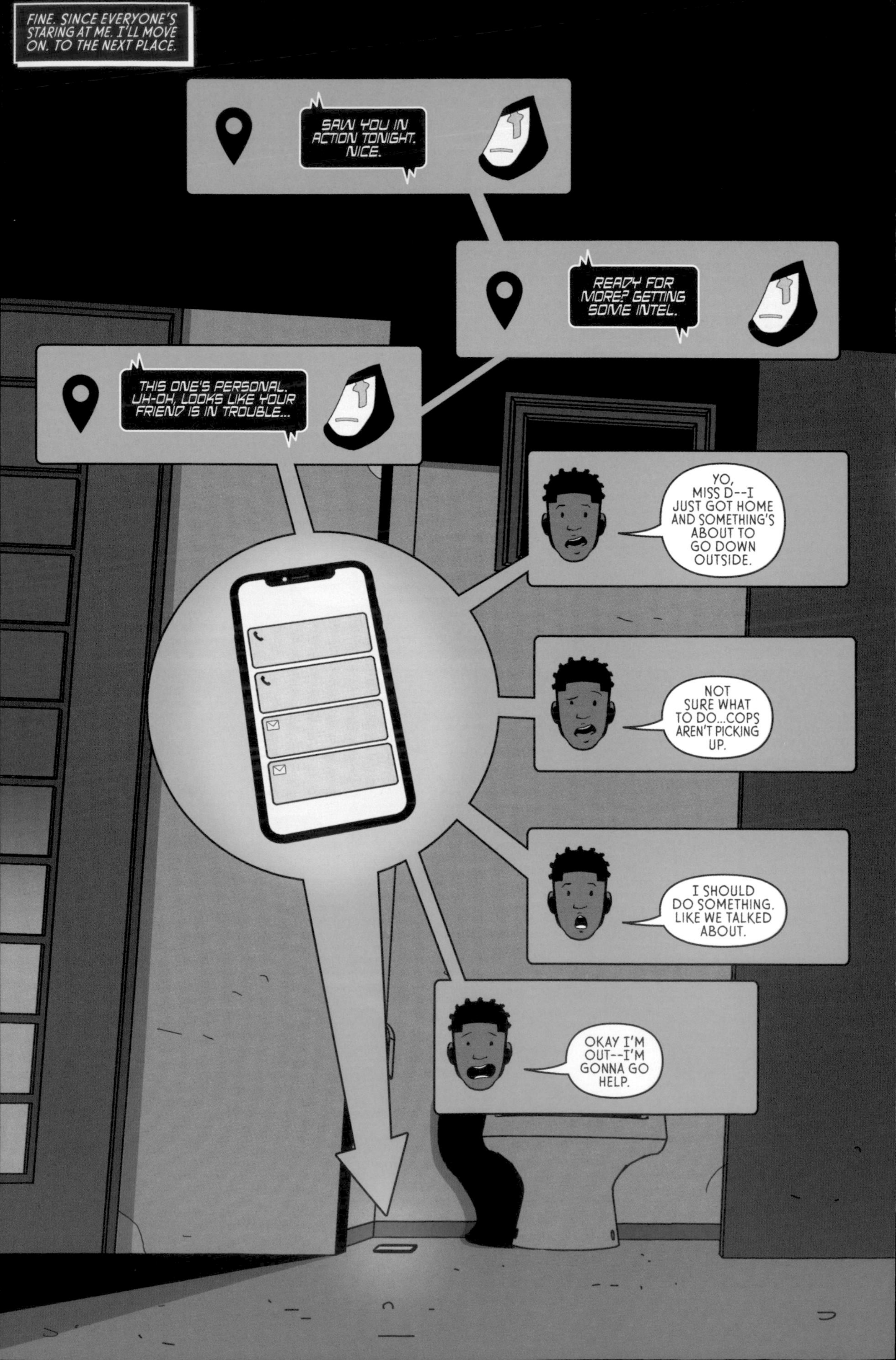
FINE. SINCE EVERYONE'S STARING AT ME. I'LL MOVE ON. TO THE NEXT PLACE.
SAW YOU IN ACTION TONIGHT. NICE.
READY FOR MORE? GETTING SOME INTEL.
THIS ONE'S PERSONAL. UH-OH, LOOKS LIKE YOUR FRIEND IS IN TROUBLE...
YO, MISS D--I JUST GOT HOME AND SOMETHING'S ABOUT TO GO DOWN OUTSIDE.
NOT SURE WHAT TO DO...COPS AREN'T PICKING UP.
I SHOULD DO SOMETHING. LIKE WE TALKED ABOUT.
OKAY I'M OUT--I'M GONNA GO HELP.

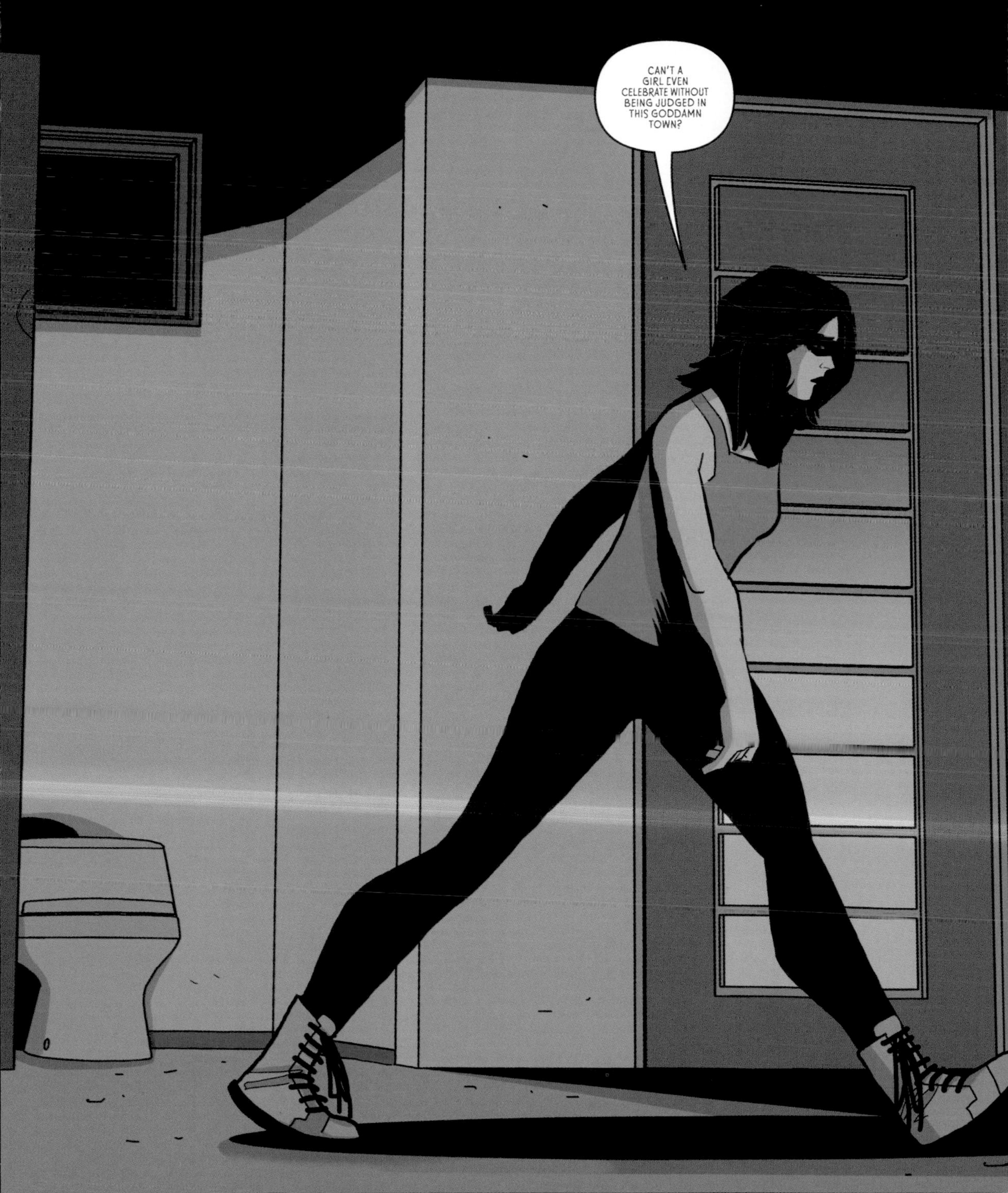
CAN'T A GIRL EVEN CELEBRATE WITHOUT BEING JUDGED IN THIS GODDAMN TOWN?

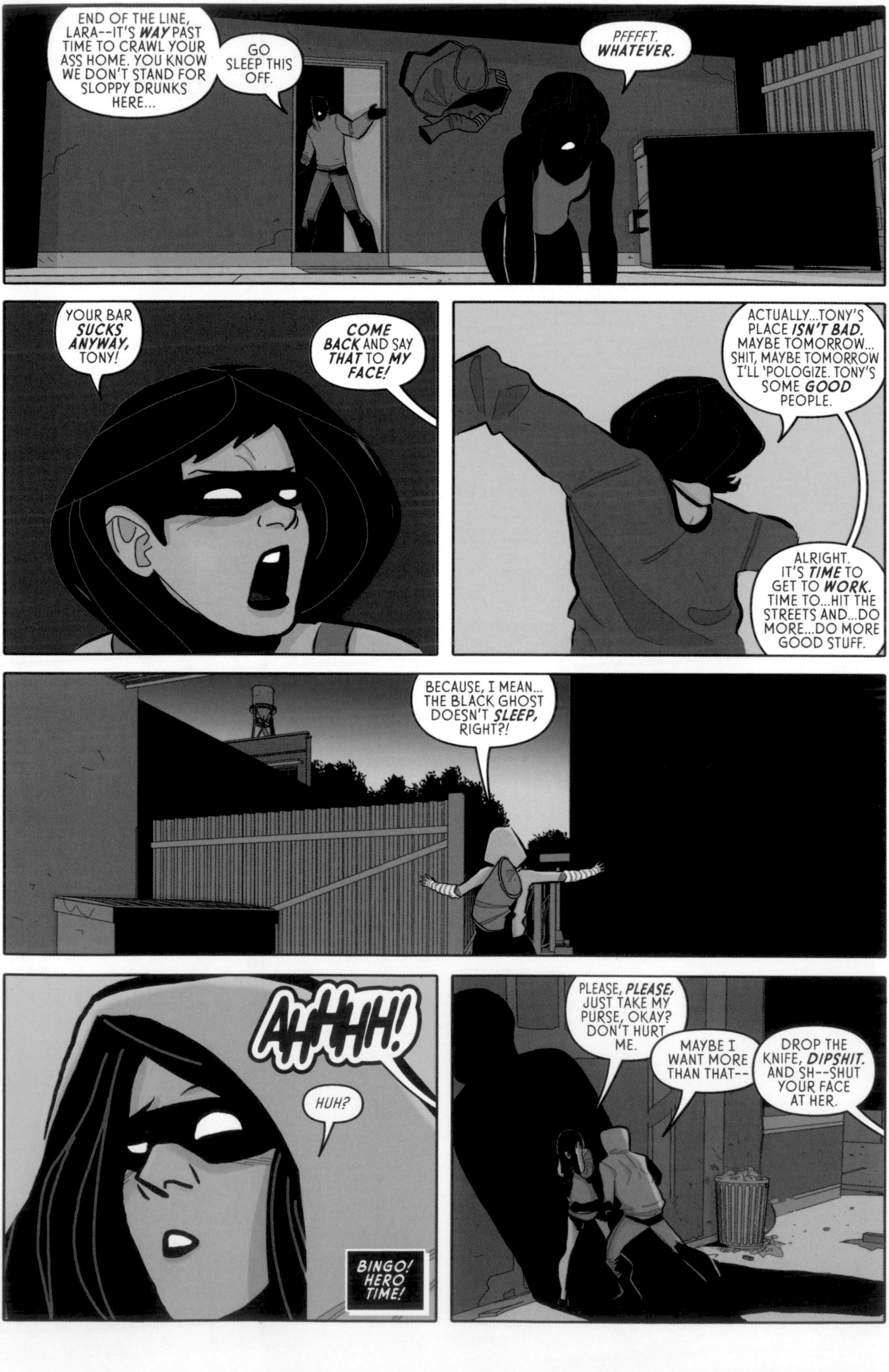
END OF THE LINE, LARA--IT'S **WAY** PAST TIME TO CRAWL YOUR ASS HOME. YOU KNOW WE DON'T STAND FOR SLOPPY DRUNKS HERE...
GO SLEEP THIS OFF.
PFFFFT. **WHATEVER.**
YOUR BAR **SUCKS ANYWAY,** TONY!
**COME BACK** AND SAY **THAT** TO **MY FACE!**
ACTUALLY...TONY'S PLACE **ISN'T BAD.** MAYBE TOMORROW... SHIT, MAYBE TOMORROW I'LL 'POLOGIZE. TONY'S SOME **GOOD** PEOPLE.
ALRIGHT. IT'S **TIME** TO GET TO **WORK.** TIME TO...HIT THE STREETS AND...DO MORE...DO MORE GOOD STUFF.
BECAUSE, I MEAN... THE BLACK GHOST DOESN'T **SLEEP,** RIGHT?!
AHHHH!
HUH?
BINGO! HERO TIME!
PLEASE, **PLEASE,** JUST TAKE MY PURSE, OKAY? DON'T HURT ME.
MAYBE I WANT MORE THAN THAT--
DROP THE KNIFE, **DIPSHIT.** AND SH--SHUT YOUR FACE AT HER.

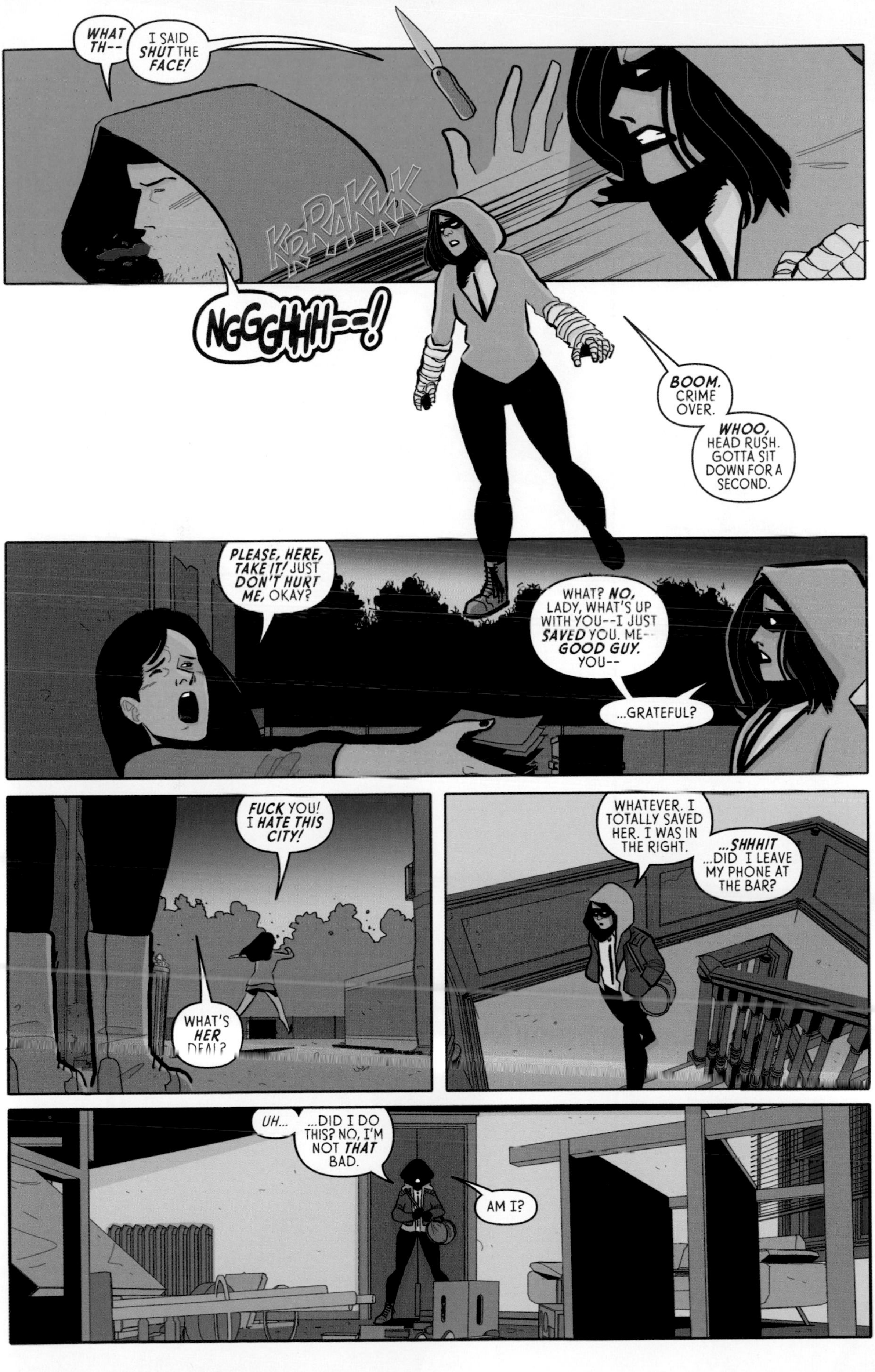
WHAT TH--
I SAID SHUT THE FACE!
KRRAKKK
NGGGHHH--!
BOOM. CRIME OVER.
WHOO, HEAD RUSH. GOTTA SIT DOWN FOR A SECOND.
PLEASE, HERE, TAKE IT! JUST DON'T HURT ME, OKAY?
WHAT? NO, LADY, WHAT'S UP WITH YOU--I JUST SAVED YOU. ME-- GOOD GUY. YOU--
...GRATEFUL?
FUCK YOU! I HATE THIS CITY!
WHAT'S HER DEAL?
WHATEVER. I TOTALLY SAVED HER. I WAS IN THE RIGHT.
...SHHHIT ...DID I LEAVE MY PHONE AT THE BAR?
UH...
...DID I DO THIS? NO, I'M NOT THAT BAD.
AM I?

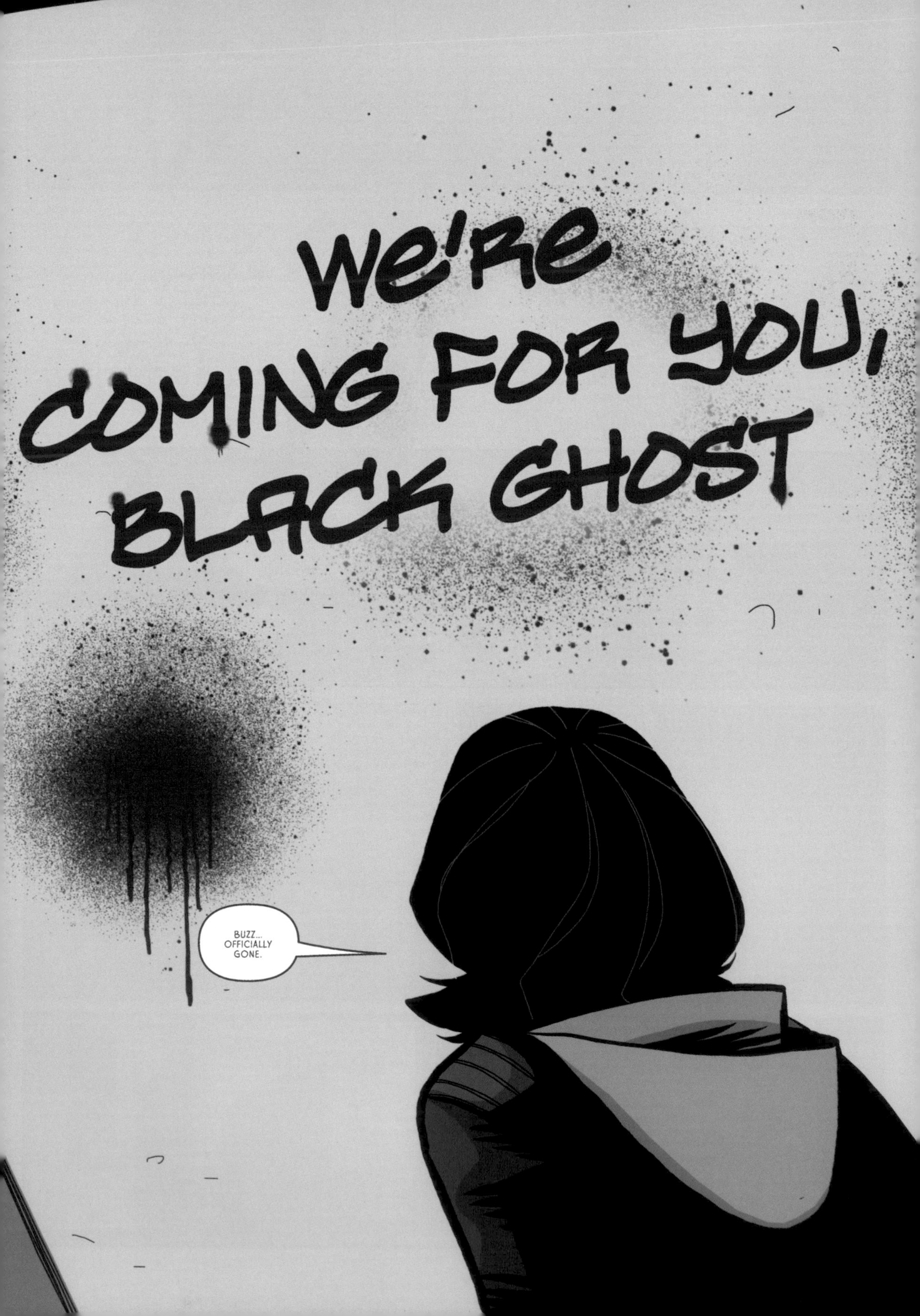
WE'RE COMING FOR YOU, BLACK GHOST
BUZZ... OFFICIALLY GONE.

# DO EVIL IN RETURN

COVER BY BILL SIENKIEWICZ

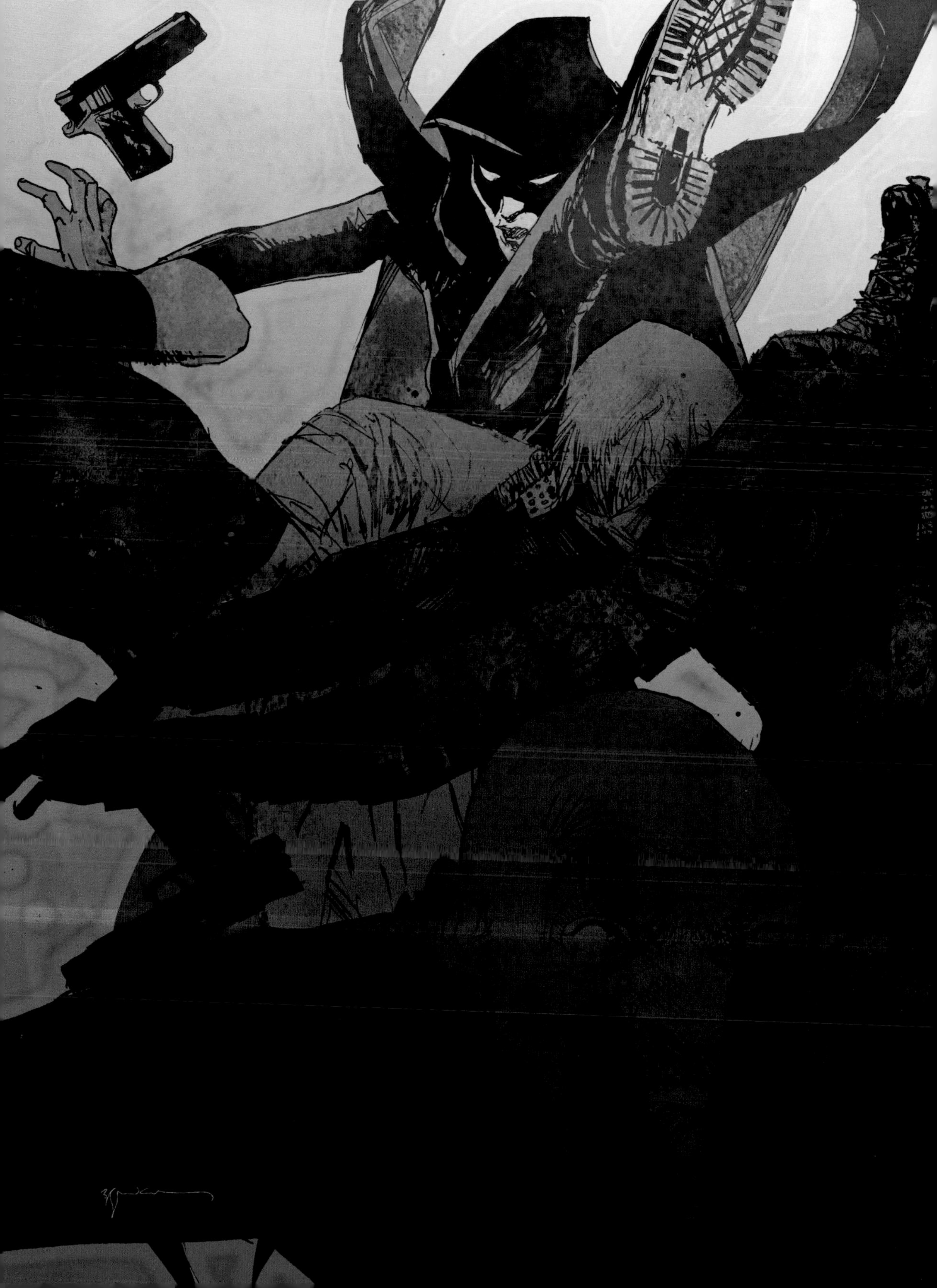

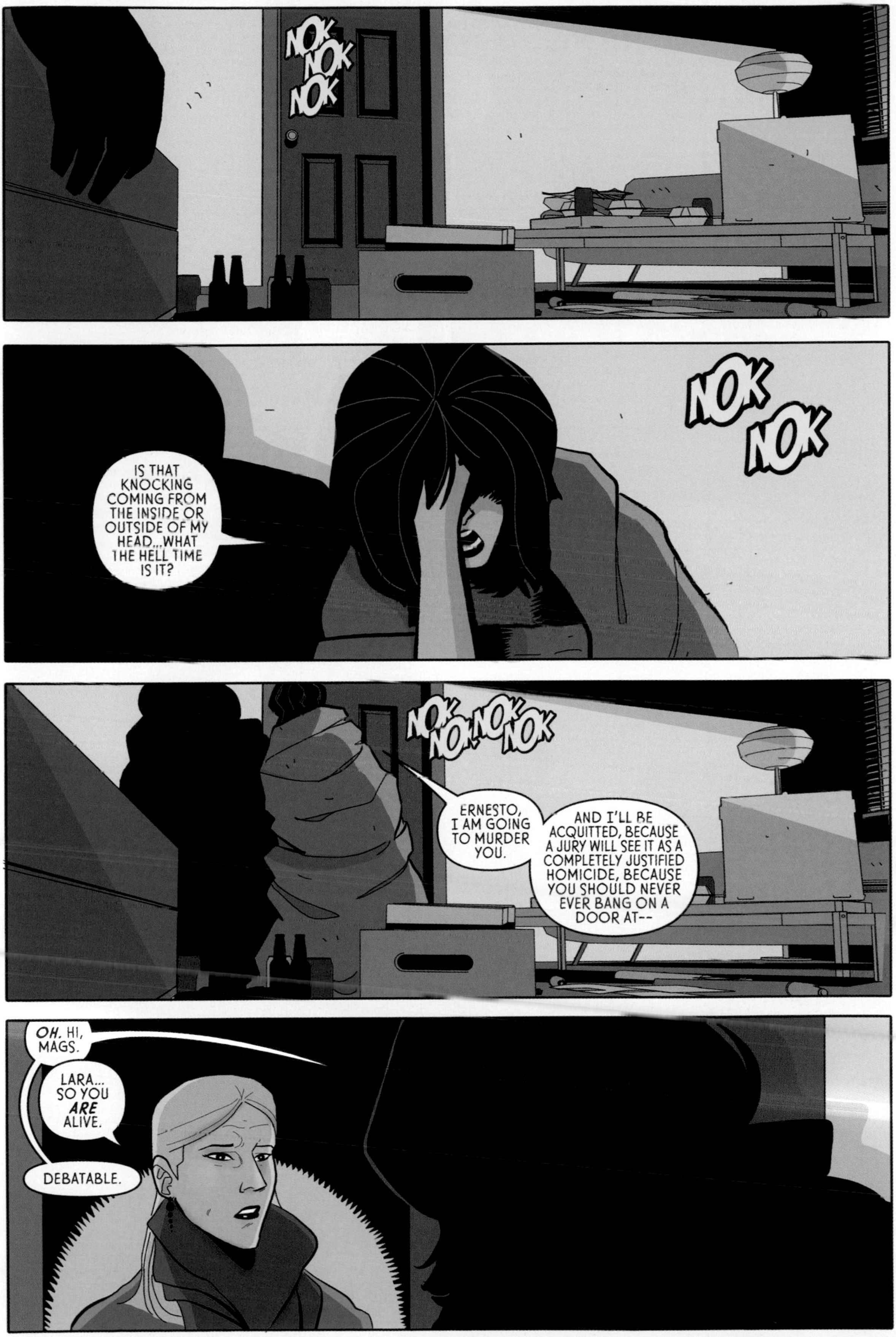
NOK NOK NOK
NOK NOK
IS THAT KNOCKING COMING FROM THE INSIDE OR OUTSIDE OF MY HEAD...WHAT THE HELL TIME IS IT?
NOK NOK NOK NOK
ERNESTO, I AM GOING TO MURDER YOU.
AND I'LL BE ACQUITTED, BECAUSE A JURY WILL SEE IT AS A COMPLETELY JUSTIFIED HOMICIDE, BECAUSE YOU SHOULD NEVER EVER BANG ON A DOOR AT--
OH. HI, MAGS.
LARA... SO YOU ARE ALIVE.
DEBATABLE.

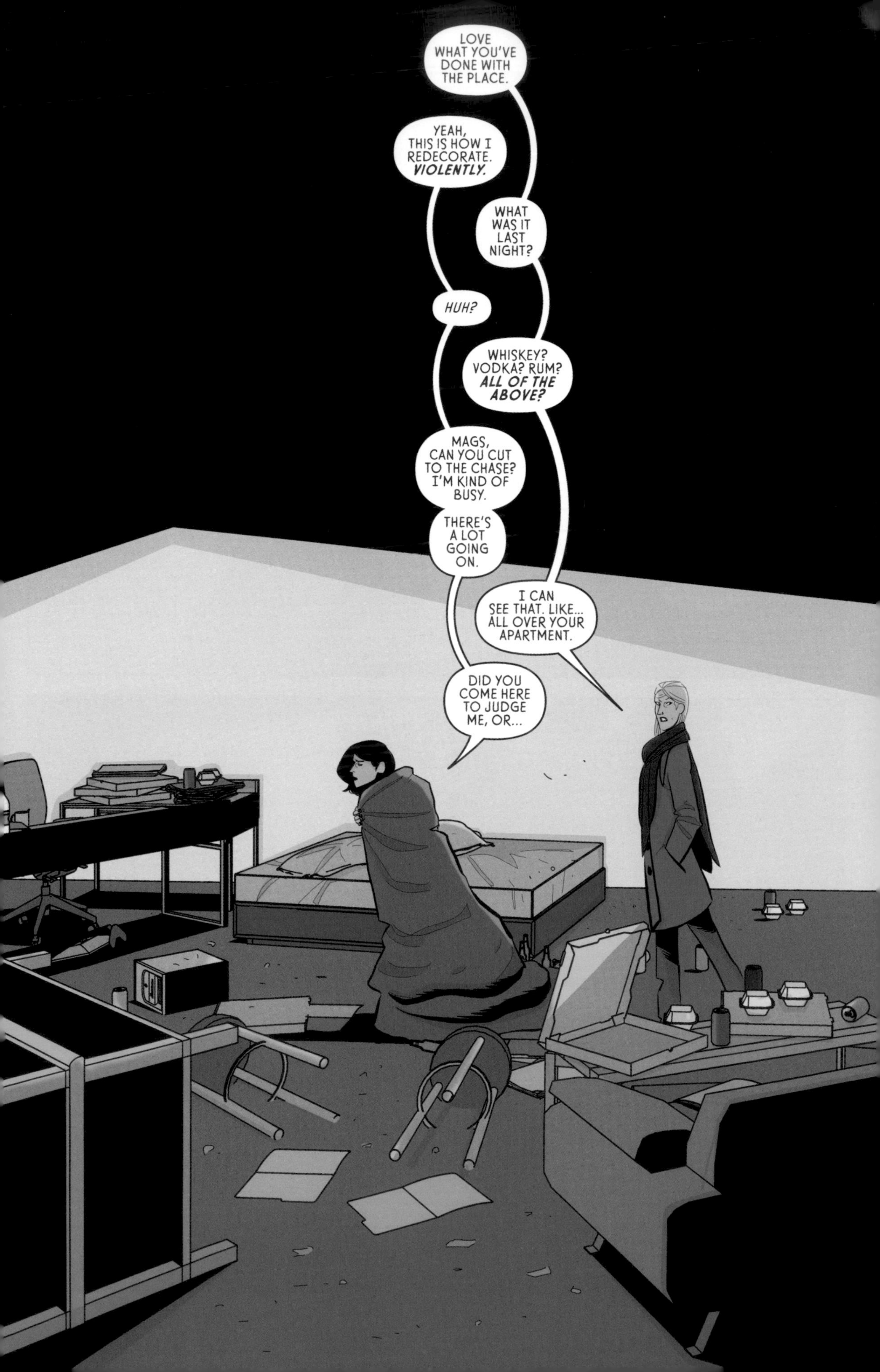
LOVE WHAT YOU'VE DONE WITH THE PLACE.
YEAH, THIS IS HOW I REDECORATE. ***VIOLENTLY.***
WHAT WAS IT LAST NIGHT?
*HUH?*
WHISKEY? VODKA? RUM? ***ALL OF THE ABOVE?***
MAGS, CAN YOU CUT TO THE CHASE? I'M KIND OF BUSY.
THERE'S A LOT GOING ON.
I CAN SEE THAT. LIKE... ALL OVER YOUR APARTMENT.
DID YOU COME HERE TO JUDGE ME, OR...

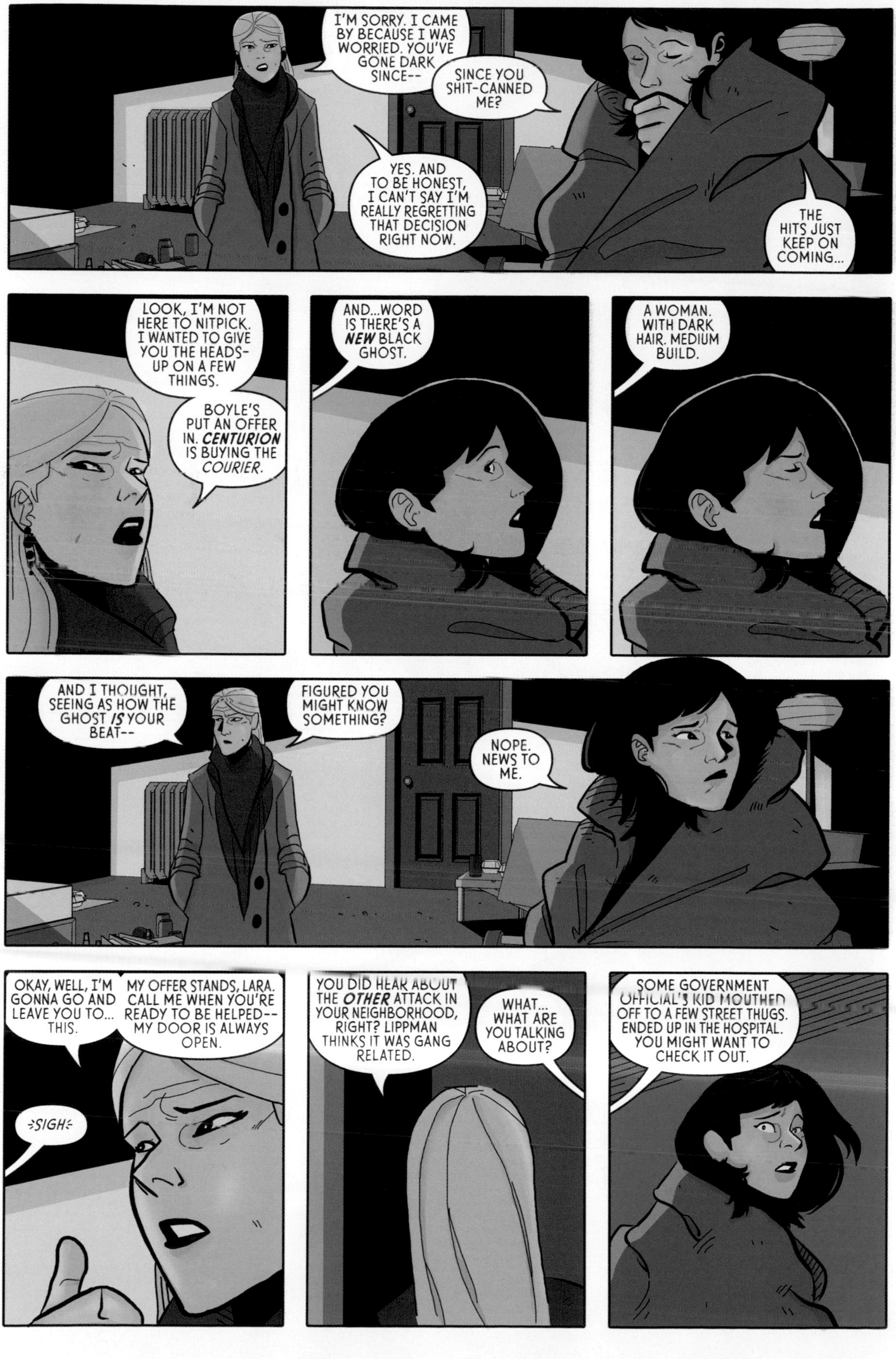

I'M SORRY. I CAME BY BECAUSE I WAS WORRIED. YOU'VE GONE DARK SINCE--
SINCE YOU SHIT-CANNED ME?
YES. AND TO BE HONEST, I CAN'T SAY I'M REALLY REGRETTING THAT DECISION RIGHT NOW.
THE HITS JUST KEEP ON COMING...
LOOK, I'M NOT HERE TO NITPICK. I WANTED TO GIVE YOU THE HEADS-UP ON A FEW THINGS.
BOYLE'S PUT AN OFFER IN. *CENTURION* IS BUYING THE *COURIER*.
AND...WORD IS THERE'S A *NEW* BLACK GHOST.
A WOMAN. WITH DARK HAIR. MEDIUM BUILD.
AND I THOUGHT, SEEING AS HOW THE GHOST *IS* YOUR BEAT--
FIGURED YOU MIGHT KNOW SOMETHING?
NOPE. NEWS TO ME.
OKAY, WELL, I'M GONNA GO AND LEAVE YOU TO... THIS.
MY OFFER STANDS, LARA. CALL ME WHEN YOU'RE READY TO BE HELPED-- MY DOOR IS ALWAYS OPEN.
SIGH
YOU DID HEAR ABOUT THE *OTHER* ATTACK IN YOUR NEIGHBORHOOD, RIGHT? LIPPMAN THINKS IT WAS GANG RELATED.
WHAT... WHAT ARE YOU TALKING ABOUT?
SOME GOVERNMENT OFFICIAL'S KID MOUTHED OFF TO A FEW STREET THUGS. ENDED UP IN THE HOSPITAL. YOU MIGHT WANT TO CHECK IT OUT.

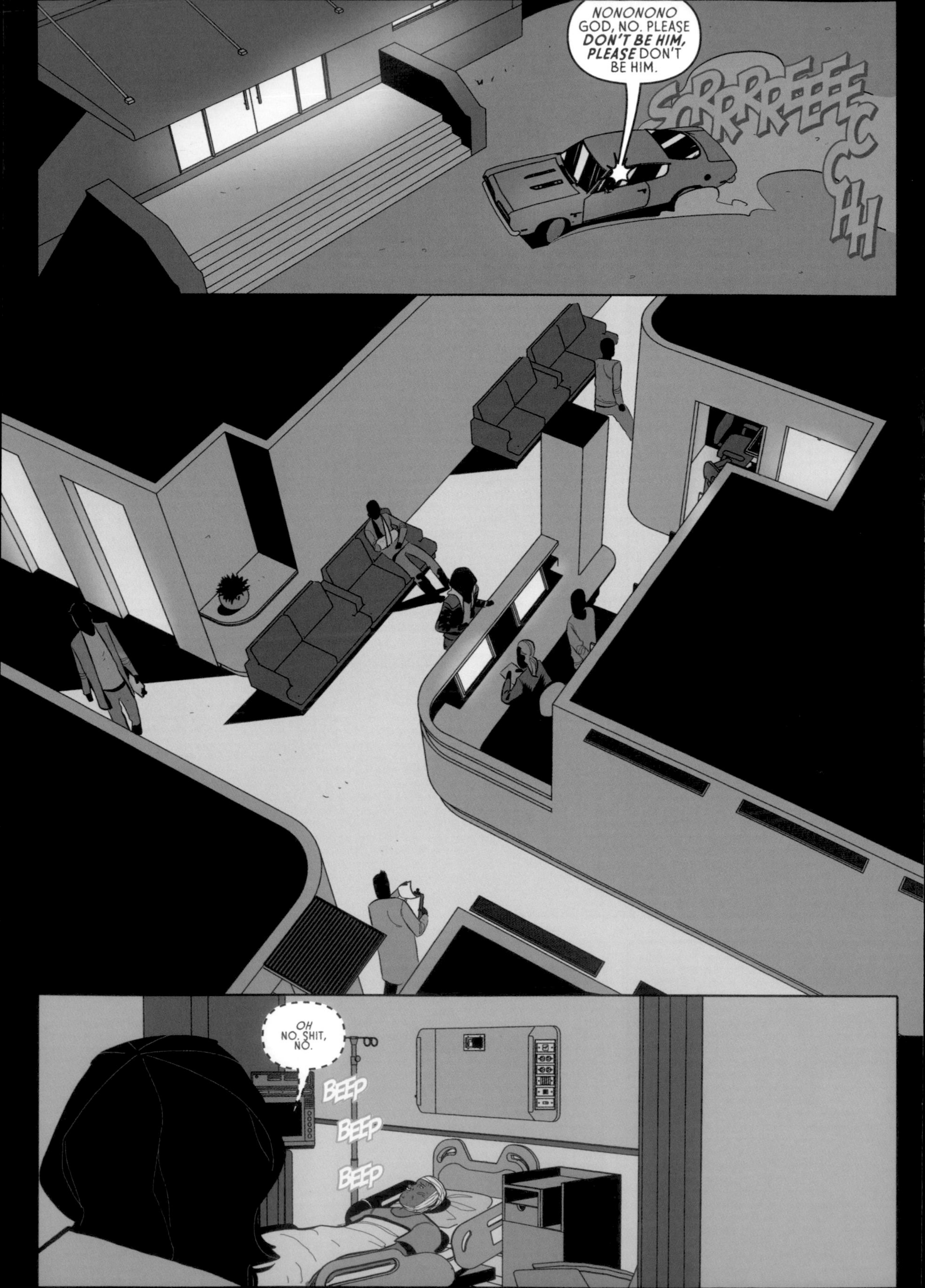
NONONONO GOD, NO. PLEASE ***DON'T BE HIM, PLEASE*** DON'T BE HIM.
SCRRREEECCHH
OH NO. SHIT, NO.
BEEP
BEEP
BEEP

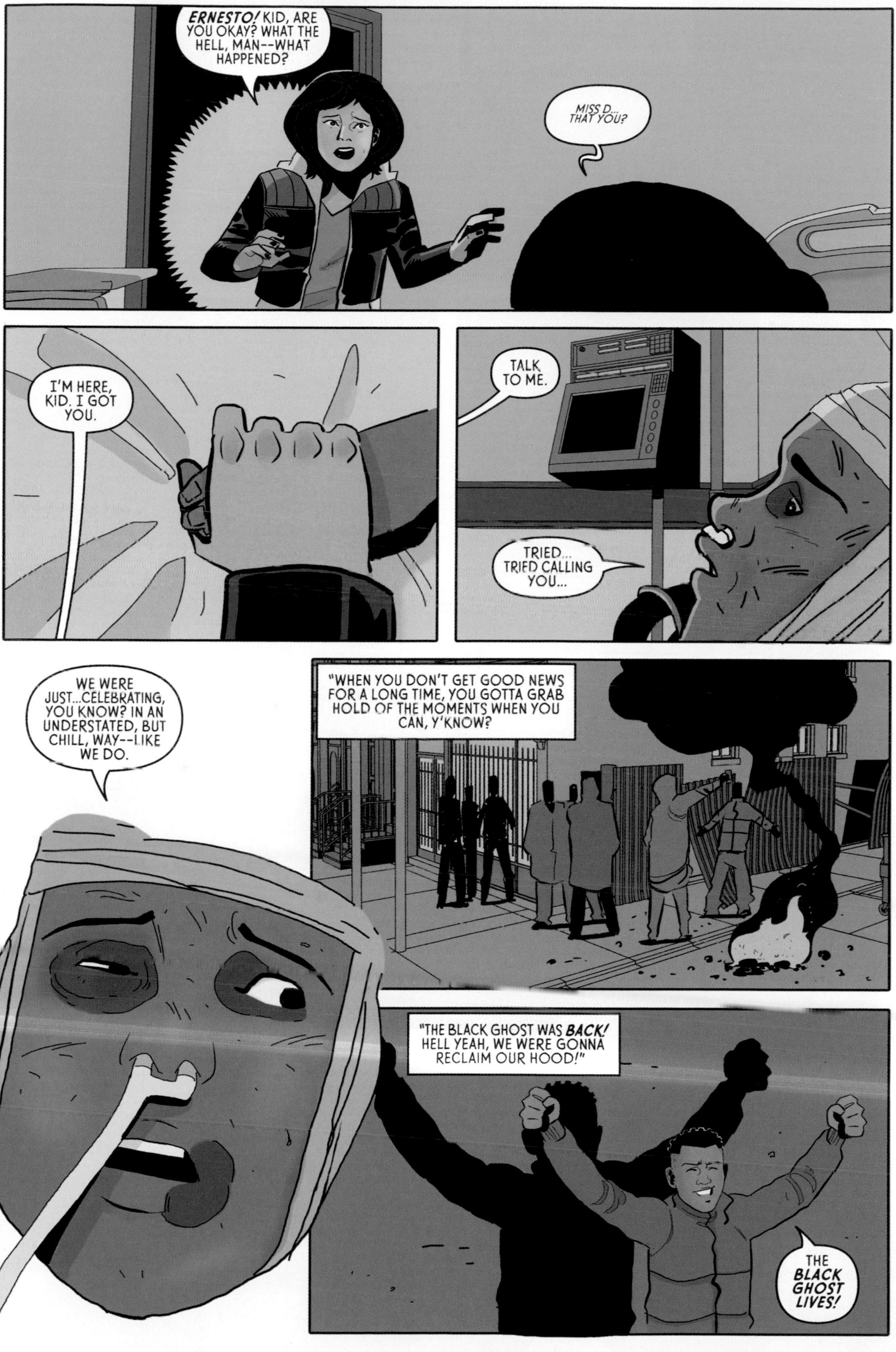
ERNESTO! KID, ARE YOU OKAY? WHAT THE HELL, MAN--WHAT HAPPENED?
MISS D... THAT YOU?
I'M HERE, KID. I GOT YOU.
TALK TO ME.
TRIED... TRIED CALLING YOU...
WE WERE JUST...CELEBRATING, YOU KNOW? IN AN UNDERSTATED, BUT CHILL, WAY--LIKE WE DO.
"WHEN YOU DON'T GET GOOD NEWS FOR A LONG TIME, YOU GOTTA GRAB HOLD OF THE MOMENTS WHEN YOU CAN, Y'KNOW?
"THE BLACK GHOST WAS BACK! HELL YEAH, WE WERE GONNA RECLAIM OUR HOOD!"
THE BLACK GHOST LIVES!

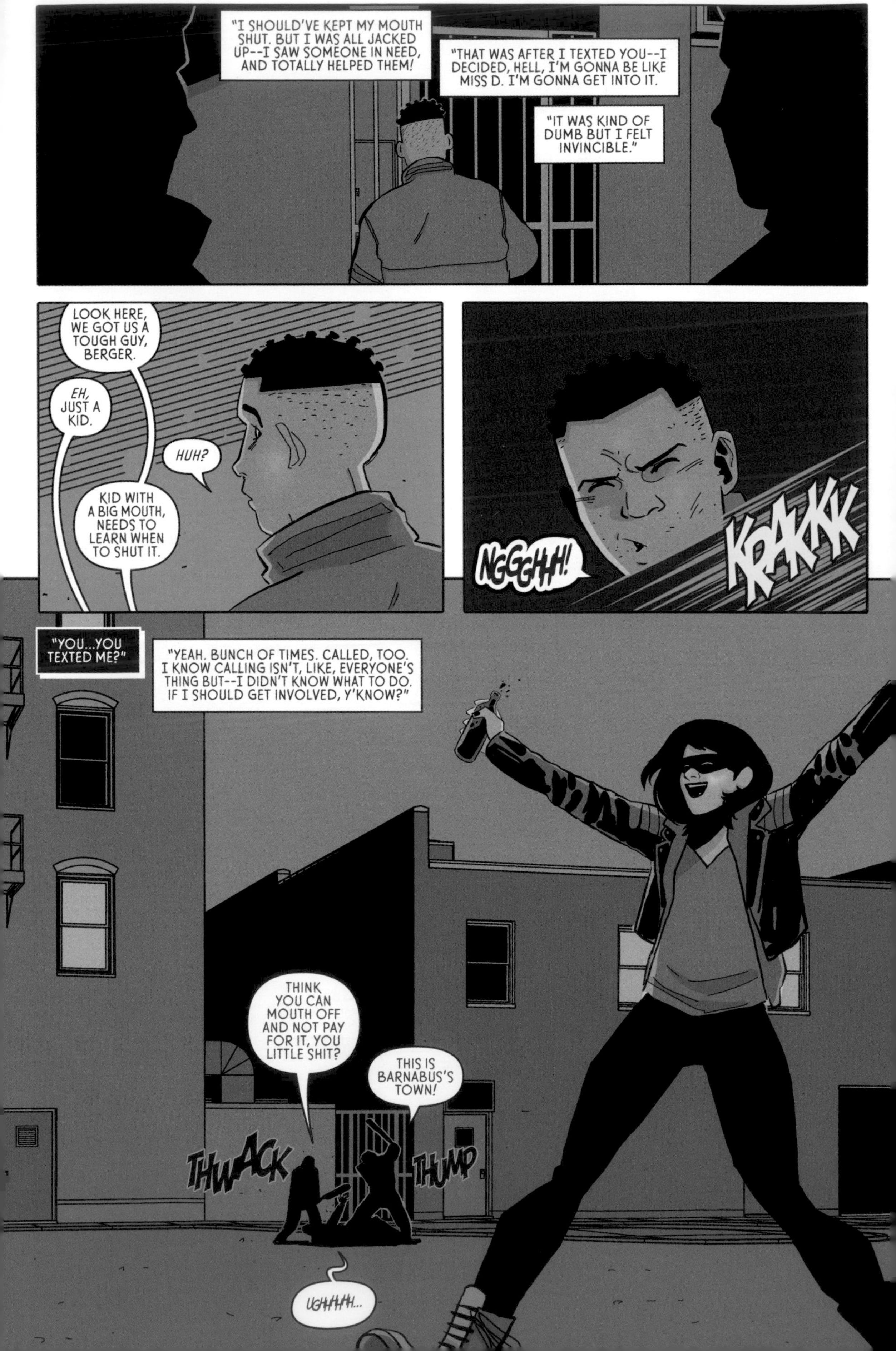
"I SHOULD'VE KEPT MY MOUTH SHUT. BUT I WAS ALL JACKED UP--I SAW SOMEONE IN NEED, AND TOTALLY HELPED THEM!
"THAT WAS AFTER I TEXTED YOU--I DECIDED, HELL, I'M GONNA BE LIKE MISS D. I'M GONNA GET INTO IT.
"IT WAS KIND OF DUMB BUT I FELT INVINCIBLE."
LOOK HERE, WE GOT US A TOUGH GUY, BERGER.
EH, JUST A KID.
HUH?
KID WITH A BIG MOUTH, NEEDS TO LEARN WHEN TO SHUT IT.
NGGGHHH!
KRAKKK
"YOU...YOU TEXTED ME?"
"YEAH. BUNCH OF TIMES. CALLED, TOO. I KNOW CALLING ISN'T, LIKE, EVERYONE'S THING BUT--I DIDN'T KNOW WHAT TO DO. IF I SHOULD GET INVOLVED, Y'KNOW?"
THINK YOU CAN MOUTH OFF AND NOT PAY FOR IT, YOU LITTLE SHIT?
THIS IS BARNABUS'S TOWN!
THWACK
THUMP
UGHHHH...

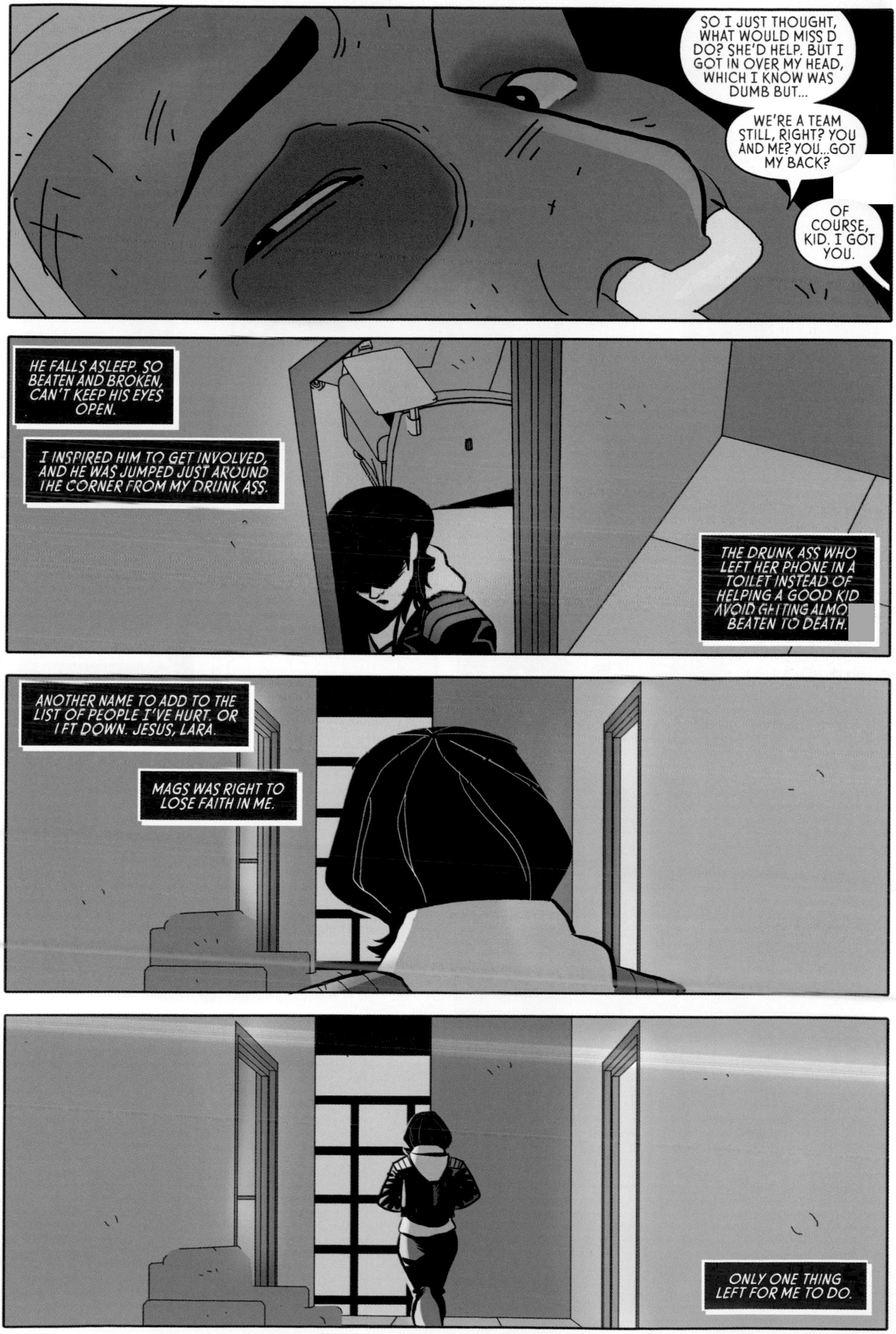
SO I JUST THOUGHT, WHAT WOULD MISS D DO? SHE'D HELP. BUT I GOT IN OVER MY HEAD, WHICH I KNOW WAS DUMB BUT...
WE'RE A TEAM STILL, RIGHT? YOU AND ME? YOU...GOT MY BACK?
OF COURSE, KID. I GOT YOU.
HE FALLS ASLEEP. SO BEATEN AND BROKEN, CAN'T KEEP HIS EYES OPEN.
I INSPIRED HIM TO GET INVOLVED, AND HE WAS JUMPED JUST AROUND THE CORNER FROM MY DRUNK ASS.
THE DRUNK ASS WHO LEFT HER PHONE IN A TOILET INSTEAD OF HELPING A GOOD KID AVOID GETTING ALMO BEATEN TO DEATH.
ANOTHER NAME TO ADD TO THE LIST OF PEOPLE I'VE HURT, OR LEFT DOWN. JESUS, LARA.
MAGS WAS RIGHT TO LOSE FAITH IN ME.
ONLY ONE THING LEFT FOR ME TO DO.

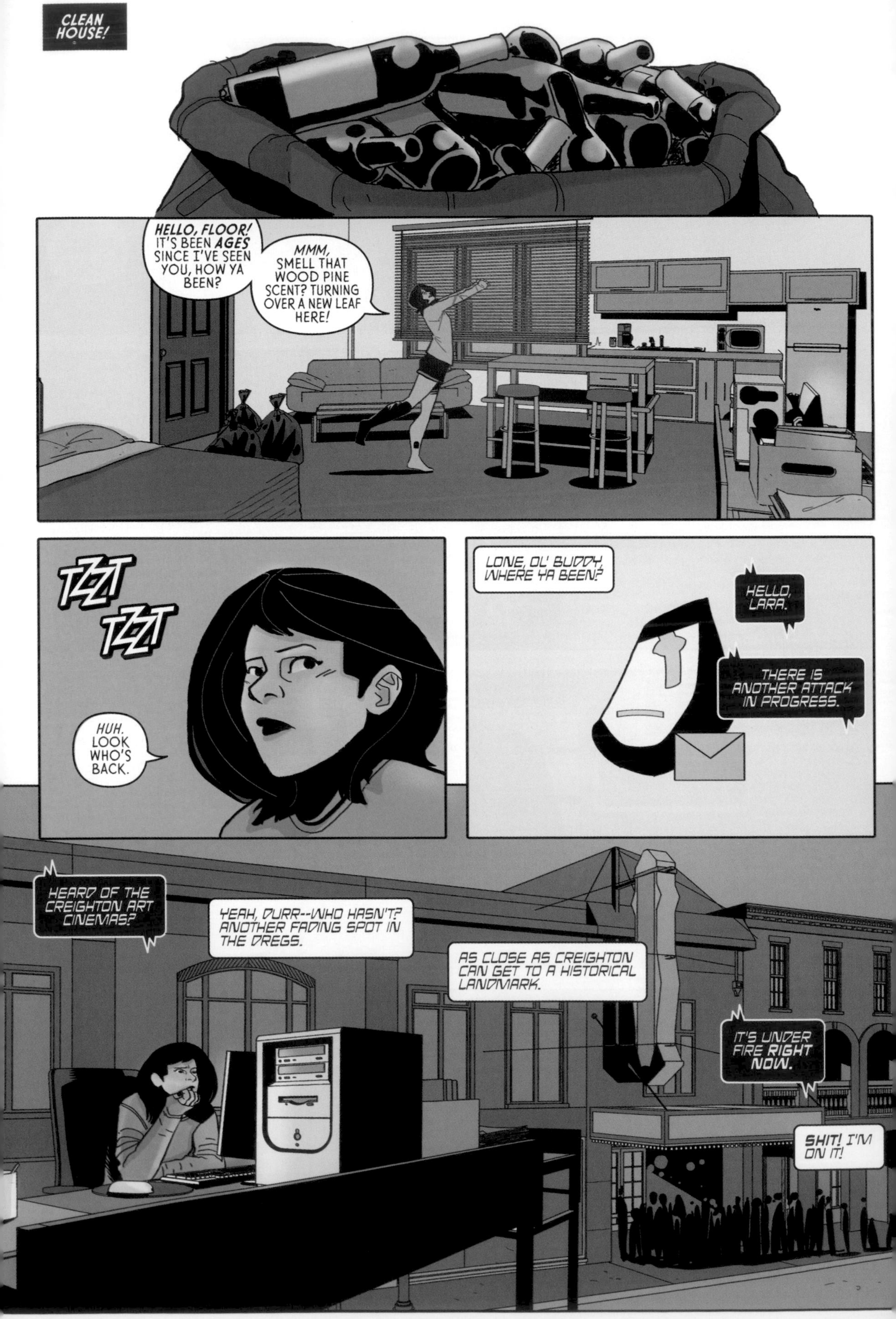
CLEAN HOUSE!
HELLO, FLOOR! IT'S BEEN AGES SINCE I'VE SEEN YOU, HOW YA BEEN?
MMM, SMELL THAT WOOD PINE SCENT? TURNING OVER A NEW LEAF HERE!
TZZT TZZT
HUH. LOOK WHO'S BACK.
LONE, OL' BUDDY, WHERE YA BEEN?
HELLO, LARA.
THERE IS ANOTHER ATTACK IN PROGRESS.
HEARD OF THE CREIGHTON ART CINEMAS?
YEAH, DURR--WHO HASN'T? ANOTHER FADING SPOT IN THE DREGS.
AS CLOSE AS CREIGHTON CAN GET TO A HISTORICAL LANDMARK.
IT'S UNDER FIRE RIGHT NOW.
SHIT! I'M ON IT!

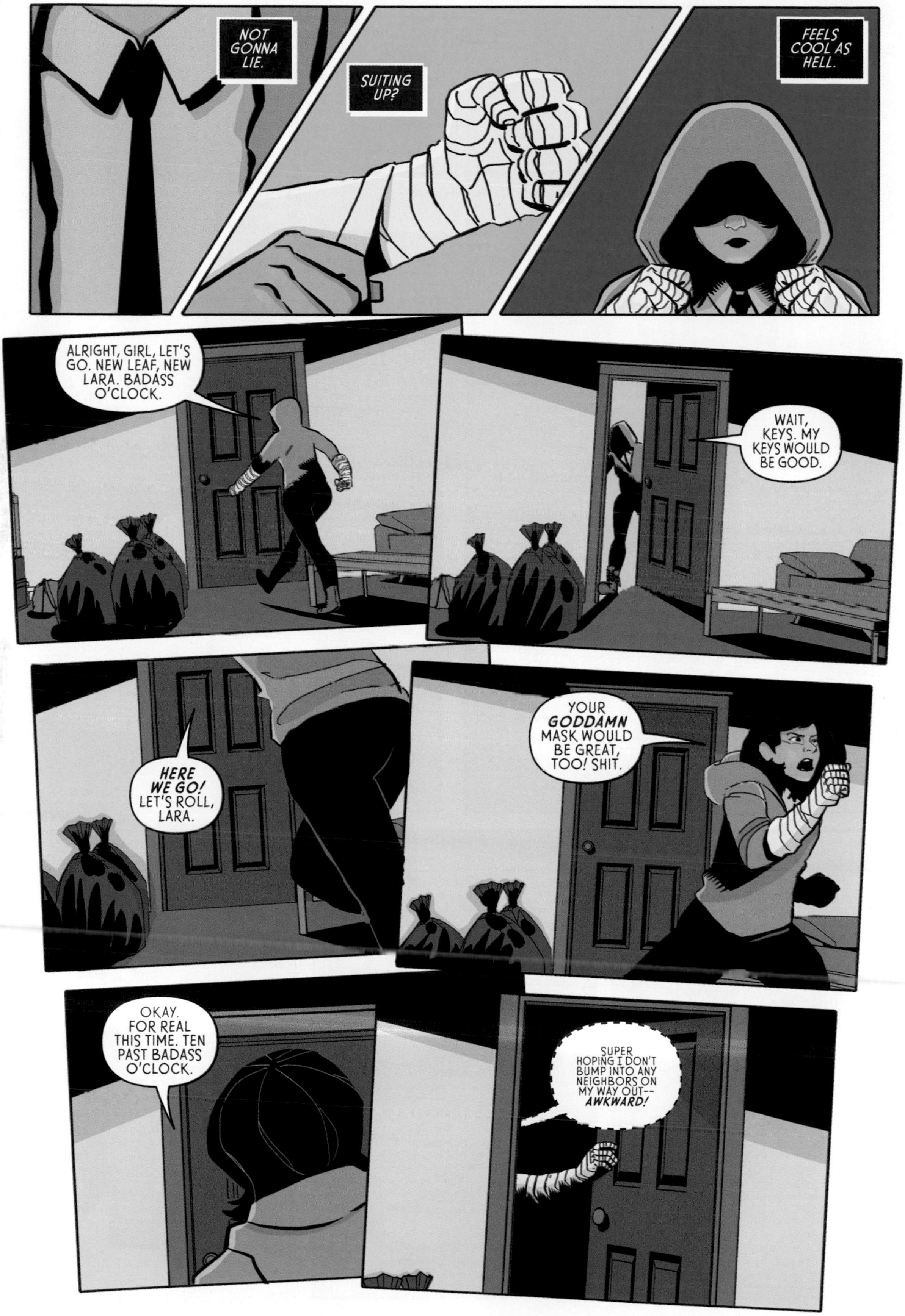
NOT GONNA LIE.
SUITING UP?
FEELS COOL AS HELL.
ALRIGHT, GIRL, LET'S GO. NEW LEAF, NEW LARA. BADASS O'CLOCK.
WAIT, KEYS. MY KEYS WOULD BE GOOD.
**HERE WE GO!** LET'S ROLL, LARA.
YOUR **GODDAMN** MASK WOULD BE GREAT, TOO! SHIT.
OKAY. FOR REAL THIS TIME. TEN PAST BADASS O'CLOCK.
SUPER HOPING I DON'T BUMP INTO ANY NEIGHBORS ON MY WAY OUT-- **AWKWARD!**

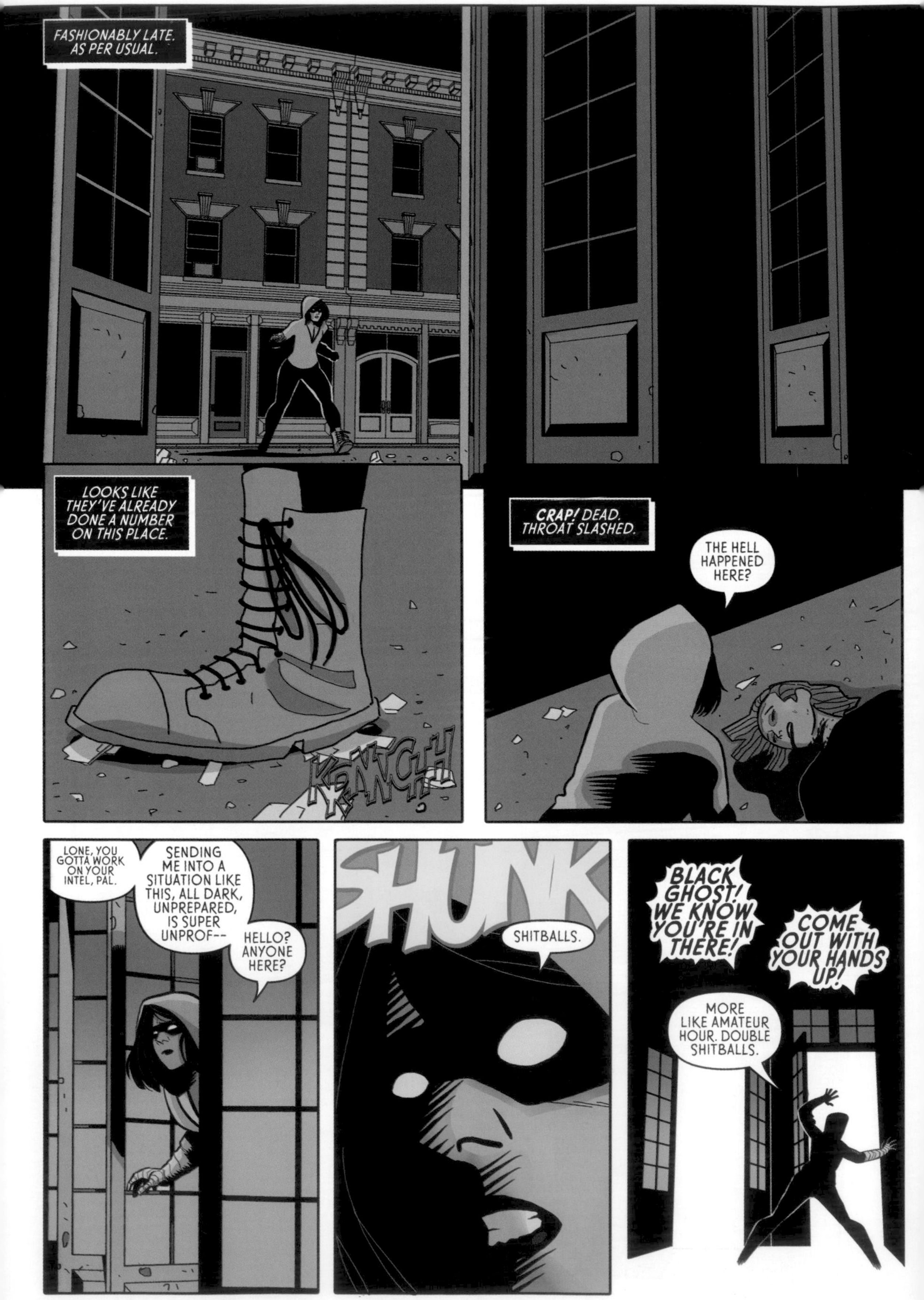
FASHIONABLY LATE. AS PER USUAL.
LOOKS LIKE THEY'VE ALREADY DONE A NUMBER ON THIS PLACE.
KRNNCHH
CRAP! DEAD. THROAT SLASHED.
THE HELL HAPPENED HERE?
LONE, YOU GOTTA WORK ON YOUR INTEL, PAL.
SENDING ME INTO A SITUATION LIKE THIS, ALL DARK, UNPREPARED, IS SUPER UNPROF--
HELLO? ANYONE HERE?
SHUNK
SHITBALLS.
BLACK GHOST! WE KNOW YOU'RE IN THERE!
COME OUT WITH YOUR HANDS UP!
MORE LIKE AMATEUR HOUR. DOUBLE SHITBALLS.

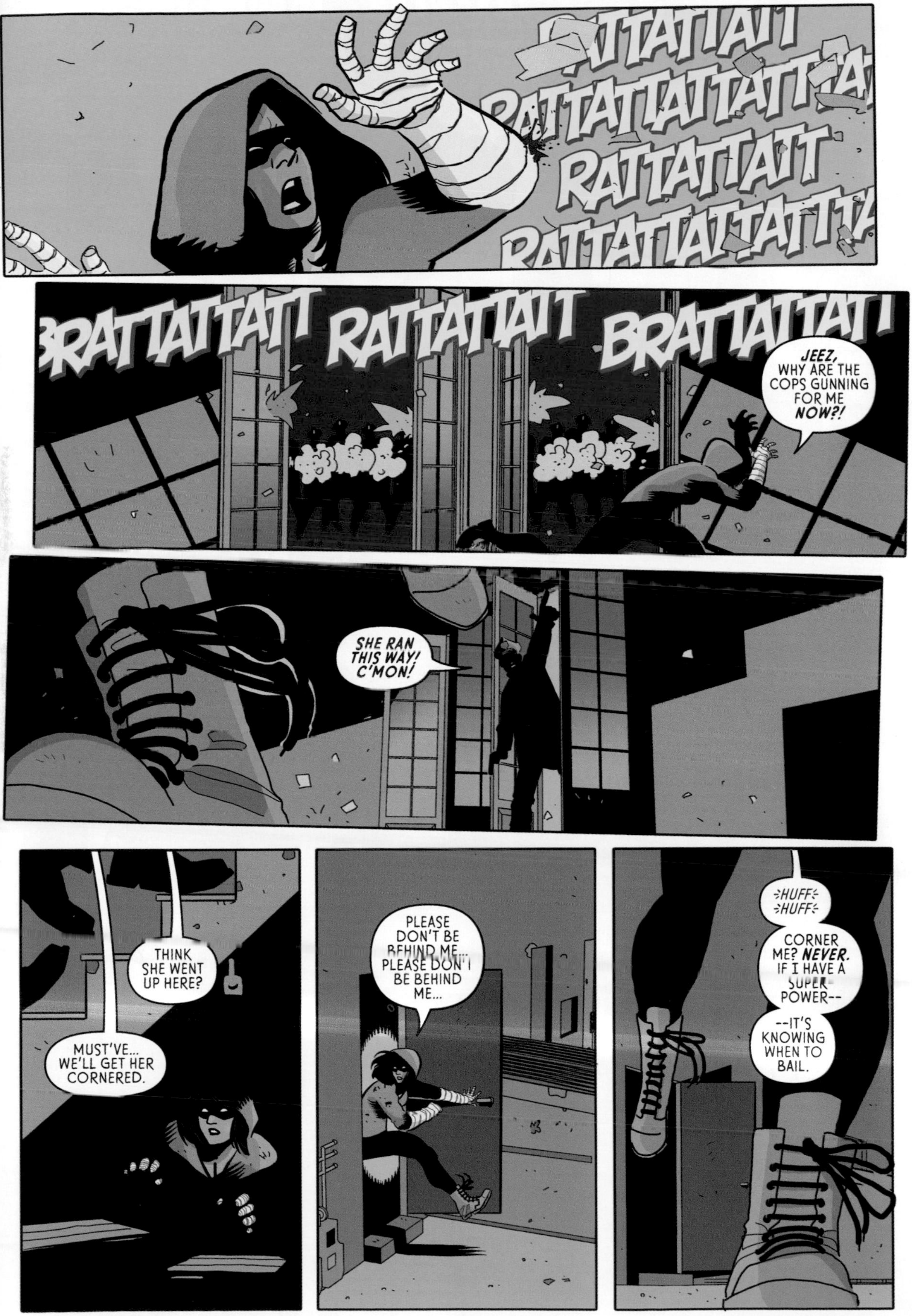
RATTATTATT
RATTATTATTATTA
RATTATTATT
RATTATTATTATTA
BRATTATTATT
RATTATTATT
BRATTATTATT
JEEZ, WHY ARE THE COPS GUNNING FOR ME NOW?!
SHE RAN THIS WAY! C'MON!
THINK SHE WENT UP HERE?
MUST'VE... WE'LL GET HER CORNERED.
PLEASE DON'T BE BEHIND ME... PLEASE DON'T BE BEHIND ME...
HUFF HUFF
CORNER ME? NEVER. IF I HAVE A SUPER-POWER--
--IT'S KNOWING WHEN TO BAIL.

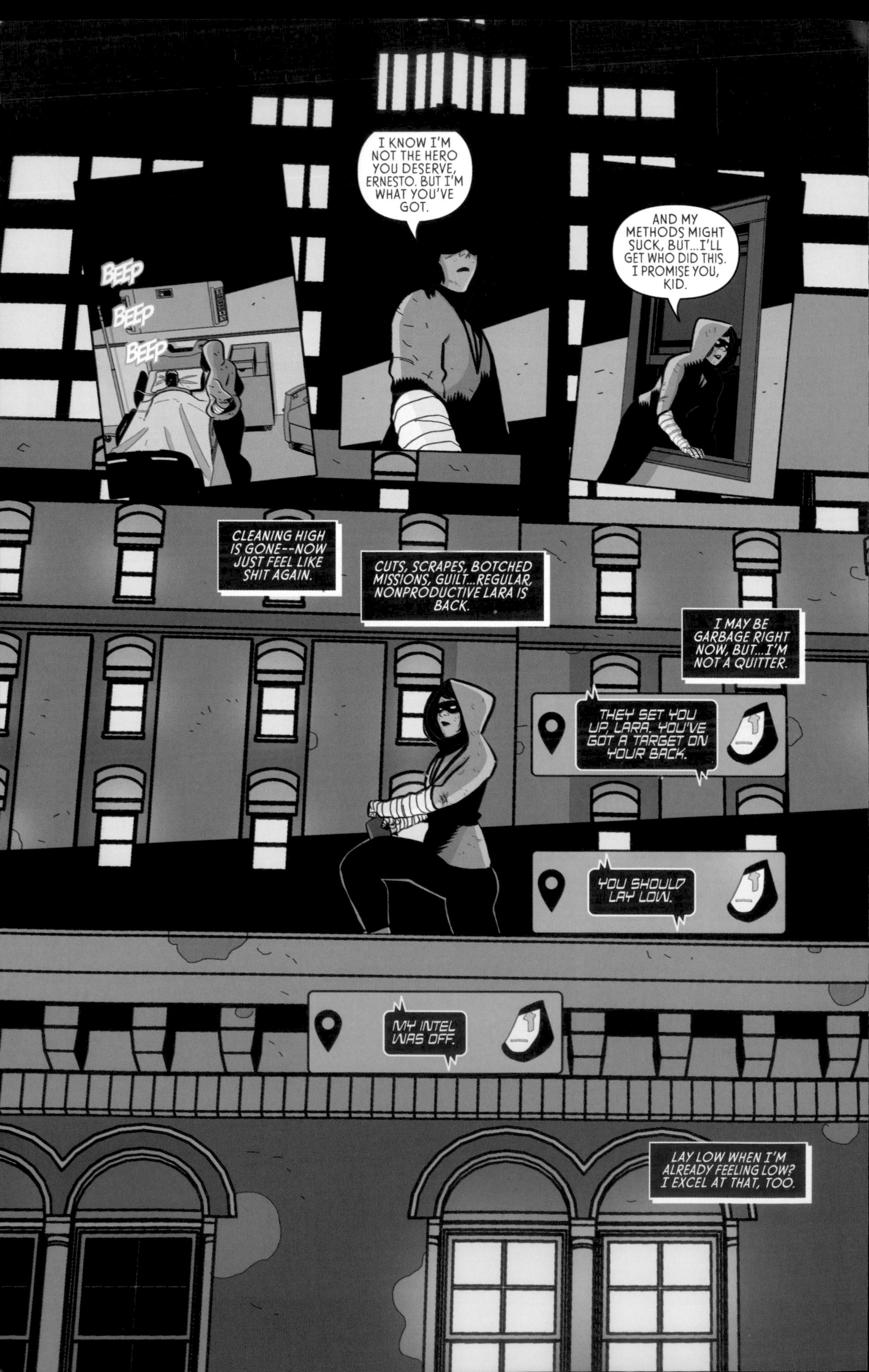
BEEP
BEEP
BEEP
I KNOW I'M NOT THE HERO YOU DESERVE, ERNESTO. BUT I'M WHAT YOU'VE GOT.
AND MY METHODS MIGHT SUCK, BUT...I'LL GET WHO DID THIS. I PROMISE YOU, KID.
CLEANING HIGH IS GONE--NOW JUST FEEL LIKE SHIT AGAIN.
CUTS, SCRAPES, BOTCHED MISSIONS, GUILT...REGULAR, NONPRODUCTIVE LARA IS BACK.
I MAY BE GARBAGE RIGHT NOW, BUT...I'M NOT A QUITTER.
THEY SET YOU UP, LARA. YOU'VE GOT A TARGET ON YOUR BACK.
YOU SHOULD LAY LOW.
MY INTEL WAS OFF.
LAY LOW WHEN I'M ALREADY FEELING LOW? I EXCEL AT THAT, TOO.

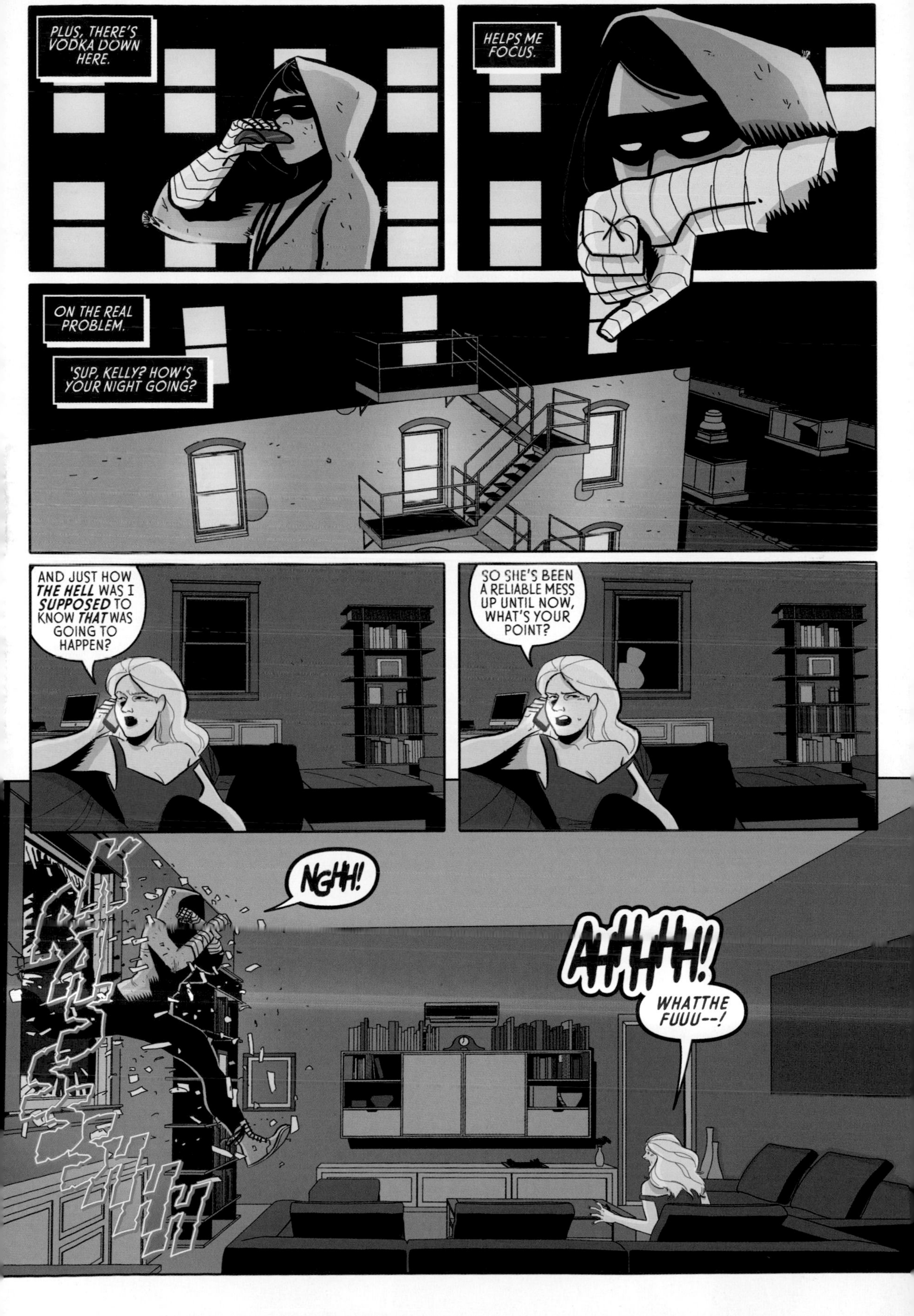
PLUS, THERE'S VODKA DOWN HERE.
HELPS ME FOCUS.
ON THE REAL PROBLEM.
'SUP, KELLY? HOW'S YOUR NIGHT GOING?
AND JUST HOW *THE HELL* WAS I *SUPPOSED* TO KNOW *THAT* WAS GOING TO HAPPEN?
SO SHE'S BEEN A RELIABLE MESS UP UNTIL NOW, WHAT'S YOUR POINT?
NGHH!
AHHHH!
WHATTHE FUUU--!

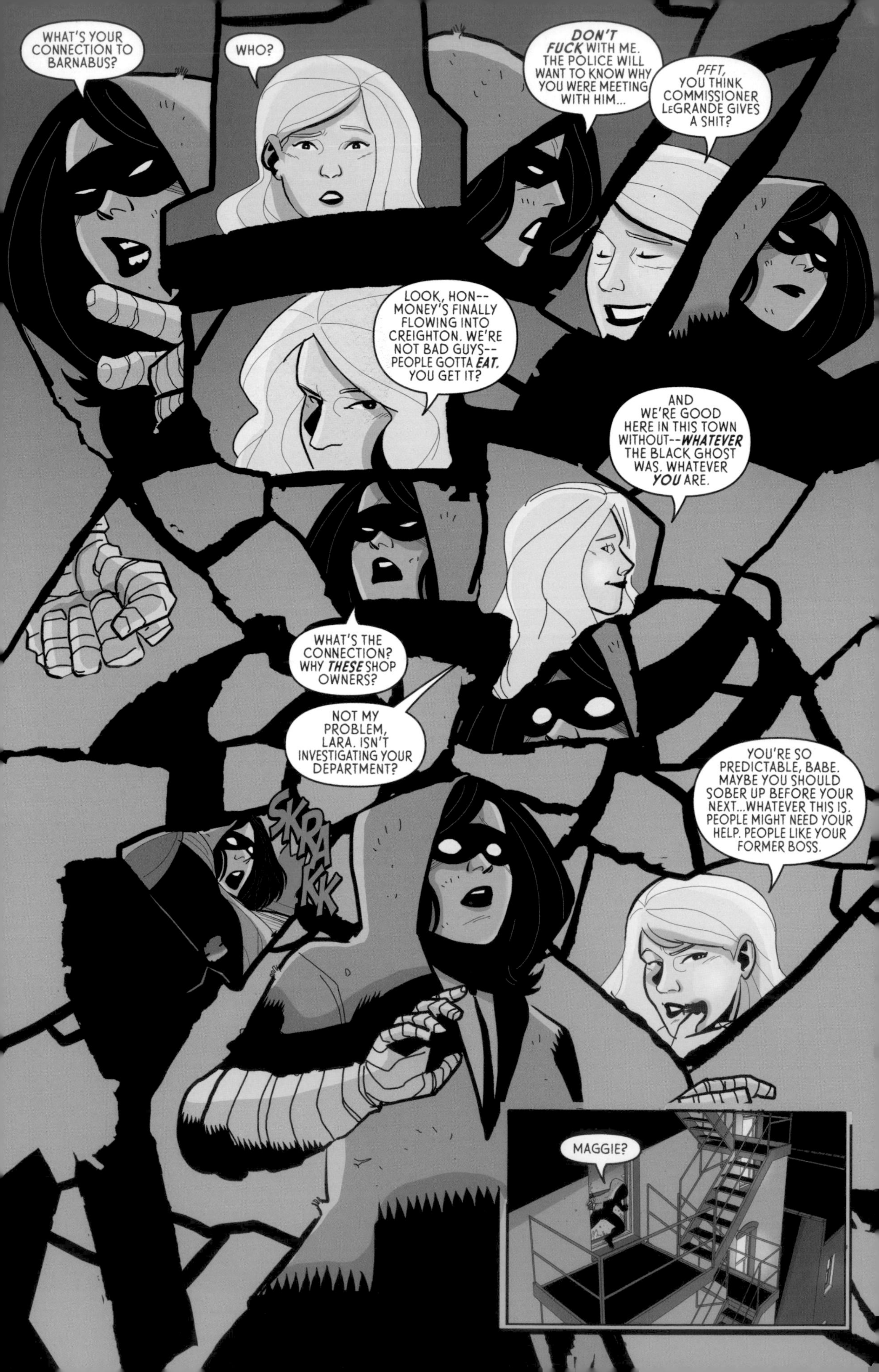
WHAT'S YOUR CONNECTION TO BARNABUS?
WHO?
***DON'T FUCK*** WITH ME. THE POLICE WILL WANT TO KNOW WHY YOU WERE MEETING WITH HIM...
*PFFT,* YOU THINK COMMISSIONER LEGRANDE GIVES A SHIT?
LOOK, HON-- MONEY'S FINALLY FLOWING INTO CREIGHTON. WE'RE NOT BAD GUYS-- PEOPLE GOTTA ***EAT.*** YOU GET IT?
AND WE'RE GOOD HERE IN THIS TOWN WITHOUT--***WHATEVER*** THE BLACK GHOST WAS. WHATEVER ***YOU*** ARE.
WHAT'S THE CONNECTION? WHY ***THESE*** SHOP OWNERS?
NOT MY PROBLEM, LARA. ISN'T INVESTIGATING YOUR DEPARTMENT?
YOU'RE SO PREDICTABLE, BABE. MAYBE YOU SHOULD SOBER UP BEFORE YOUR NEXT...WHATEVER THIS IS. PEOPLE MIGHT NEED YOUR HELP. PEOPLE LIKE YOUR FORMER BOSS.
SKRAKK
MAGGIE?

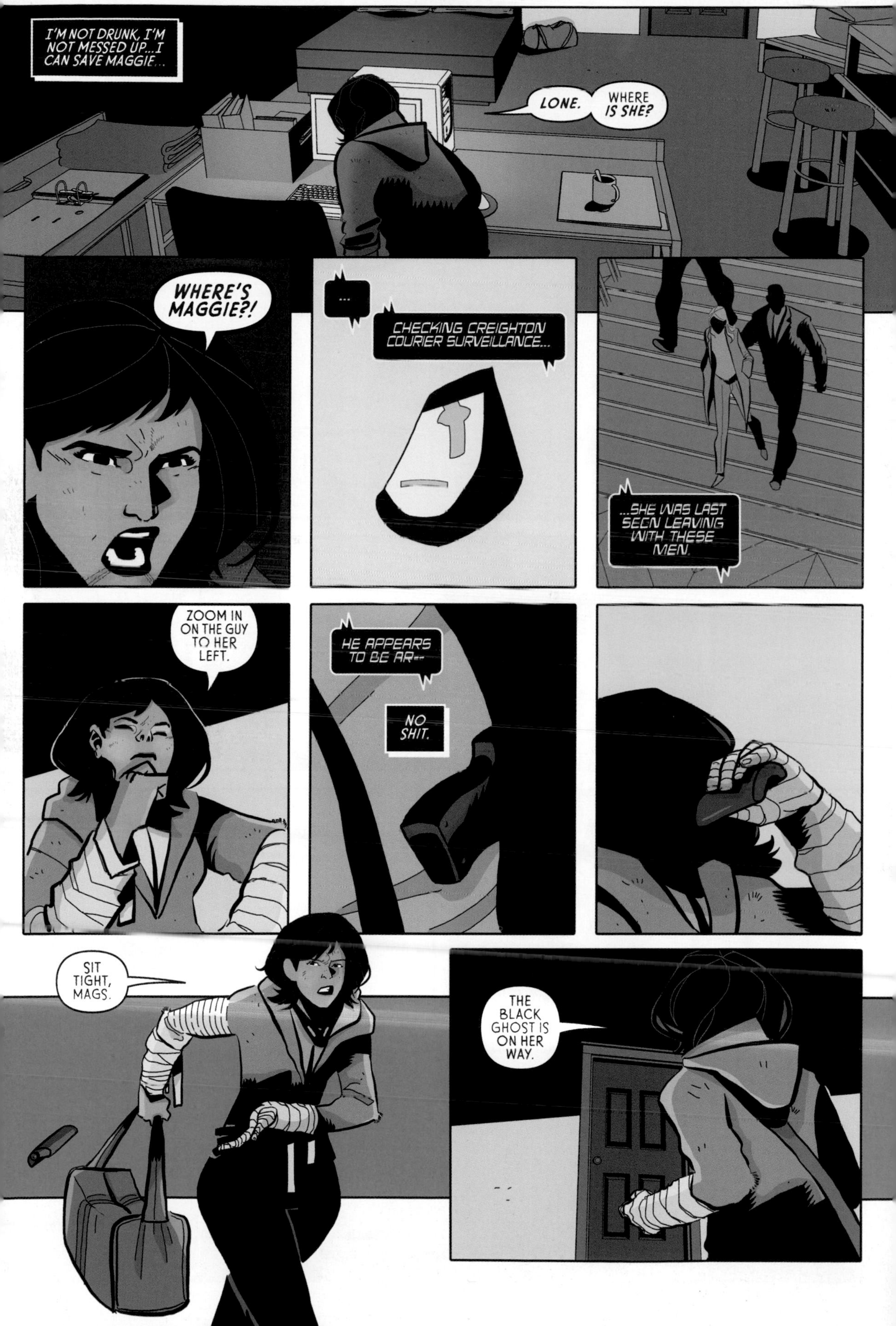
I'M NOT DRUNK, I'M NOT MESSED UP...I CAN SAVE MAGGIE...
LONE.
WHERE IS SHE?
WHERE'S MAGGIE?!
...
CHECKING CREIGHTON COURIER SURVEILLANCE...
...SHE WAS LAST SEEN LEAVING WITH THESE MEN.
ZOOM IN ON THE GUY TO HER LEFT.
HE APPEARS TO BE AR--
NO SHIT.
SIT TIGHT, MAGS.
THE BLACK GHOST IS ON HER WAY.

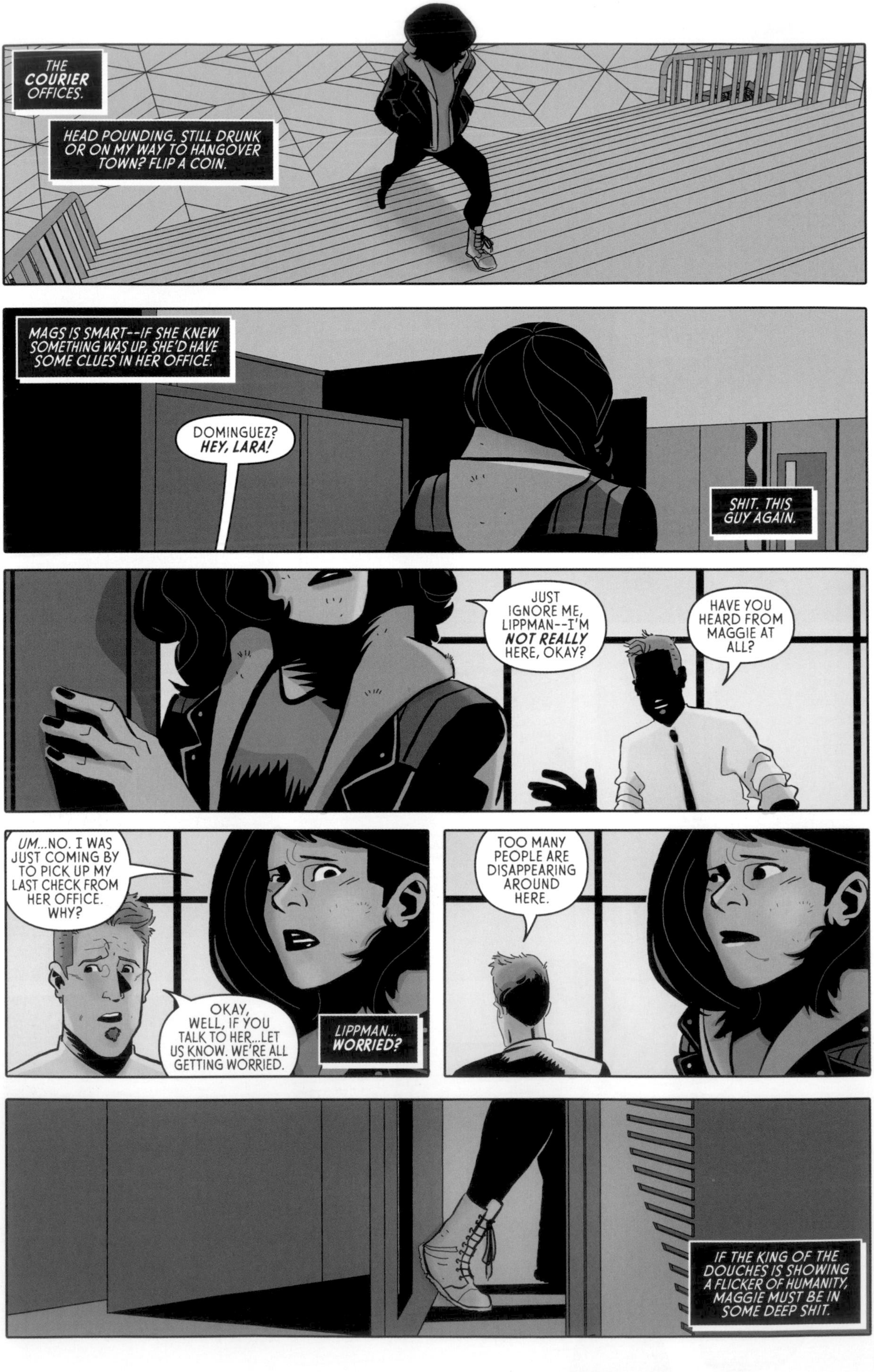
THE COURIER OFFICES.
HEAD POUNDING. STILL DRUNK OR ON MY WAY TO HANGOVER TOWN? FLIP A COIN.
MAGS IS SMART--IF SHE KNEW SOMETHING WAS UP, SHE'D HAVE SOME CLUES IN HER OFFICE.
DOMINGUEZ? HEY, LARA!
SHIT. THIS GUY AGAIN.
JUST IGNORE ME, LIPPMAN--I'M NOT REALLY HERE, OKAY?
HAVE YOU HEARD FROM MAGGIE AT ALL?
UM...NO. I WAS JUST COMING BY TO PICK UP MY LAST CHECK FROM HER OFFICE. WHY?
OKAY, WELL, IF YOU TALK TO HER...LET US KNOW. WE'RE ALL GETTING WORRIED.
LIPPMAN... WORRIED?
TOO MANY PEOPLE ARE DISAPPEARING AROUND HERE.
IF THE KING OF THE DOUCHES IS SHOWING A FLICKER OF HUMANITY, MAGGIE MUST BE IN SOME DEEP SHIT.

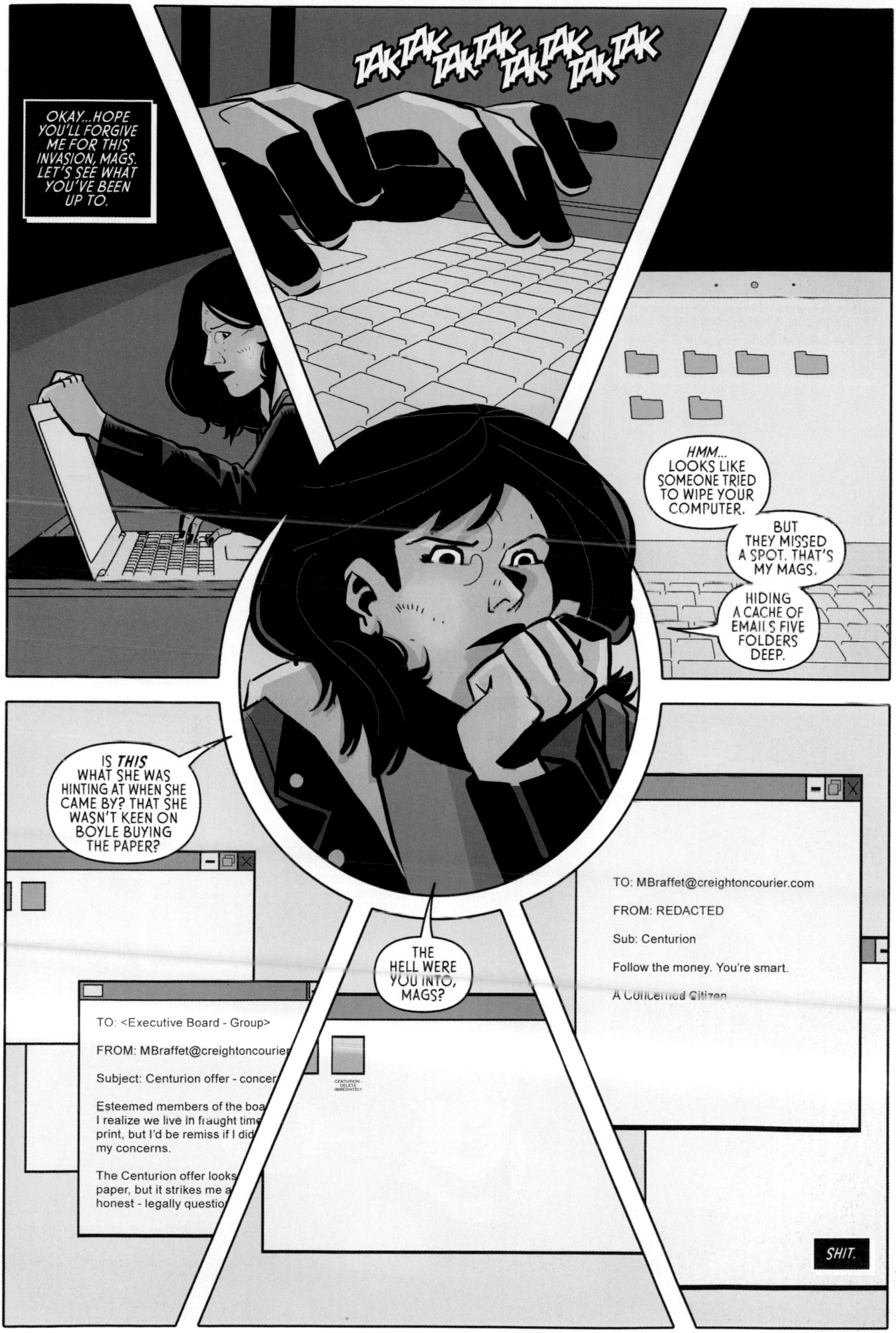
OKAY...HOPE YOU'LL FORGIVE ME FOR THIS INVASION, MAGS. LET'S SEE WHAT YOU'VE BEEN UP TO.
TAKTAK TAKTAK TAKTAK TAKTAK
HMM... LOOKS LIKE SOMEONE TRIED TO WIPE YOUR COMPUTER.
BUT THEY MISSED A SPOT. THAT'S MY MAGS.
HIDING A CACHE OF EMAILS FIVE FOLDERS DEEP.
IS THIS WHAT SHE WAS HINTING AT WHEN SHE CAME BY? THAT SHE WASN'T KEEN ON BOYLE BUYING THE PAPER?
TO: MBraffet@creightoncourier.com
FROM: REDACTED
Sub: Centurion
Follow the money. You're smart.
A Concerned Citizen
THE HELL WERE YOU INTO, MAGS?
TO: <Executive Board - Group>
FROM: MBraffet@creightoncourier
Subject: Centurion offer - concer
Esteemed members of the boa
I realize we live in fraught time
print, but I'd be remiss if I did
my concerns.
The Centurion offer looks
paper, but it strikes me a
honest - legally questio
CENTURION - DELETE IMMEDIATELY
SHIT.

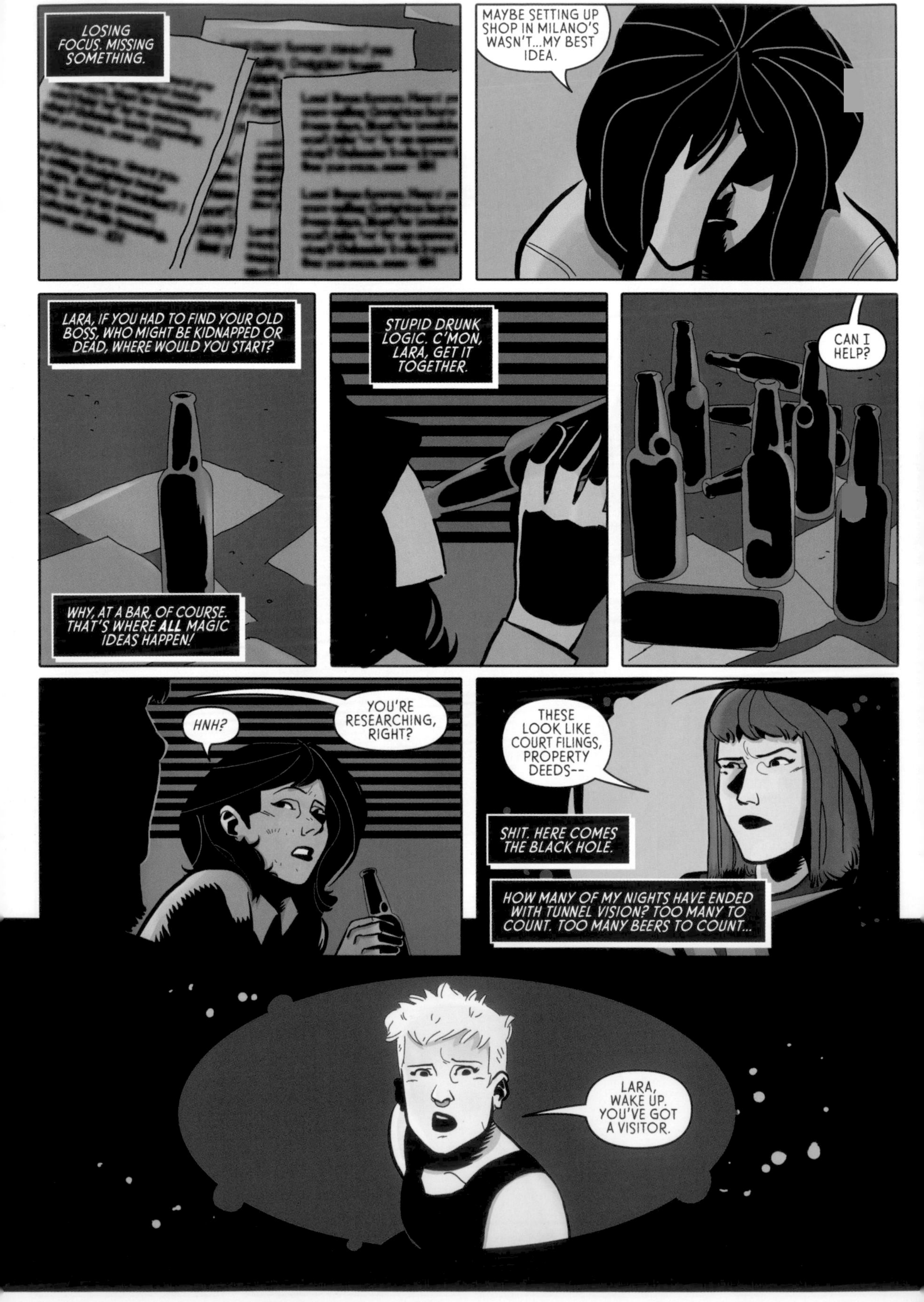
LOSING FOCUS. MISSING SOMETHING.
MAYBE SETTING UP SHOP IN MILANO'S WASN'T...MY BEST IDEA.
LARA, IF YOU HAD TO FIND YOUR OLD BOSS, WHO MIGHT BE KIDNAPPED OR DEAD, WHERE WOULD YOU START?
WHY, AT A BAR, OF COURSE. THAT'S WHERE ALL MAGIC IDEAS HAPPEN!
STUPID DRUNK LOGIC. C'MON, LARA, GET IT TOGETHER.
CAN I HELP?
YOU'RE RESEARCHING, RIGHT?
HNH?
THESE LOOK LIKE COURT FILINGS, PROPERTY DEEDS--
SHIT. HERE COMES THE BLACK HOLE.
HOW MANY OF MY NIGHTS HAVE ENDED WITH TUNNEL VISION? TOO MANY TO COUNT. TOO MANY BEERS TO COUNT...
LARA, WAKE UP. YOU'VE GOT A VISITOR.

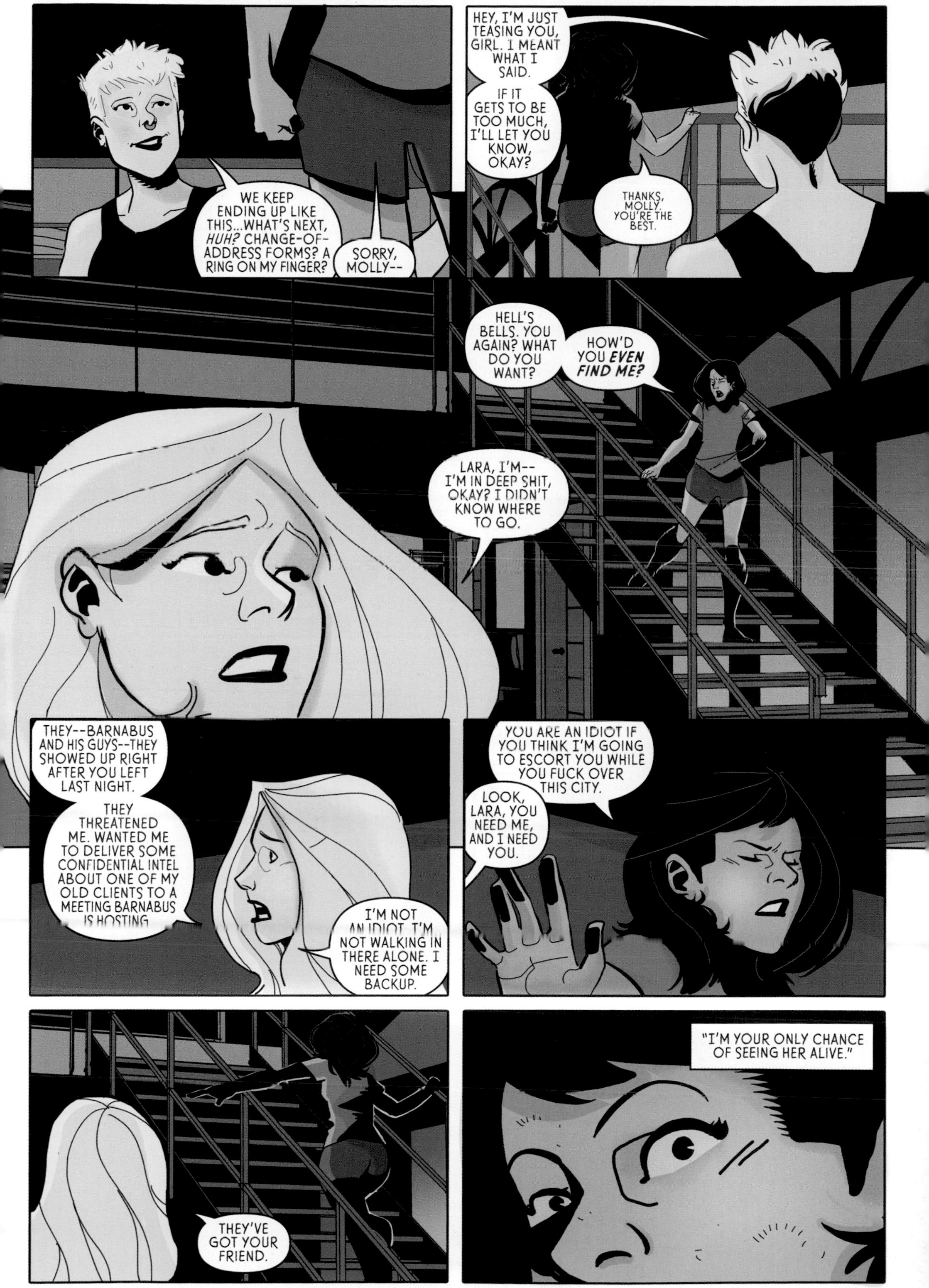
WE KEEP ENDING UP LIKE THIS...WHAT'S NEXT, *HUH?* CHANGE-OF-ADDRESS FORMS? A RING ON MY FINGER?
SORRY, MOLLY--
HEY, I'M JUST TEASING YOU, GIRL. I MEANT WHAT I SAID.
IF IT GETS TO BE TOO MUCH, I'LL LET YOU KNOW, OKAY?
THANKS, MOLLY. YOU'RE THE BEST.
HELL'S BELLS. YOU AGAIN? WHAT DO YOU WANT?
HOW'D YOU ***EVEN FIND ME?***
LARA, I'M-- I'M IN DEEP SHIT, OKAY? I DIDN'T KNOW WHERE TO GO.
THEY--BARNABUS AND HIS GUYS--THEY SHOWED UP RIGHT AFTER YOU LEFT LAST NIGHT.
THEY THREATENED ME. WANTED ME TO DELIVER SOME CONFIDENTIAL INTEL ABOUT ONE OF MY OLD CLIENTS TO A MEETING BARNABUS IS HOSTING.
I'M NOT AN IDIOT. I'M NOT WALKING IN THERE ALONE. I NEED SOME BACKUP.
YOU ARE AN IDIOT IF YOU THINK I'M GOING TO ESCORT YOU WHILE YOU FUCK OVER THIS CITY.
LOOK, LARA, YOU NEED ME, AND I NEED YOU.
THEY'VE GOT YOUR FRIEND.
"I'M YOUR ONLY CHANCE OF SEEING HER ALIVE."

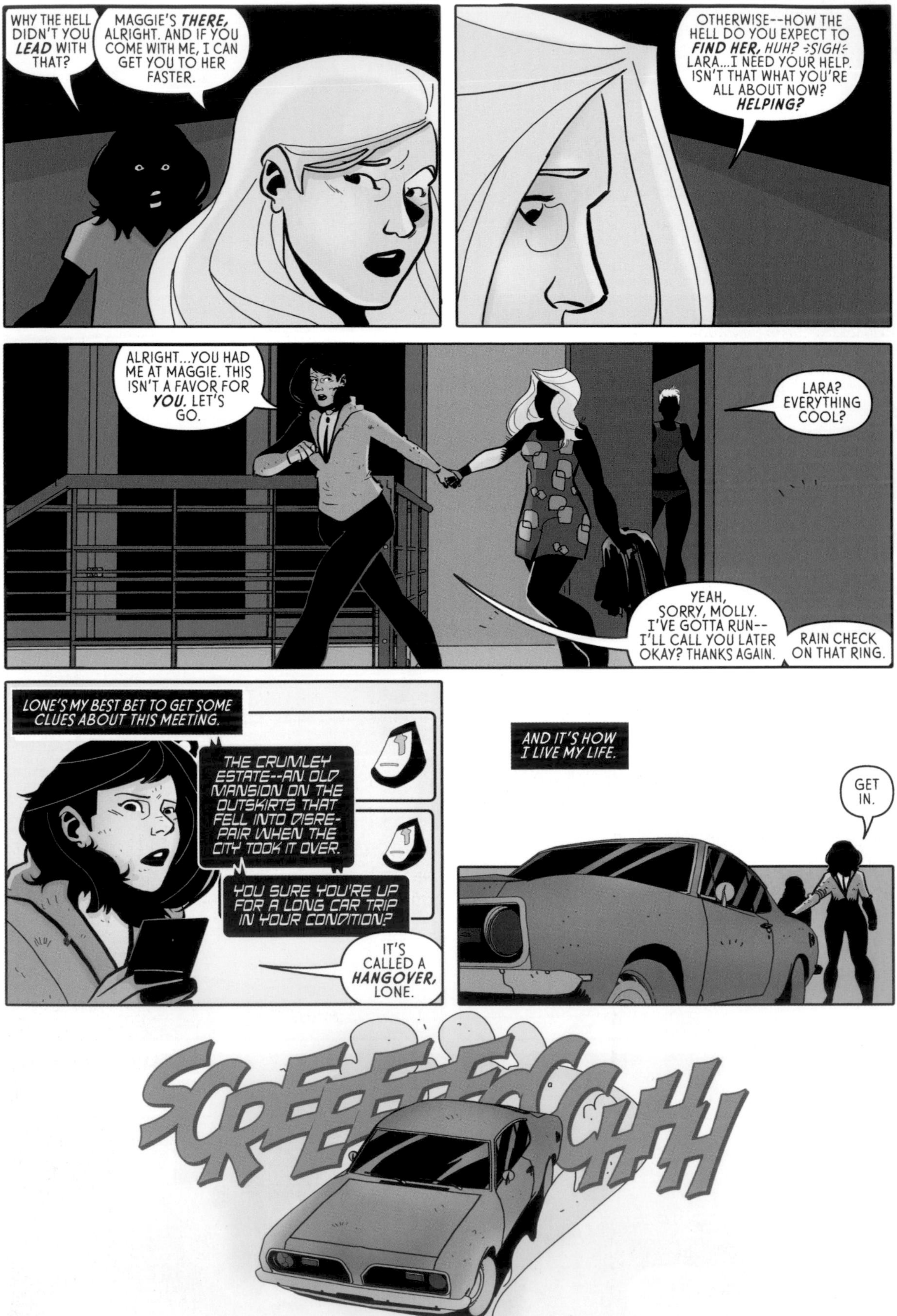
WHY THE HELL DIDN'T YOU LEAD WITH THAT?
MAGGIE'S THERE, ALRIGHT. AND IF YOU COME WITH ME, I CAN GET YOU TO HER FASTER.
OTHERWISE--HOW THE HELL DO YOU EXPECT TO FIND HER, HUH? ⪢SIGH⪡ LARA...I NEED YOUR HELP. ISN'T THAT WHAT YOU'RE ALL ABOUT NOW? HELPING?
ALRIGHT...YOU HAD ME AT MAGGIE. THIS ISN'T A FAVOR FOR YOU. LET'S GO.
LARA? EVERYTHING COOL?
YEAH, SORRY, MOLLY. I'VE GOTTA RUN-- I'LL CALL YOU LATER OKAY? THANKS AGAIN.
RAIN CHECK ON THAT RING.
LONE'S MY BEST BET TO GET SOME CLUES ABOUT THIS MEETING.
THE CRUMLEY ESTATE--AN OLD MANSION ON THE OUTSKIRTS THAT FELL INTO DISREPAIR WHEN THE CITY TOOK IT OVER.
YOU SURE YOU'RE UP FOR A LONG CAR TRIP IN YOUR CONDITION?
IT'S CALLED A HANGOVER, LONE.
AND IT'S HOW I LIVE MY LIFE.
GET IN.
SCREEEEECCHHH

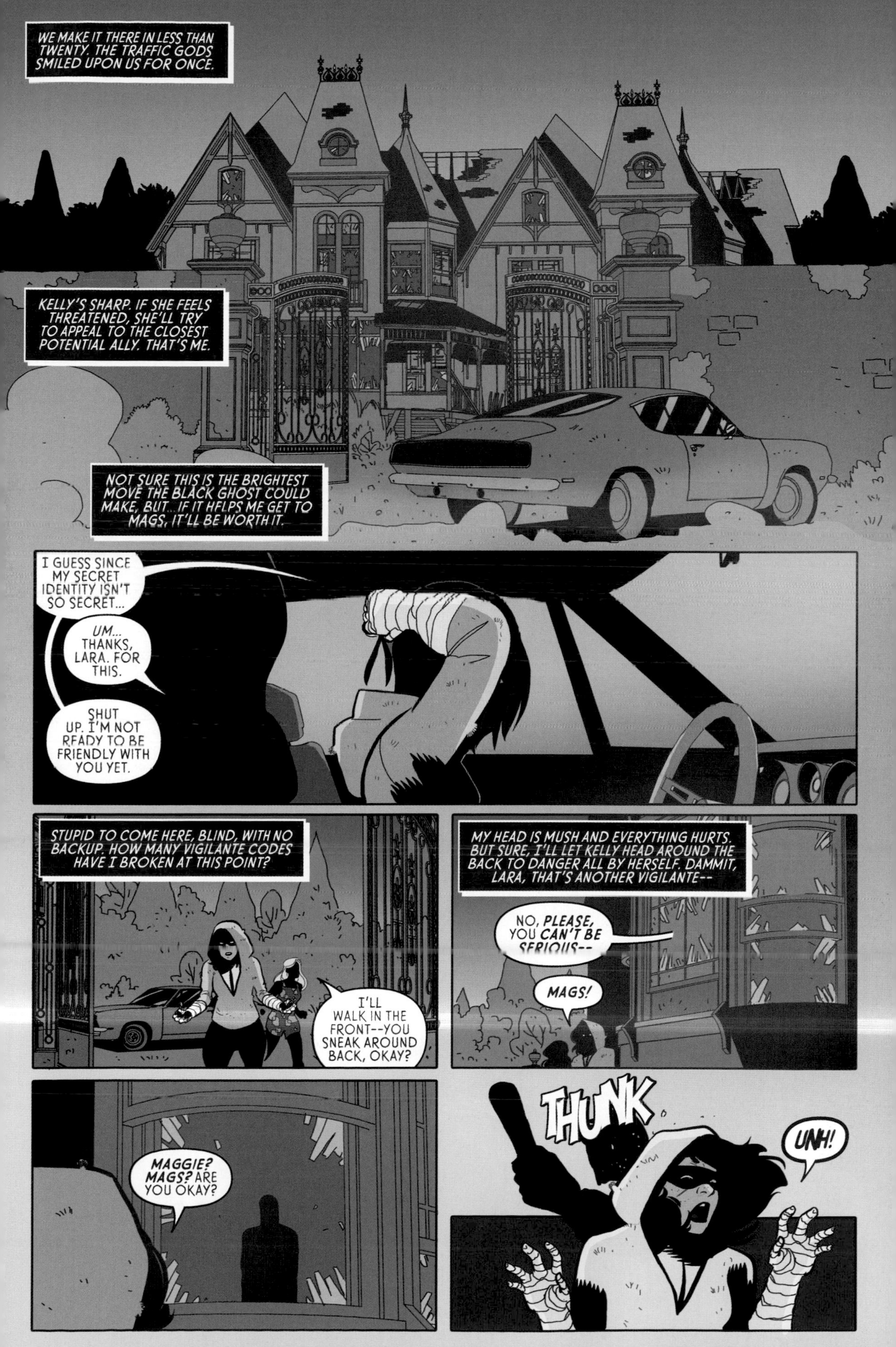
WE MAKE IT THERE IN LESS THAN TWENTY. THE TRAFFIC GODS SMILED UPON US FOR ONCE.
KELLY'S SHARP. IF SHE FEELS THREATENED, SHE'LL TRY TO APPEAL TO THE CLOSEST POTENTIAL ALLY. THAT'S ME.
NOT SURE THIS IS THE BRIGHTEST MOVE THE BLACK GHOST COULD MAKE, BUT... IF IT HELPS ME GET TO MAGS, IT'LL BE WORTH IT.
I GUESS SINCE MY SECRET IDENTITY ISN'T SO SECRET...
UM... THANKS, LARA. FOR THIS.
SHUT UP. I'M NOT READY TO BE FRIENDLY WITH YOU YET.
STUPID TO COME HERE, BLIND, WITH NO BACKUP. HOW MANY VIGILANTE CODES HAVE I BROKEN AT THIS POINT?
I'LL WALK IN THE FRONT--YOU SNEAK AROUND BACK, OKAY?
MY HEAD IS MUSH AND EVERYTHING HURTS. BUT SURE, I'LL LET KELLY HEAD AROUND THE BACK TO DANGER ALL BY HERSELF. DAMMIT, LARA, THAT'S ANOTHER VIGILANTE--
NO, PLEASE, YOU CAN'T BE SERIOUS--
MAGS!
MAGGIE? MAGS? ARE YOU OKAY?
THUNK
UNH!

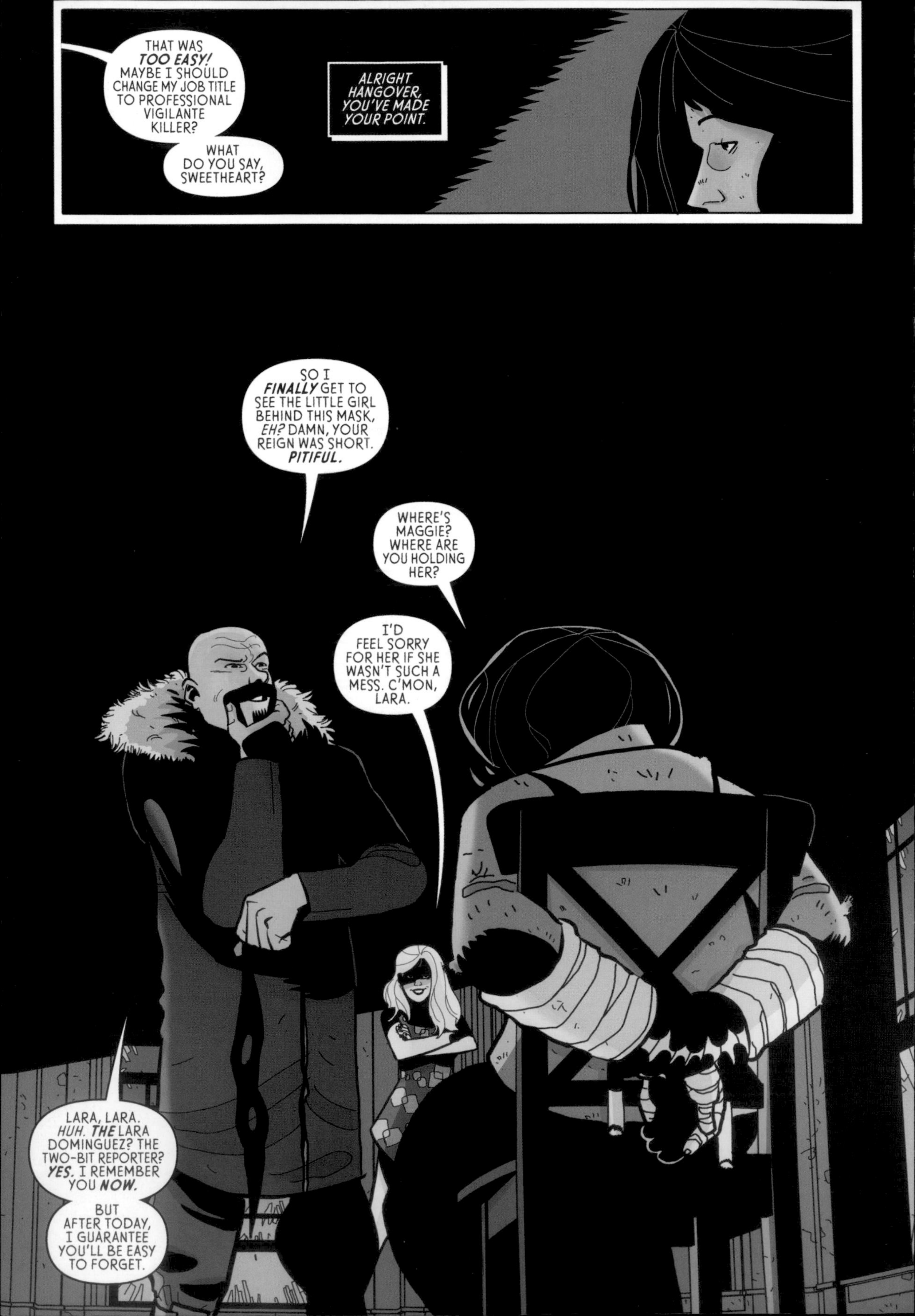

THAT WAS TOO EASY! MAYBE I SHOULD CHANGE MY JOB TITLE TO PROFESSIONAL VIGILANTE KILLER?
WHAT DO YOU SAY, SWEETHEART?
ALRIGHT HANGOVER, YOU'VE MADE YOUR POINT.
SO I FINALLY GET TO SEE THE LITTLE GIRL BEHIND THIS MASK, EH? DAMN, YOUR REIGN WAS SHORT. PITIFUL.
WHERE'S MAGGIE? WHERE ARE YOU HOLDING HER?
I'D FEEL SORRY FOR HER IF SHE WASN'T SUCH A MESS. C'MON, LARA.
LARA, LARA. HUH. THE LARA DOMINGUEZ? THE TWO-BIT REPORTER? YES. I REMEMBER YOU NOW.
BUT AFTER TODAY, I GUARANTEE YOU'LL BE EASY TO FORGET.

# CHAPTER 5
## A STRANGER IN MY GRAVE
COVER BY MONICA GALLAGHER

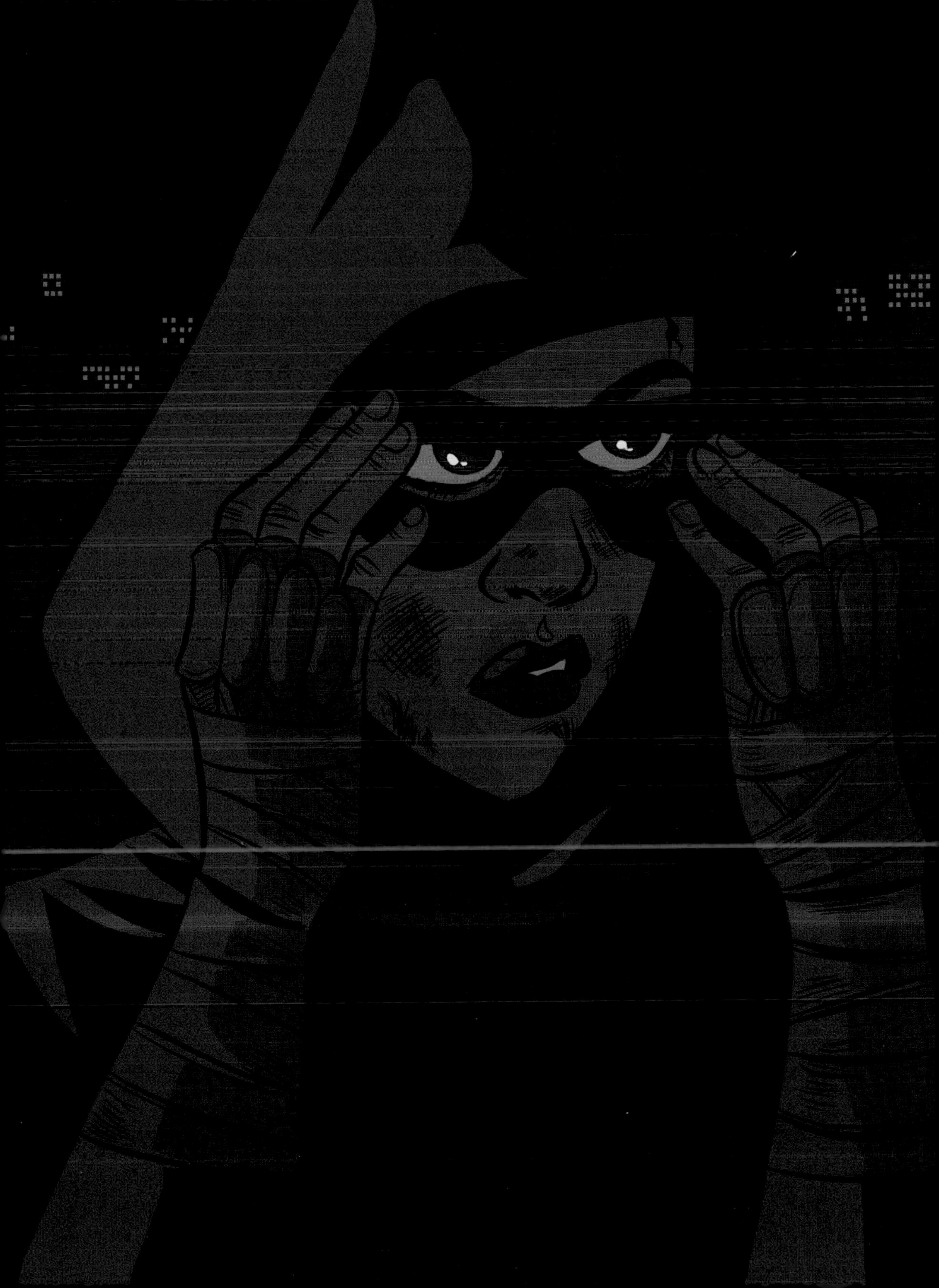

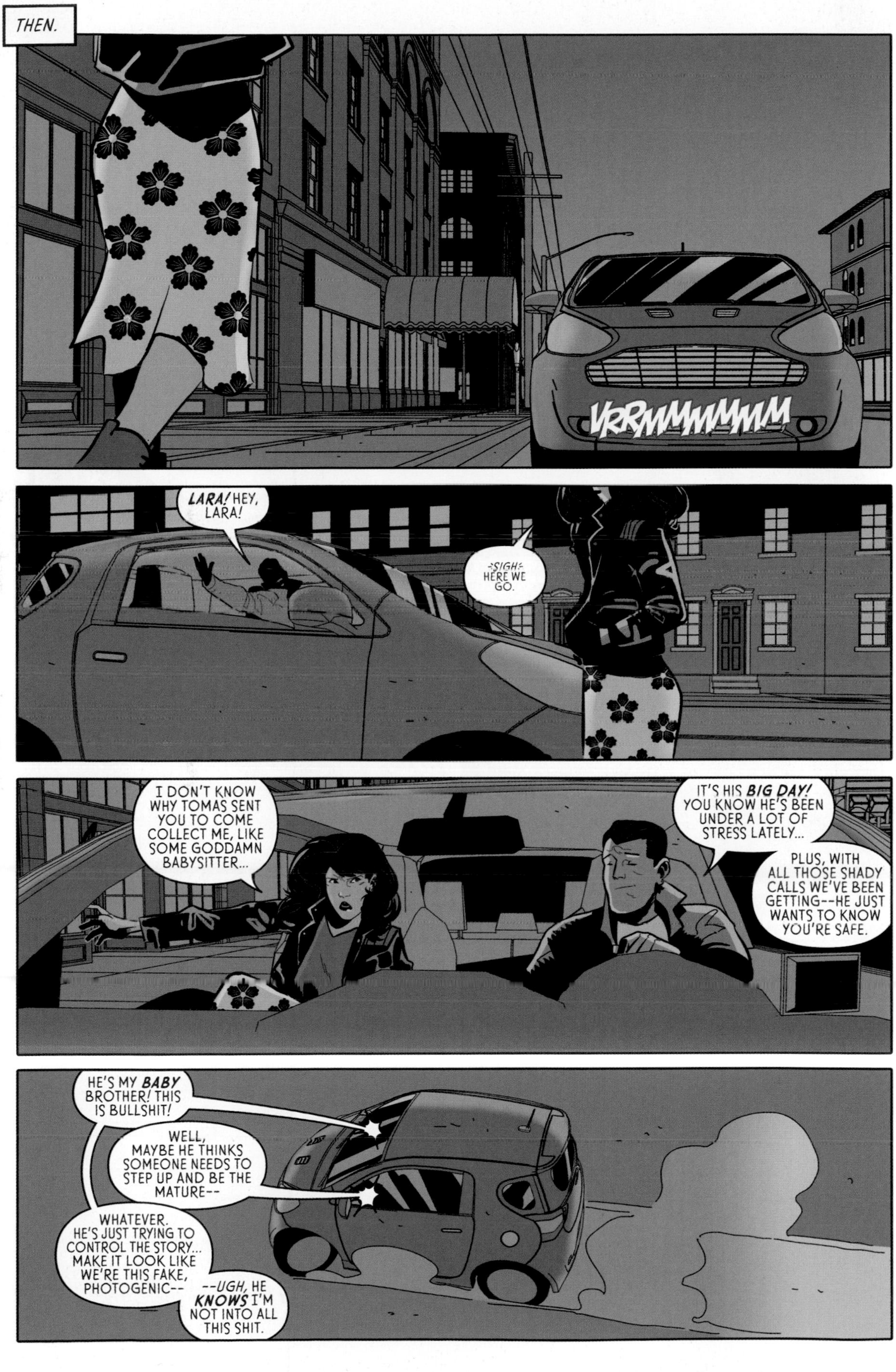
THEN.
VRRMMMMMM
LARA! HEY, LARA!
*SIGH* HERE WE GO.
I DON'T KNOW WHY TOMAS SENT YOU TO COME COLLECT ME, LIKE SOME GODDAMN BABYSITTER...
IT'S HIS **BIG DAY!** YOU KNOW HE'S BEEN UNDER A LOT OF STRESS LATELY...
PLUS, WITH ALL THOSE SHADY CALLS WE'VE BEEN GETTING--HE JUST WANTS TO KNOW YOU'RE SAFE.
HE'S MY **BABY** BROTHER! THIS IS BULLSHIT!
WELL, MAYBE HE THINKS SOMEONE NEEDS TO STEP UP AND BE THE MATURE--
WHATEVER. HE'S JUST TRYING TO CONTROL THE STORY... MAKE IT LOOK LIKE WE'RE THIS FAKE, PHOTOGENIC--
--*UGH,* HE **KNOWS** I'M NOT INTO ALL THIS SHIT.

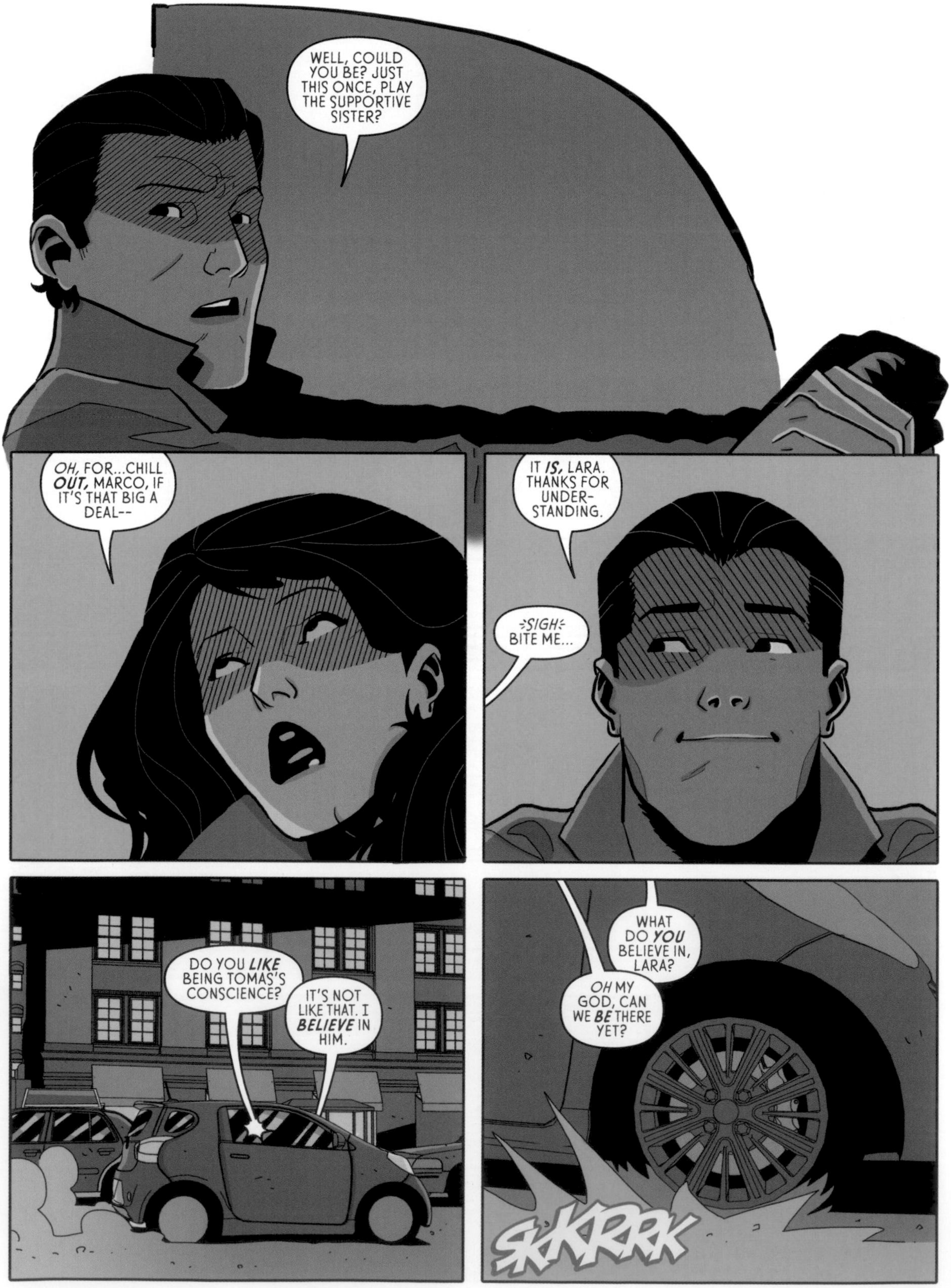
WELL, COULD YOU BE? JUST THIS ONCE, PLAY THE SUPPORTIVE SISTER?
OH, FOR...CHILL OUT, MARCO, IF IT'S THAT BIG A DEAL--
IT IS, LARA. THANKS FOR UNDER-STANDING.
SIGH BITE ME...
DO YOU LIKE BEING TOMAS'S CONSCIENCE?
IT'S NOT LIKE THAT. I BELIEVE IN HIM.
WHAT DO YOU BELIEVE IN, LARA?
OH MY GOD, CAN WE BE THERE YET?
SKKRRRK

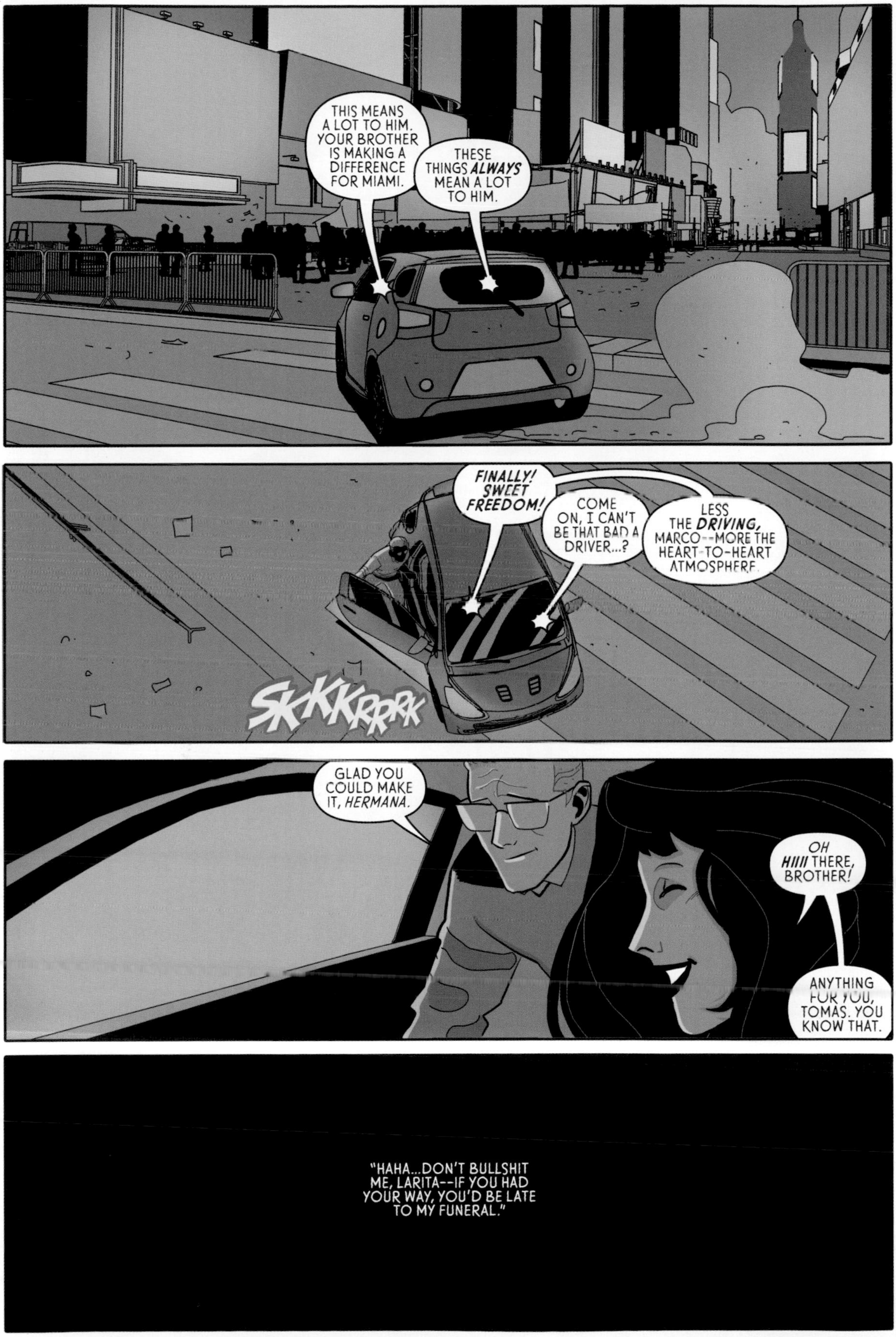
THIS MEANS A LOT TO HIM. YOUR BROTHER IS MAKING A DIFFERENCE FOR MIAMI.
THESE THINGS ***ALWAYS*** MEAN A LOT TO HIM.
***FINALLY! SWEET FREEDOM!***
COME ON, I CAN'T BE THAT BAD A DRIVER...?
LESS THE ***DRIVING,*** MARCO--MORE THE HEART-TO-HEART ATMOSPHERE.
SKKKRRRK
GLAD YOU COULD MAKE IT, *HERMANA.*
*OH* ***HIIII*** THERE, BROTHER!
ANYTHING FOR YOU, TOMAS. YOU KNOW THAT.
"HAHA...DON'T BULLSHIT ME, LARITA--IF YOU HAD YOUR WAY, YOU'D BE LATE TO MY FUNERAL."

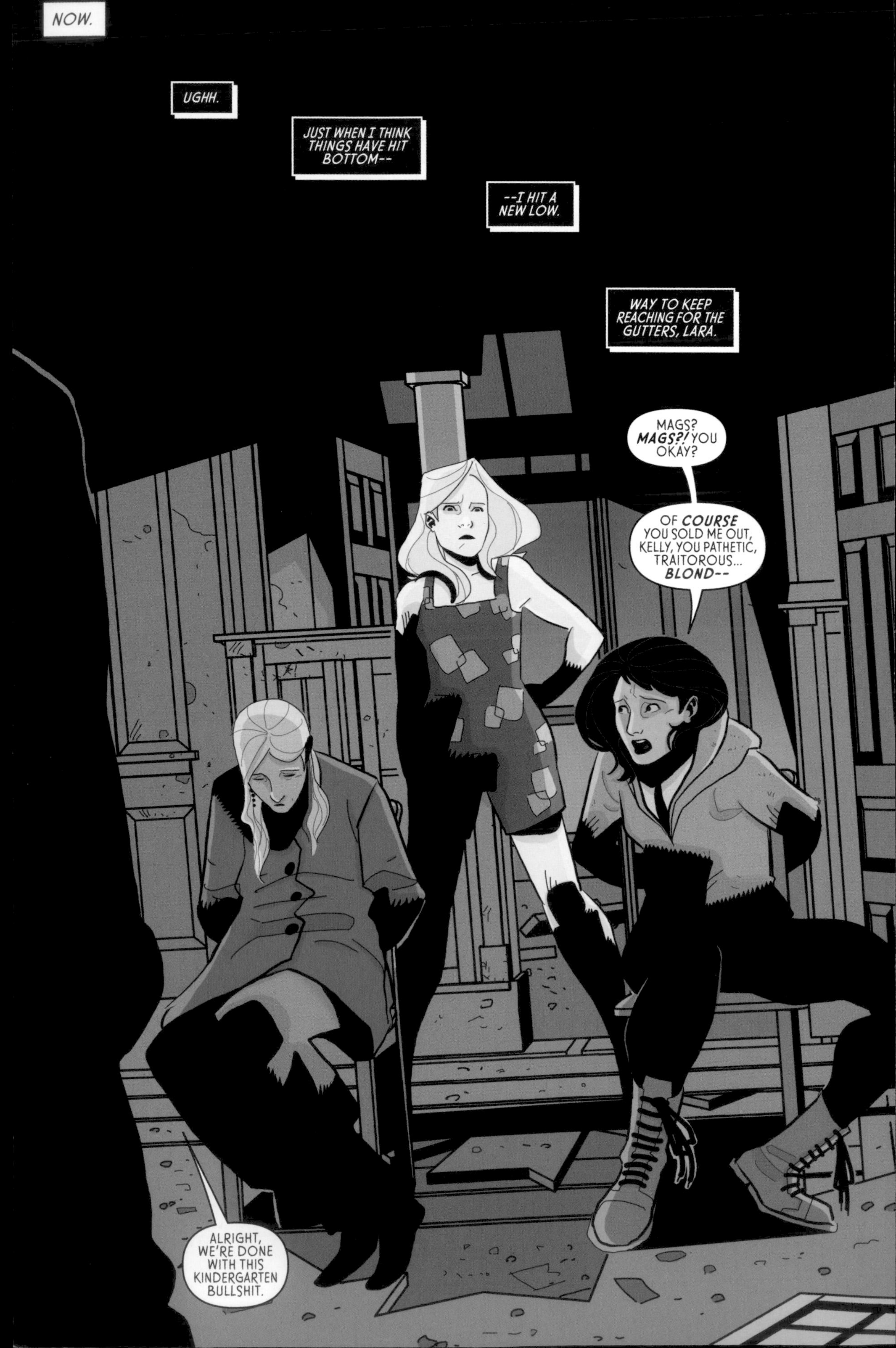
NOW.
UGHH.
JUST WHEN I THINK THINGS HAVE HIT BOTTOM--
--I HIT A NEW LOW.
WAY TO KEEP REACHING FOR THE GUTTERS, LARA.
MAGS? MAGS?! YOU OKAY?
OF COURSE YOU SOLD ME OUT, KELLY, YOU PATHETIC, TRAITOROUS... BLOND--
ALRIGHT, WE'RE DONE WITH THIS KINDERGARTEN BULLSHIT.

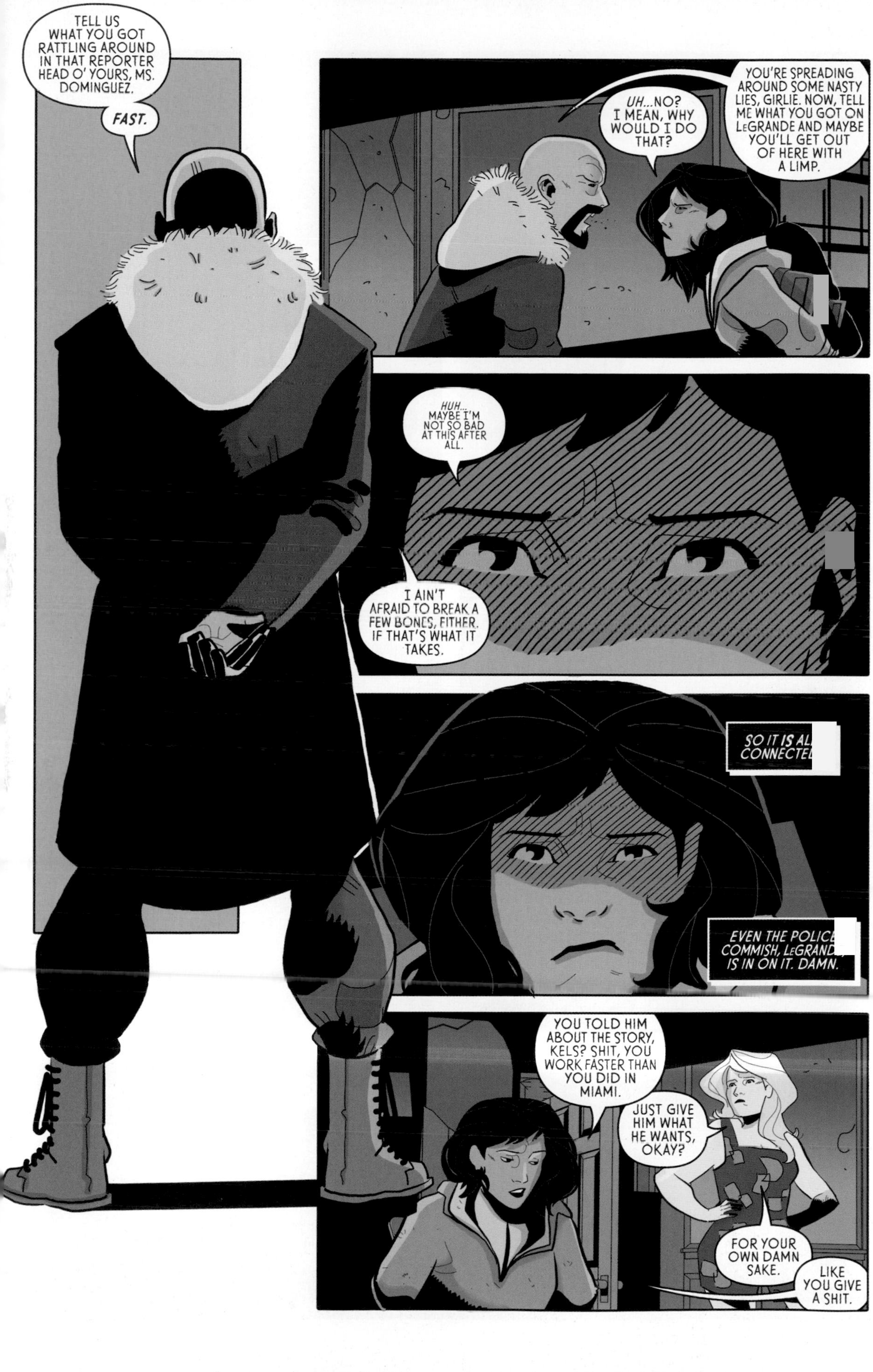
TELL US WHAT YOU GOT RATTLING AROUND IN THAT REPORTER HEAD O' YOURS, MS. DOMINGUEZ.
FAST.
YOU'RE SPREADING AROUND SOME NASTY LIES, GIRLIE. NOW, TELL ME WHAT YOU GOT ON LEGRANDE AND MAYBE YOU'LL GET OUT OF HERE WITH A LIMP.
UH...NO? I MEAN, WHY WOULD I DO THAT?
HUH... MAYBE I'M NOT SO BAD AT THIS AFTER ALL.
I AIN'T AFRAID TO BREAK A FEW BONES, FITHER. IF THAT'S WHAT IT TAKES.
SO IT IS AL
CONNECTE
EVEN THE POLICE COMMISH, LEGRAND IS IN ON IT. DAMN.
YOU TOLD HIM ABOUT THE STORY, KELS? SHIT, YOU WORK FASTER THAN YOU DID IN MIAMI.
JUST GIVE HIM WHAT HE WANTS, OKAY?
FOR YOUR OWN DAMN SAKE.
LIKE YOU GIVE A SHIT.

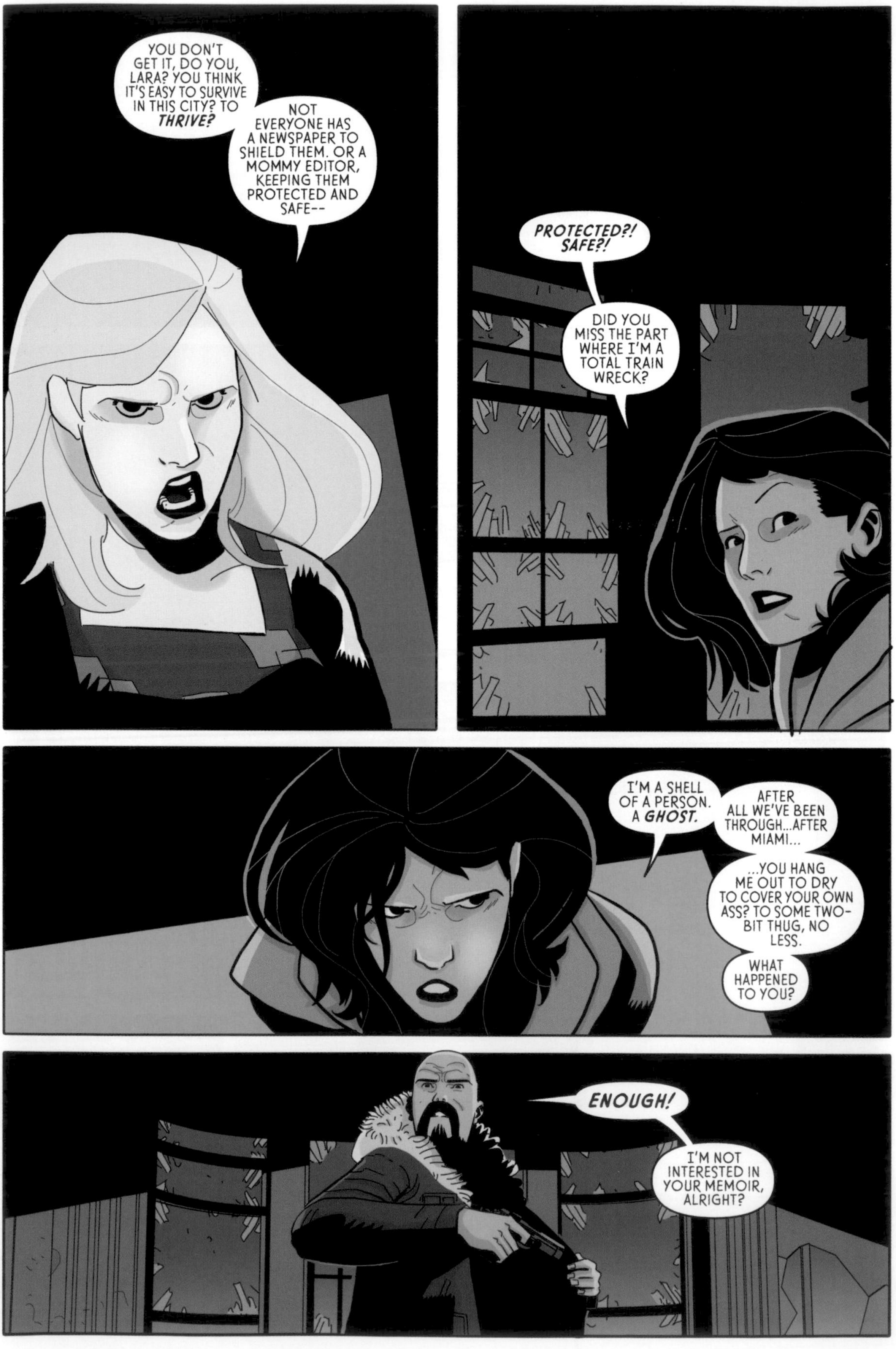
YOU DON'T GET IT, DO YOU, LARA? YOU THINK IT'S EASY TO SURVIVE IN THIS CITY? TO *THRIVE?*
NOT EVERYONE HAS A NEWSPAPER TO SHIELD THEM. OR A MOMMY EDITOR, KEEPING THEM PROTECTED AND SAFE--
*PROTECTED?! SAFE?!*
DID YOU MISS THE PART WHERE I'M A TOTAL TRAIN WRECK?
I'M A SHELL OF A PERSON. A *GHOST.*
AFTER ALL WE'VE BEEN THROUGH...AFTER MIAMI...
...YOU HANG ME OUT TO DRY TO COVER YOUR OWN ASS? TO SOME TWO-BIT THUG, NO LESS.
WHAT HAPPENED TO YOU?
*ENOUGH!*
I'M NOT INTERESTED IN YOUR MEMOIR, ALRIGHT?

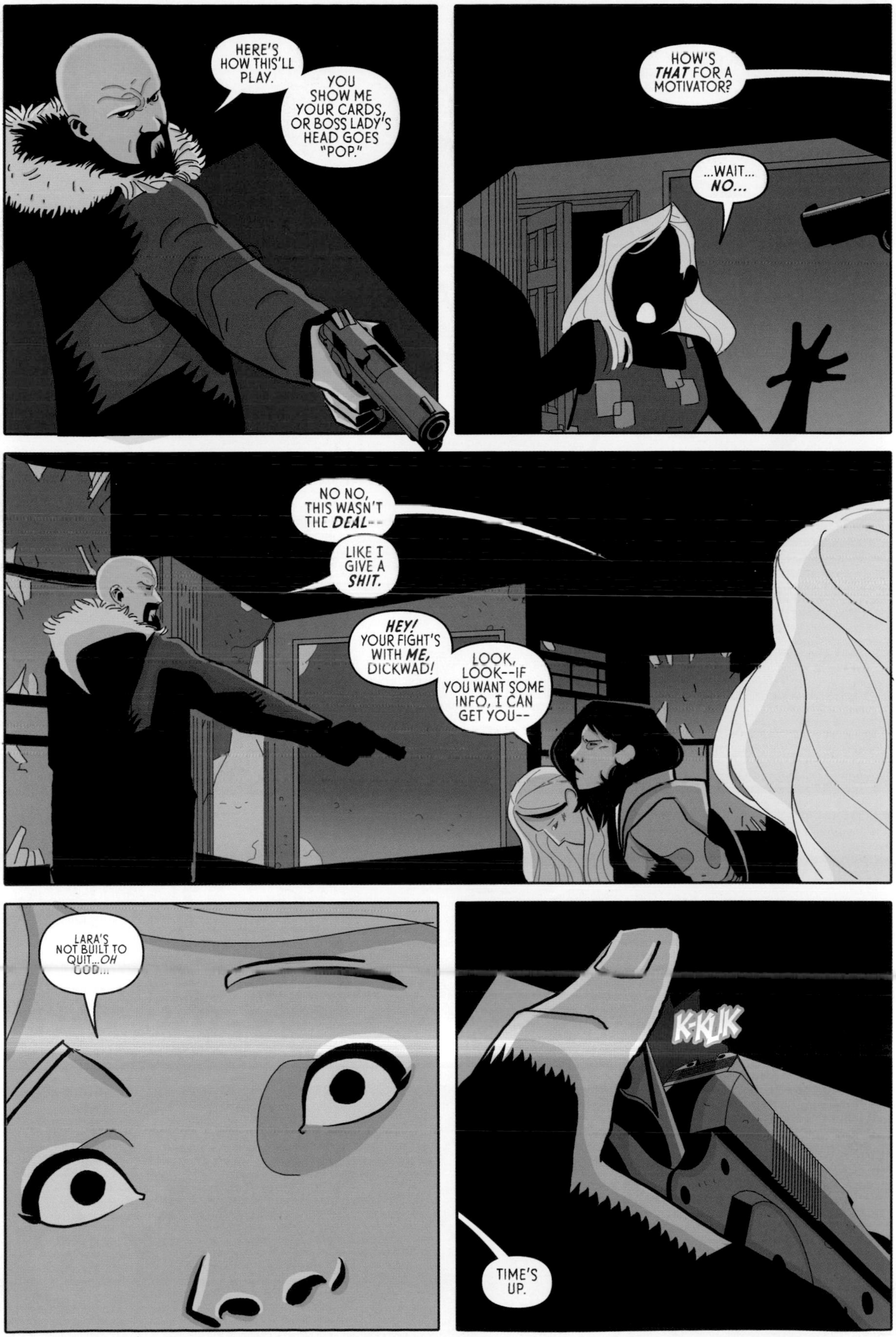
HERE'S HOW THIS'LL PLAY.
YOU SHOW ME YOUR CARDS, OR BOSS LADY'S HEAD GOES "POP."
HOW'S *THAT* FOR A MOTIVATOR?
...WAIT... *NO...*
NO NO, THIS WASN'T THE *DEAL*--
LIKE I GIVE A *SHIT.*
*HEY!* YOUR FIGHT'S WITH *ME,* DICKWAD!
LOOK, LOOK--IF YOU WANT SOME INFO, I CAN GET YOU--
LARA'S NOT BUILT TO QUIT...*OH* GOD...
K-KLIK
TIME'S UP.

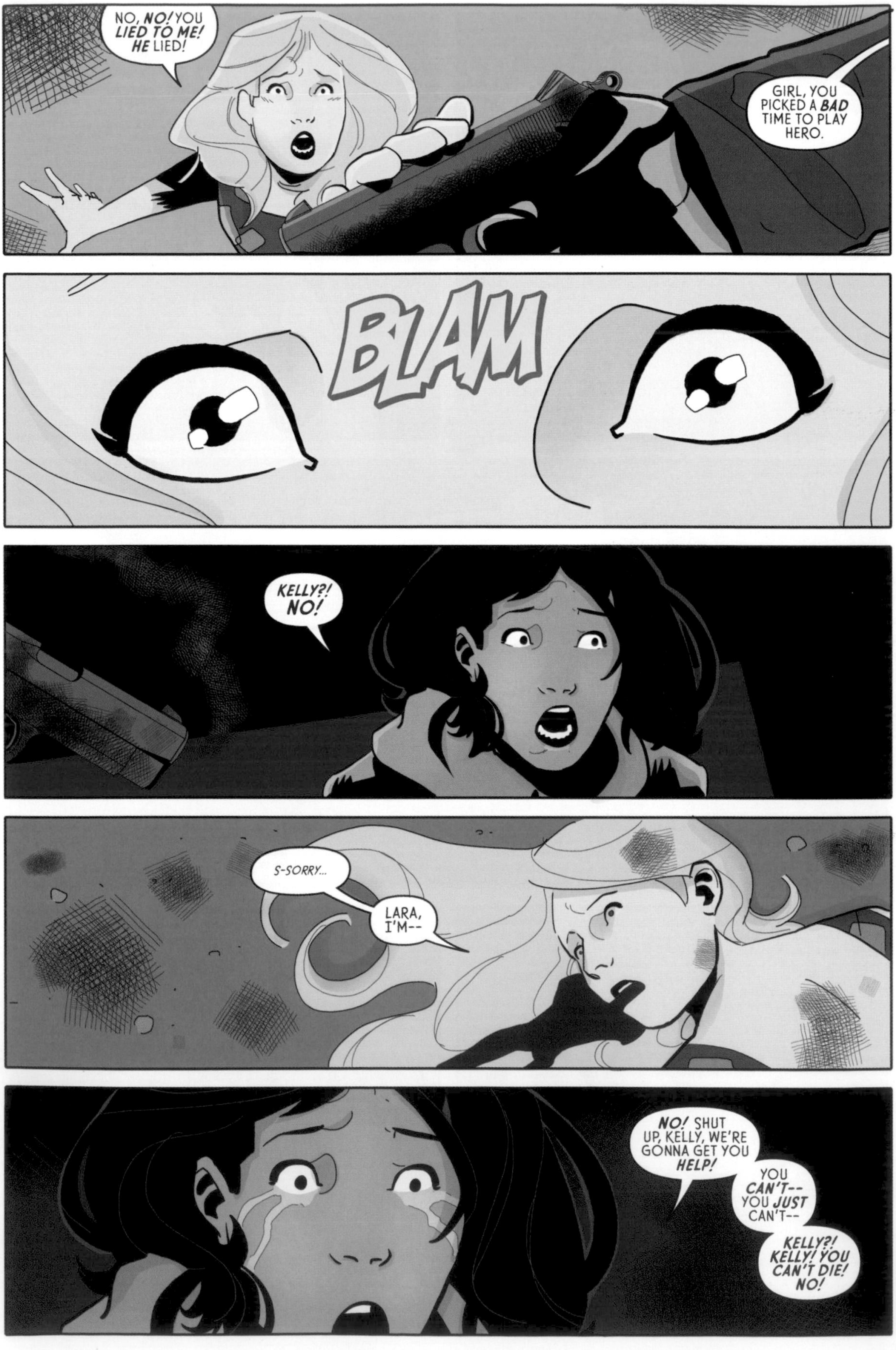
NO, **NO!** YOU **LIED TO ME! HE** LIED!
GIRL, YOU PICKED A **BAD** TIME TO PLAY HERO.
BLAM
KELLY?! NO!
S-SORRY...
LARA, I'M--
**NO!** SHUT UP, KELLY, WE'RE GONNA GET YOU **HELP!**
YOU **CAN'T--** YOU **JUST** CAN'T--
KELLY?! KELLY! YOU CAN'T DIE! NO!

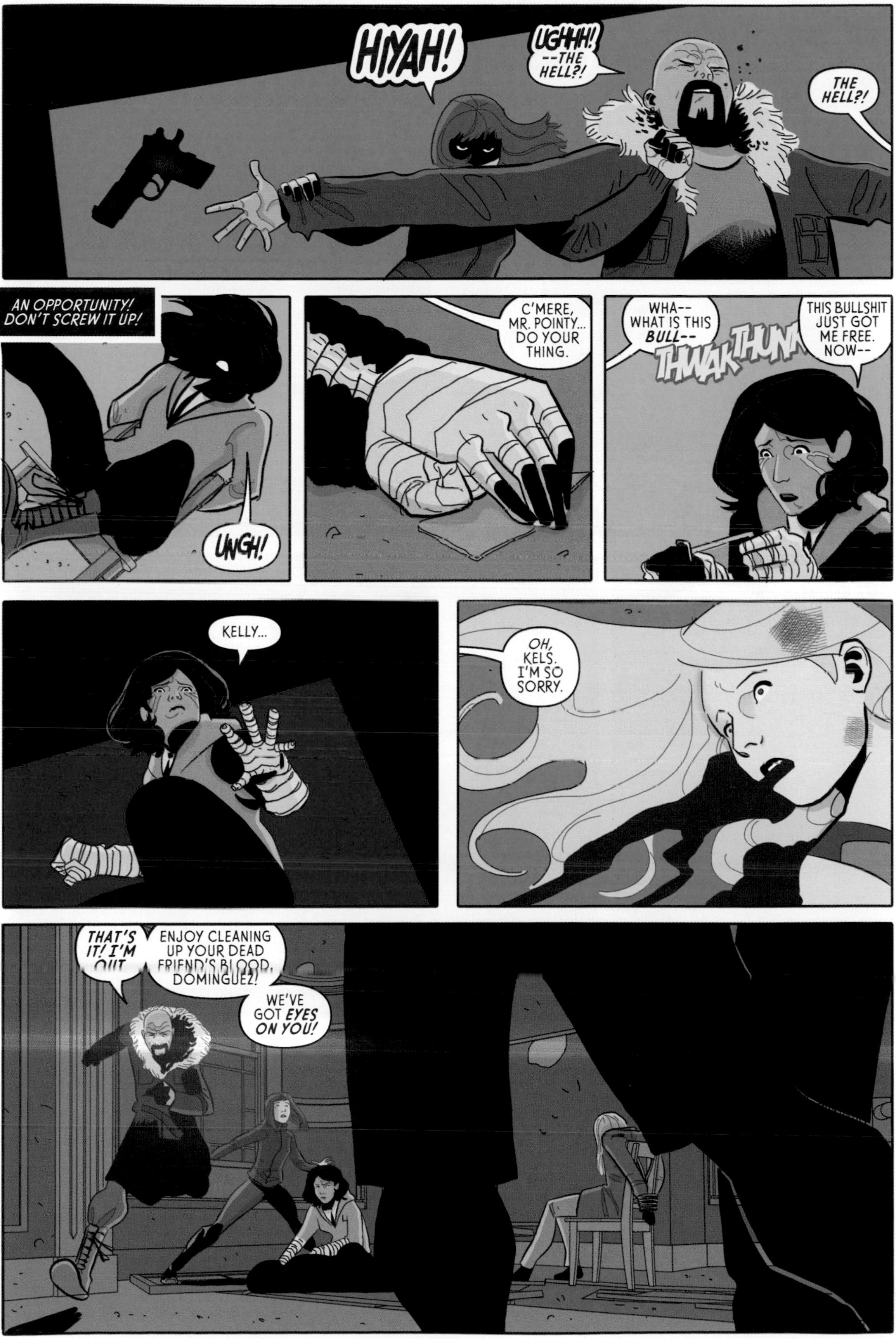
HIYAH!
UGHHH! --THE HELL?!
THE HELL?!
AN OPPORTUNITY! DON'T SCREW IT UP!
UNGH!
C'MERE, MR. POINTY... DO YOUR THING.
WHA-- WHAT IS THIS BULL--
THWAK THUNK
THIS BULLSHIT JUST GOT ME FREE. NOW--
KELLY...
OH, KELS. I'M SO SORRY.
THAT'S IT! I'M OUT.
ENJOY CLEANING UP YOUR DEAD FRIEND'S BLOOD, DOMINGUEZ!
WE'VE GOT EYES ON YOU!

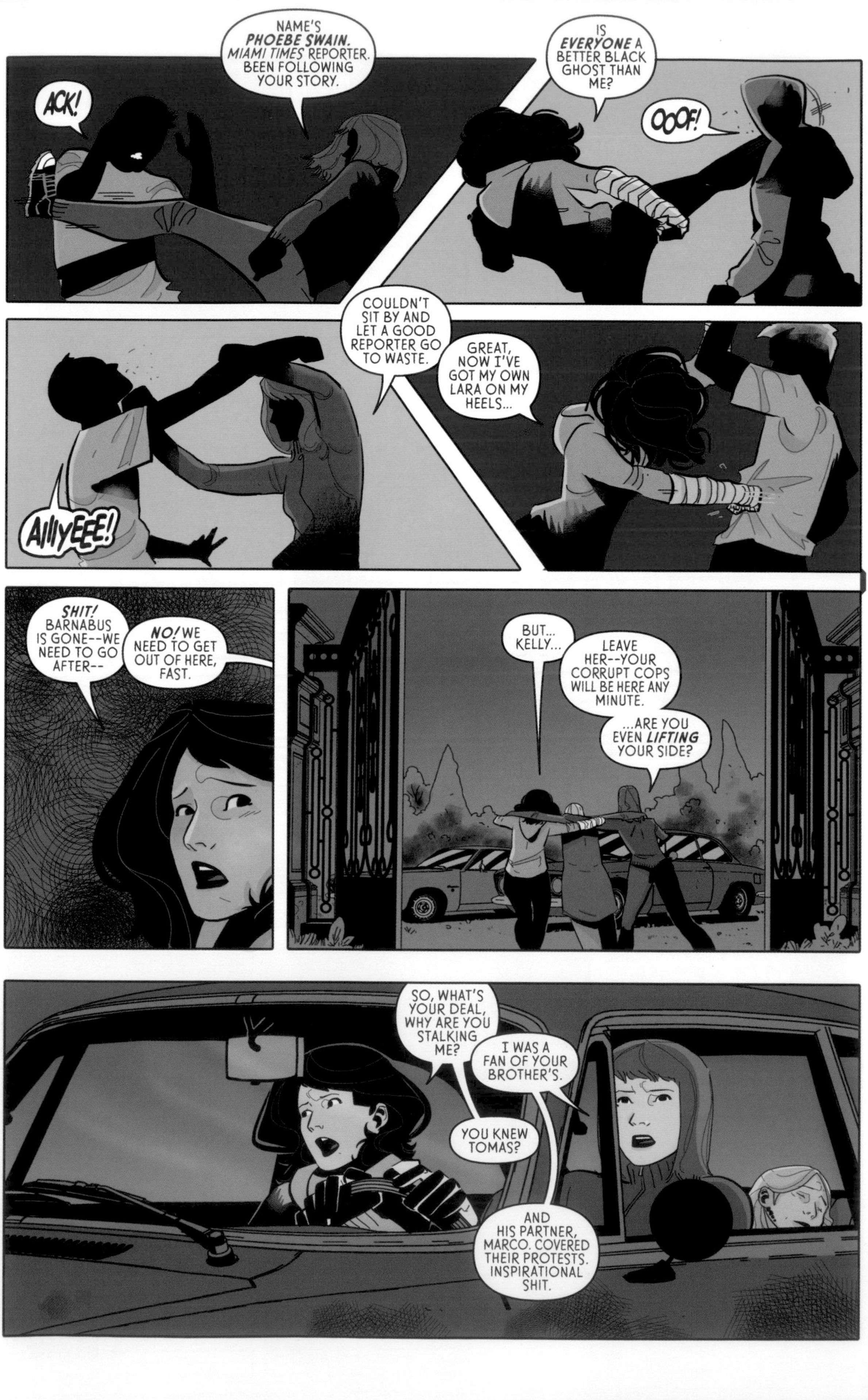
ACK!
NAME'S *PHOEBE SWAIN.* *MIAMI TIMES* REPORTER. BEEN FOLLOWING YOUR STORY.
IS *EVERYONE* A BETTER BLACK GHOST THAN ME?
OOOF!
COULDN'T SIT BY AND LET A GOOD REPORTER GO TO WASTE.
AIIIYEEE!
GREAT, NOW I'VE GOT MY OWN LARA ON MY HEELS...
*SHIT!* BARNABUS IS GONE--WE NEED TO GO AFTER--
*NO!* WE NEED TO GET OUT OF HERE, FAST.
BUT... KELLY...
LEAVE HER--YOUR CORRUPT COPS WILL BE HERE ANY MINUTE.
...ARE YOU EVEN *LIFTING* YOUR SIDE?
SO, WHAT'S YOUR DEAL, WHY ARE YOU STALKING ME?
I WAS A FAN OF YOUR BROTHER'S.
YOU KNEW TOMAS?
AND HIS PARTNER, MARCO. COVERED THEIR PROTESTS. INSPIRATIONAL SHIT.

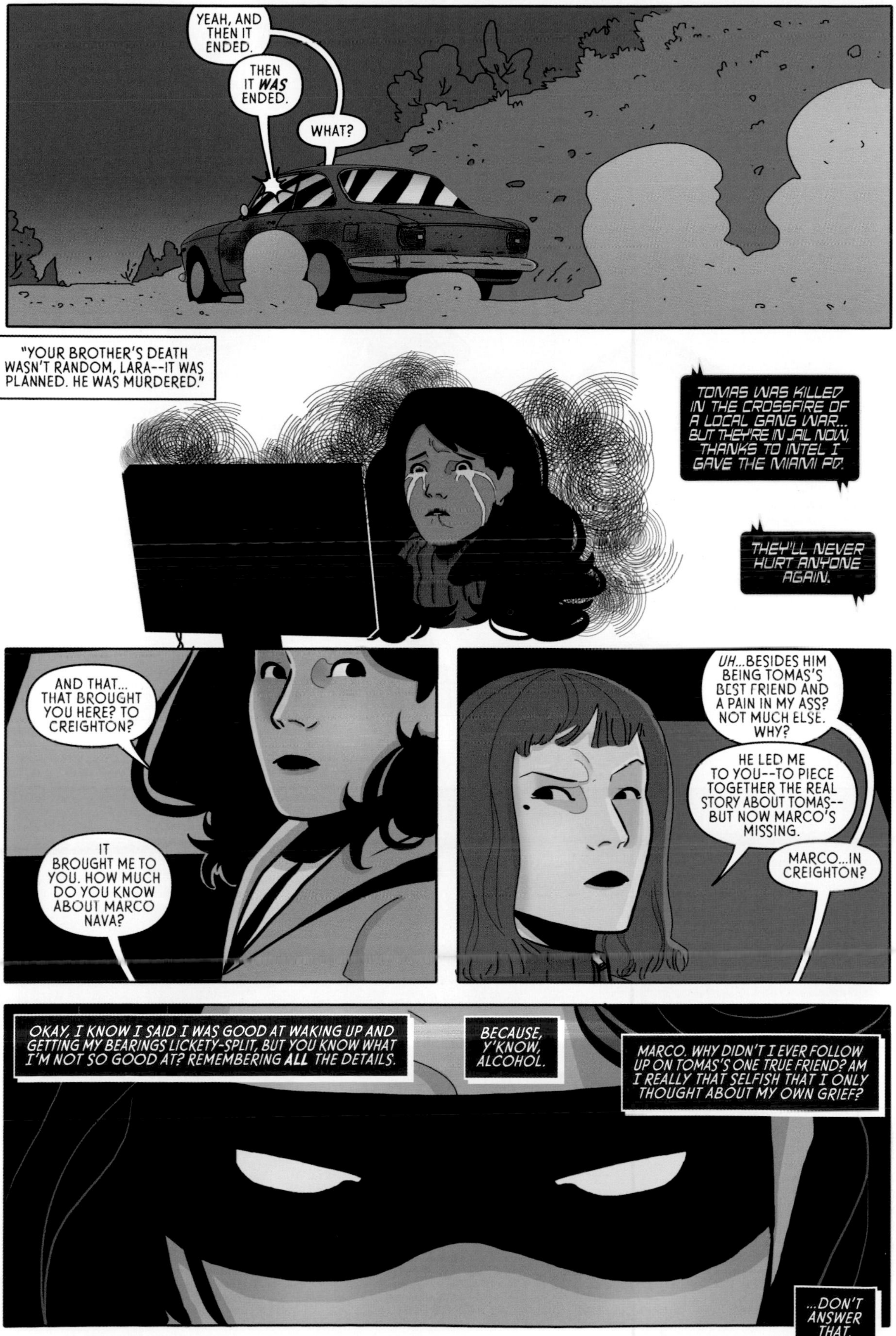

YEAH, AND THEN IT ENDED.
THEN IT WAS ENDED.
WHAT?
"YOUR BROTHER'S DEATH WASN'T RANDOM, LARA--IT WAS PLANNED. HE WAS MURDERED."
TOMAS WAS KILLED IN THE CROSSFIRE OF A LOCAL GANG WAR... BUT THEY'RE IN JAIL NOW, THANKS TO INTEL I GAVE THE MIAMI PD.
THEY'LL NEVER HURT ANYONE AGAIN.
AND THAT... THAT BROUGHT YOU HERE? TO CREIGHTON?
IT BROUGHT ME TO YOU. HOW MUCH DO YOU KNOW ABOUT MARCO NAVA?
UH...BESIDES HIM BEING TOMAS'S BEST FRIEND AND A PAIN IN MY ASS? NOT MUCH ELSE. WHY?
HE LED ME TO YOU--TO PIECE TOGETHER THE REAL STORY ABOUT TOMAS--BUT NOW MARCO'S MISSING.
MARCO...IN CREIGHTON?
OKAY, I KNOW I SAID I WAS GOOD AT WAKING UP AND GETTING MY BEARINGS LICKETY-SPLIT, BUT YOU KNOW WHAT I'M NOT SO GOOD AT? REMEMBERING ALL THE DETAILS.
BECAUSE, Y'KNOW, ALCOHOL.
MARCO. WHY DIDN'T I EVER FOLLOW UP ON TOMAS'S ONE TRUE FRIEND? AM I REALLY THAT SELFISH THAT I ONLY THOUGHT ABOUT MY OWN GRIEF?
...DON'T ANSWER THAT.

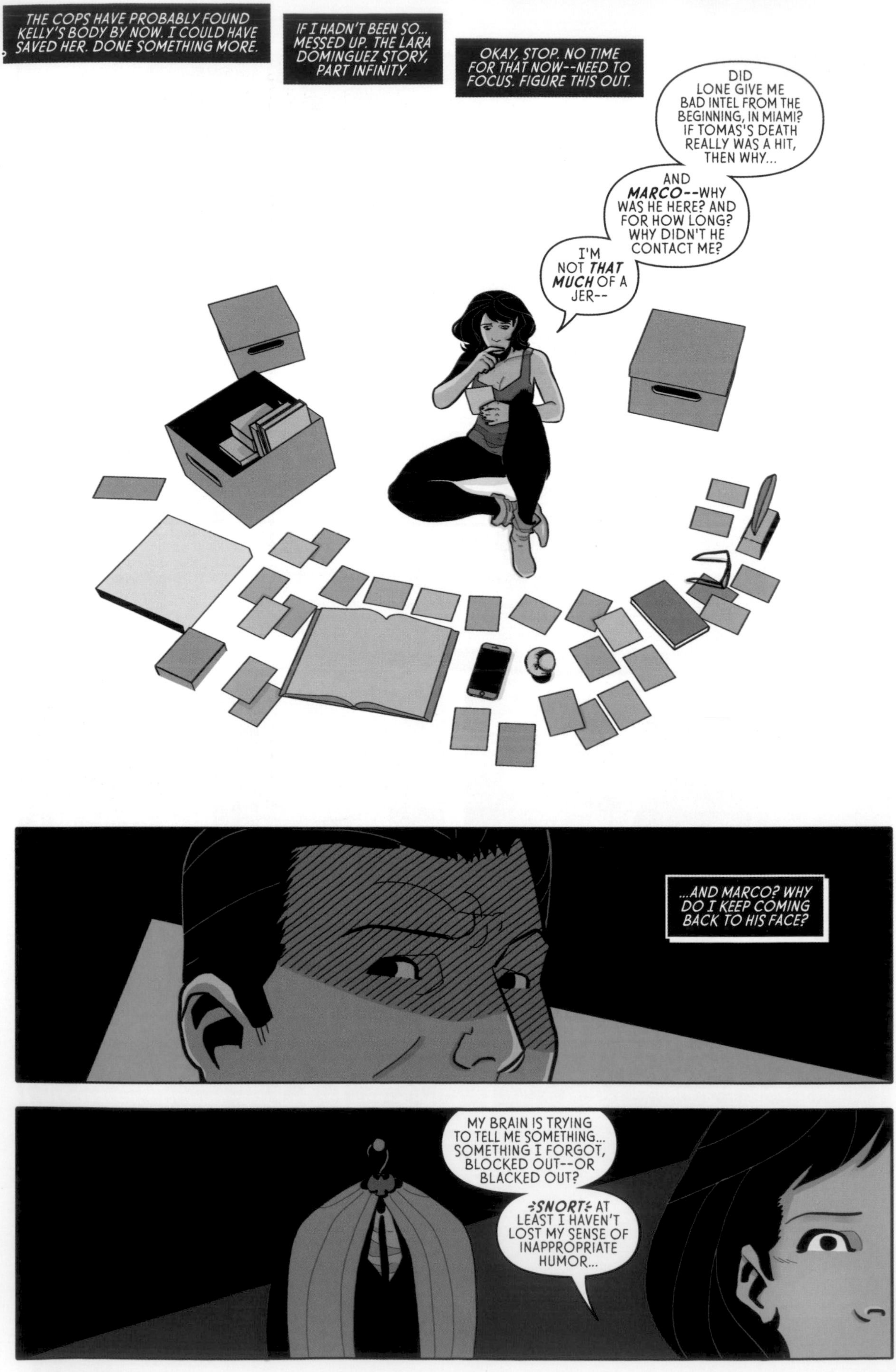
THE COPS HAVE PROBABLY FOUND KELLY'S BODY BY NOW. I COULD HAVE SAVED HER. DONE SOMETHING MORE.
IF I HADN'T BEEN SO... MESSED UP. THE LARA DOMINGUEZ STORY, PART INFINITY.
OKAY, STOP. NO TIME FOR THAT NOW--NEED TO FOCUS. FIGURE THIS OUT.
DID LONE GIVE ME BAD INTEL FROM THE BEGINNING, IN MIAMI? IF TOMAS'S DEATH REALLY WAS A HIT, THEN WHY...
AND ***MARCO***--WHY WAS HE HERE? AND FOR HOW LONG? WHY DIDN'T HE CONTACT ME?
I'M NOT ***THAT MUCH*** OF A JER--
...AND MARCO? WHY DO I KEEP COMING BACK TO HIS FACE?
MY BRAIN IS TRYING TO TELL ME SOMETHING... SOMETHING I FORGOT, BLOCKED OUT--OR BLACKED OUT?
*SNORT* AT LEAST I HAVEN'T LOST MY SENSE OF INAPPROPRIATE HUMOR...

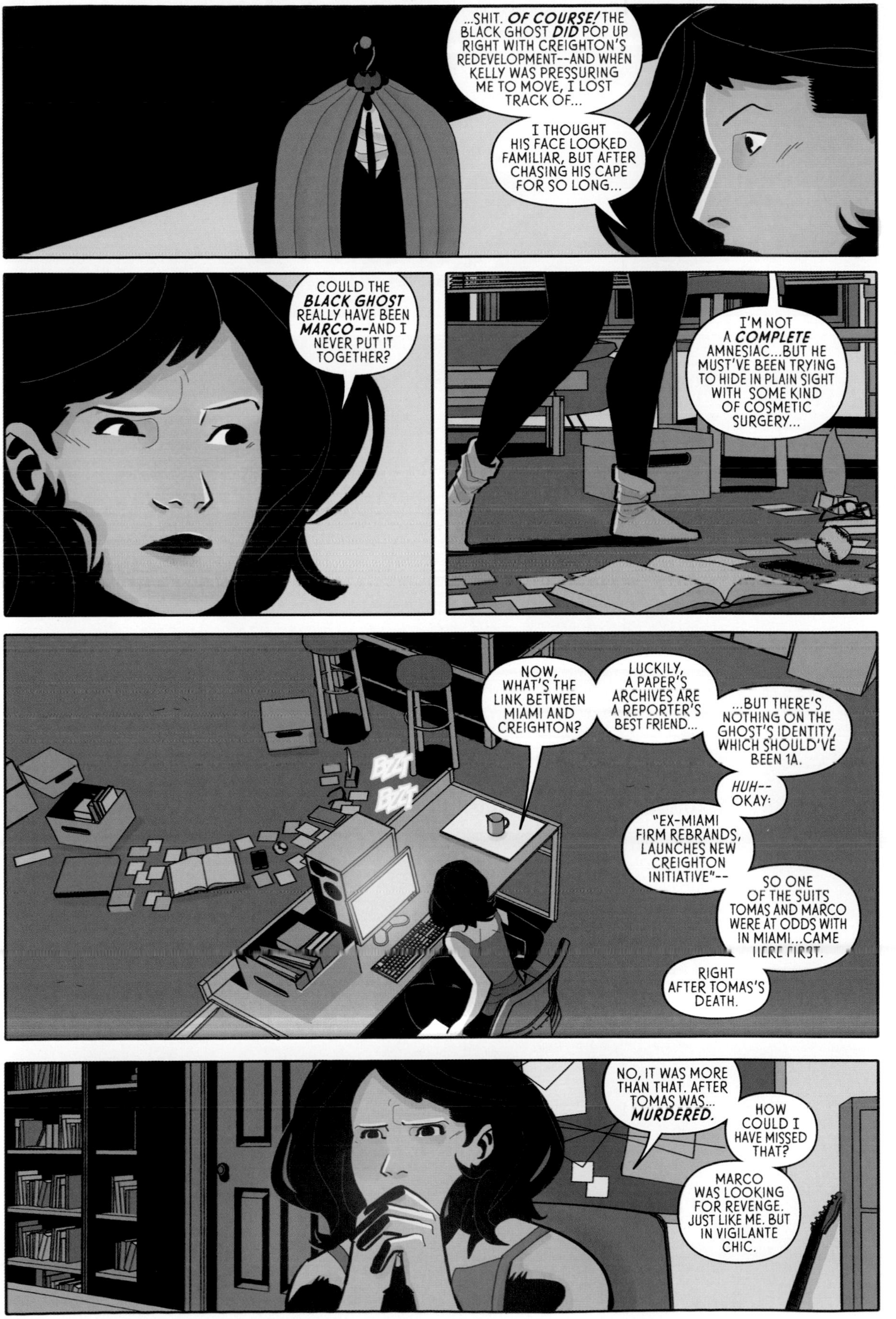
...SHIT. OF COURSE! THE BLACK GHOST DID POP UP RIGHT WITH CREIGHTON'S REDEVELOPMENT--AND WHEN KELLY WAS PRESSURING ME TO MOVE, I LOST TRACK OF...
I THOUGHT HIS FACE LOOKED FAMILIAR, BUT AFTER CHASING HIS CAPE FOR SO LONG...
COULD THE BLACK GHOST REALLY HAVE BEEN MARCO--AND I NEVER PUT IT TOGETHER?
I'M NOT A COMPLETE AMNESIAC...BUT HE MUST'VE BEEN TRYING TO HIDE IN PLAIN SIGHT WITH SOME KIND OF COSMETIC SURGERY...
NOW, WHAT'S THE LINK BETWEEN MIAMI AND CREIGHTON?
LUCKILY, A PAPER'S ARCHIVES ARE A REPORTER'S BEST FRIEND...
...BUT THERE'S NOTHING ON THE GHOST'S IDENTITY, WHICH SHOULD'VE BEEN 1A.
BZZT BZZT
HUH--OKAY:
"EX-MIAMI FIRM REBRANDS, LAUNCHES NEW CREIGHTON INITIATIVE"--
SO ONE OF THE SUITS TOMAS AND MARCO WERE AT ODDS WITH IN MIAMI...CAME HERE FIRST.
RIGHT AFTER TOMAS'S DEATH.
NO, IT WAS MORE THAN THAT. AFTER TOMAS WAS... MURDERED.
HOW COULD I HAVE MISSED THAT?
MARCO WAS LOOKING FOR REVENGE. JUST LIKE ME. BUT IN VIGILANTE CHIC.

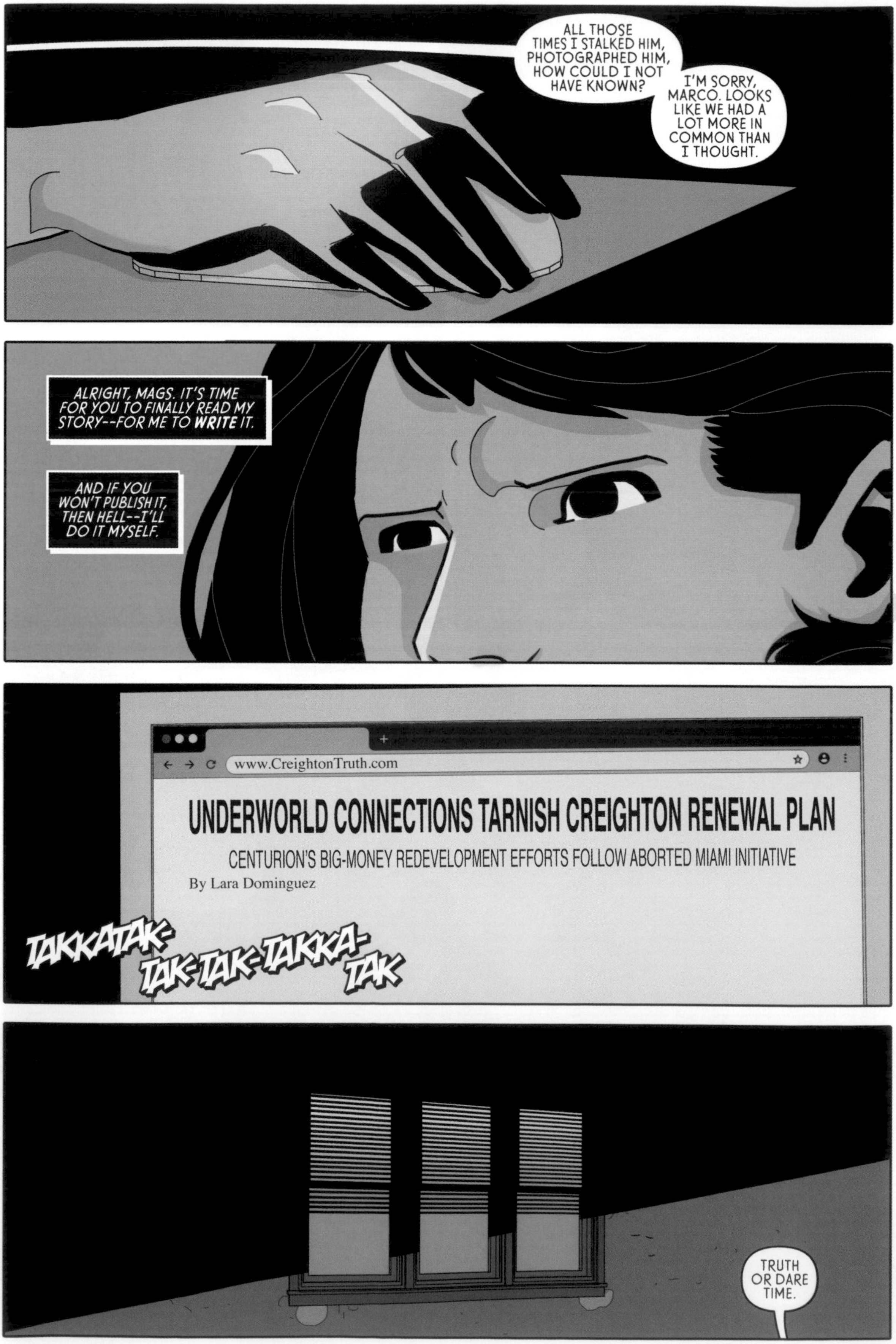
ALL THOSE TIMES I STALKED HIM, PHOTOGRAPHED HIM, HOW COULD I NOT HAVE KNOWN?
I'M SORRY, MARCO. LOOKS LIKE WE HAD A LOT MORE IN COMMON THAN I THOUGHT.
ALRIGHT, MAGS. IT'S TIME FOR YOU TO FINALLY READ MY STORY--FOR ME TO **WRITE** IT.
AND IF YOU WON'T PUBLISH IT, THEN HELL--I'LL DO IT MYSELF.
www.CreightonTruth.com
UNDERWORLD CONNECTIONS TARNISH CREIGHTON RENEWAL PLAN
CENTURION'S BIG-MONEY REDEVELOPMENT EFFORTS FOLLOW ABORTED MIAMI INITIATIVE
By Lara Dominguez
TAKKATAK-TAK-TAK-TAKKA-TAK
TRUTH OR DARE TIME.

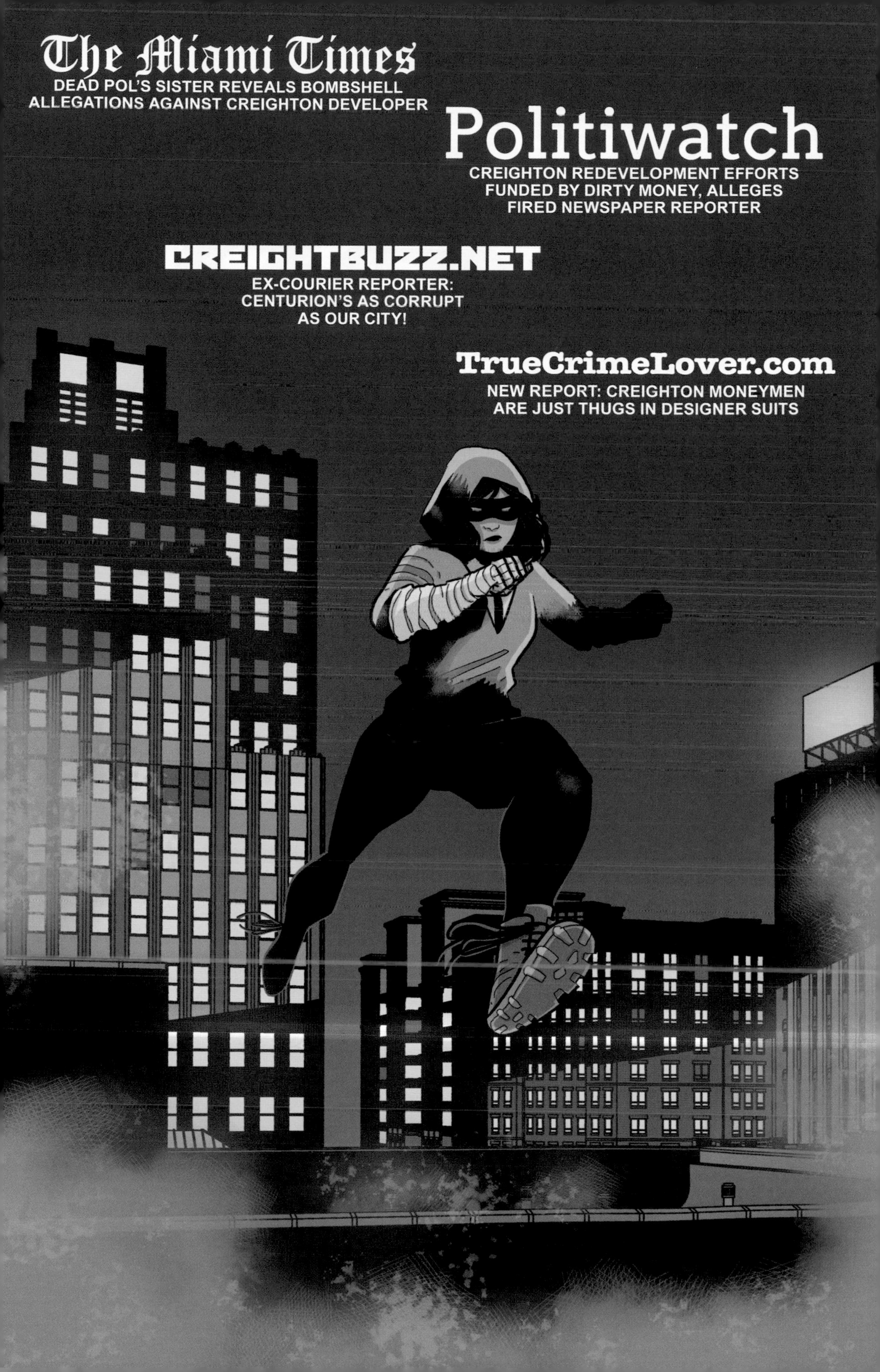
The Miami Times
DEAD POL'S SISTER REVEALS BOMBSHELL ALLEGATIONS AGAINST CREIGHTON DEVELOPER
Politiwatch
CREIGHTON REDEVELOPMENT EFFORTS FUNDED BY DIRTY MONEY, ALLEGES FIRED NEWSPAPER REPORTER
CREIGHTBUZZ.NET
EX-COURIER REPORTER: CENTURION'S AS CORRUPT AS OUR CITY!
TrueCrimeLover.com
NEW REPORT: CREIGHTON MONEYMEN ARE JUST THUGS IN DESIGNER SUITS

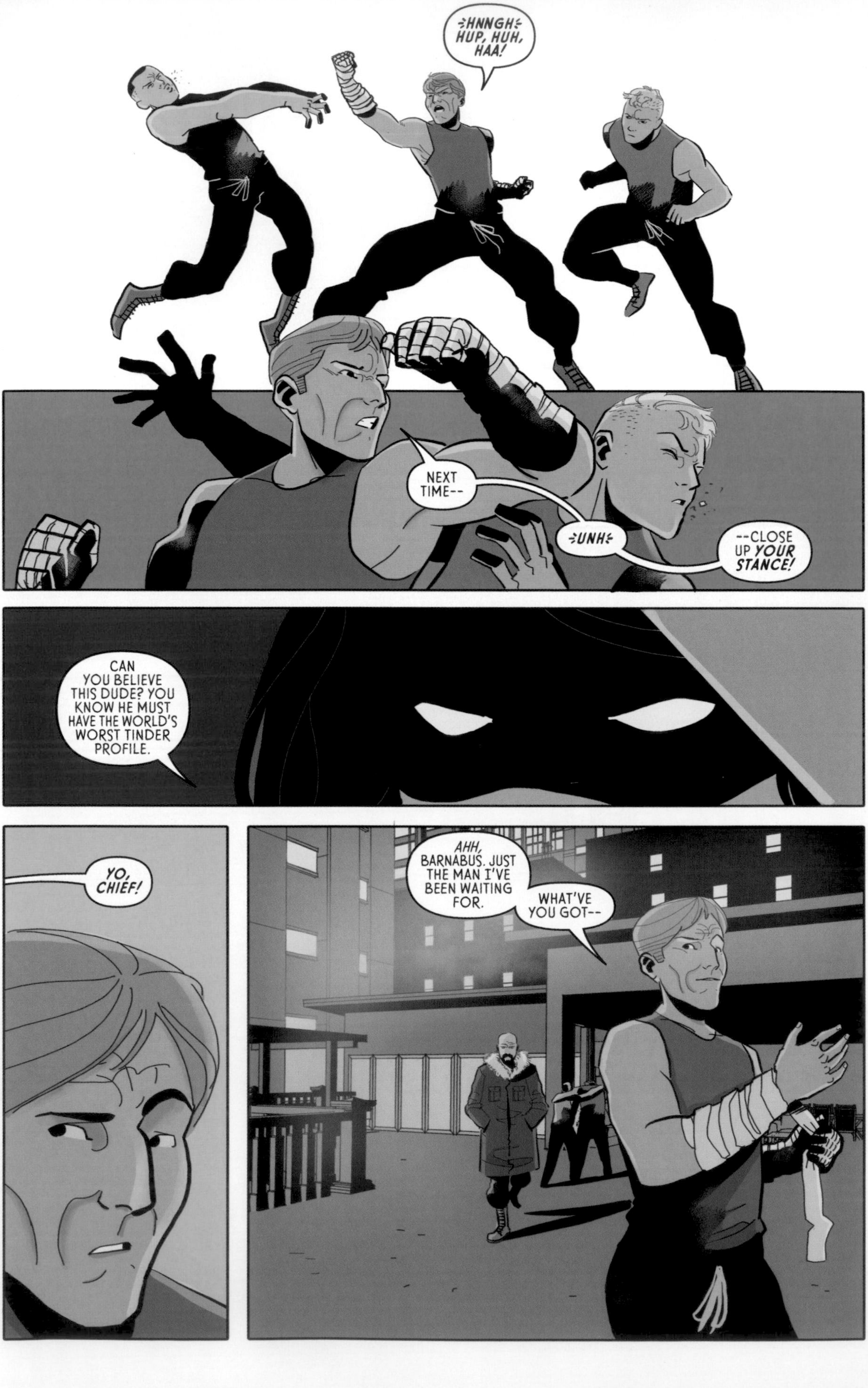
HNNGH HUP, HUH, HAA!
NEXT TIME--
UNH
--CLOSE UP YOUR STANCE!
CAN YOU BELIEVE THIS DUDE? YOU KNOW HE MUST HAVE THE WORLD'S WORST TINDER PROFILE.
YO, CHIEF!
AHH, BARNABUS. JUST THE MAN I'VE BEEN WAITING FOR.
WHAT'VE YOU GOT--

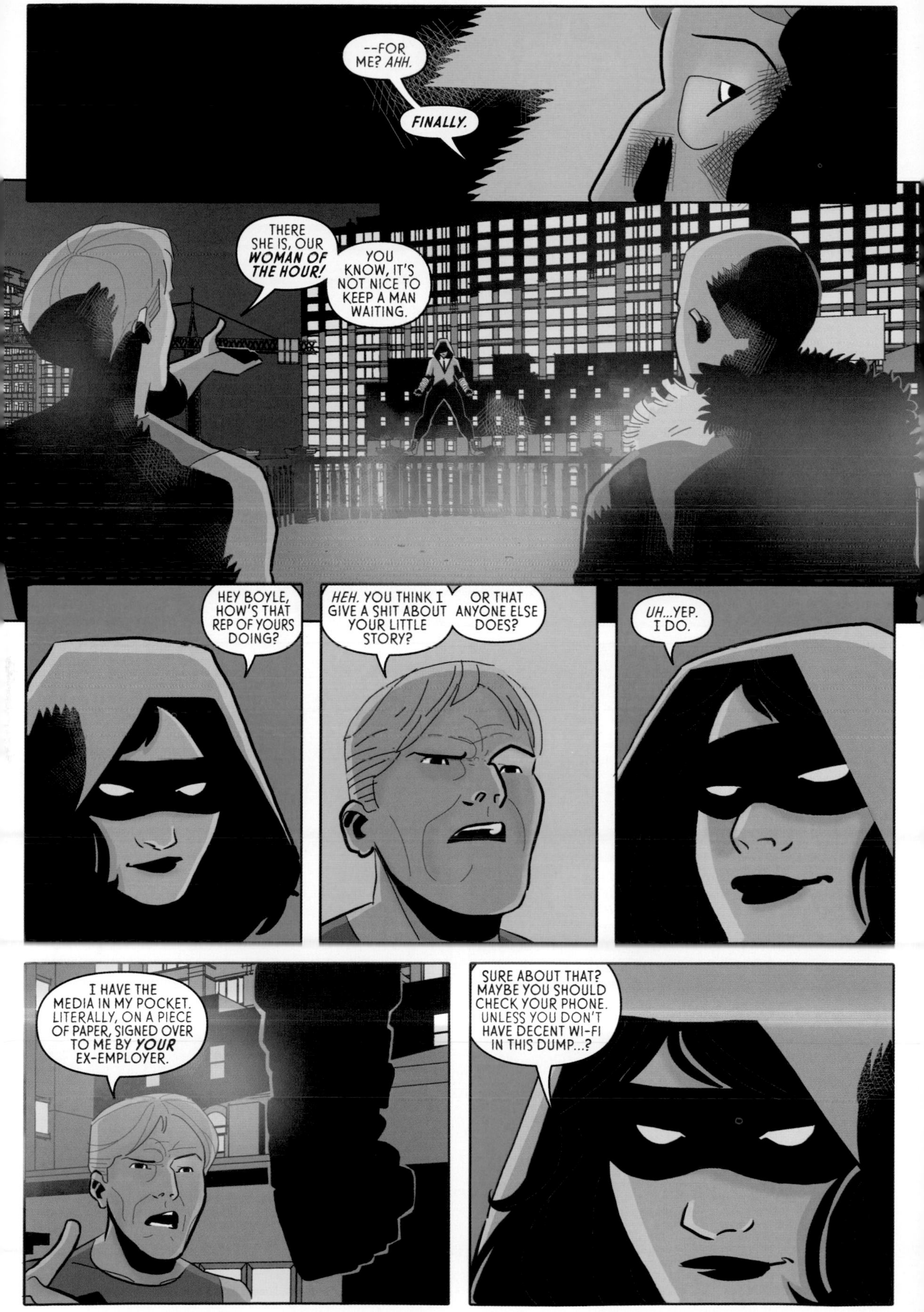
--FOR ME? *AHH.*
***FINALLY.***
THERE SHE IS, OUR ***WOMAN OF THE HOUR!***
YOU KNOW, IT'S NOT NICE TO KEEP A MAN WAITING.
HEY BOYLE, HOW'S THAT REP OF YOURS DOING?
*HEH.* YOU THINK I GIVE A SHIT ABOUT YOUR LITTLE STORY?
OR THAT ANYONE ELSE DOES?
*UH*...YEP. I DO.
I HAVE THE MEDIA IN MY POCKET. LITERALLY, ON A PIECE OF PAPER, SIGNED OVER TO ME BY ***YOUR*** EX-EMPLOYER.
SURE ABOUT THAT? MAYBE YOU SHOULD CHECK YOUR PHONE. UNLESS YOU DON'T HAVE DECENT WI-FI IN THIS DUMP...?

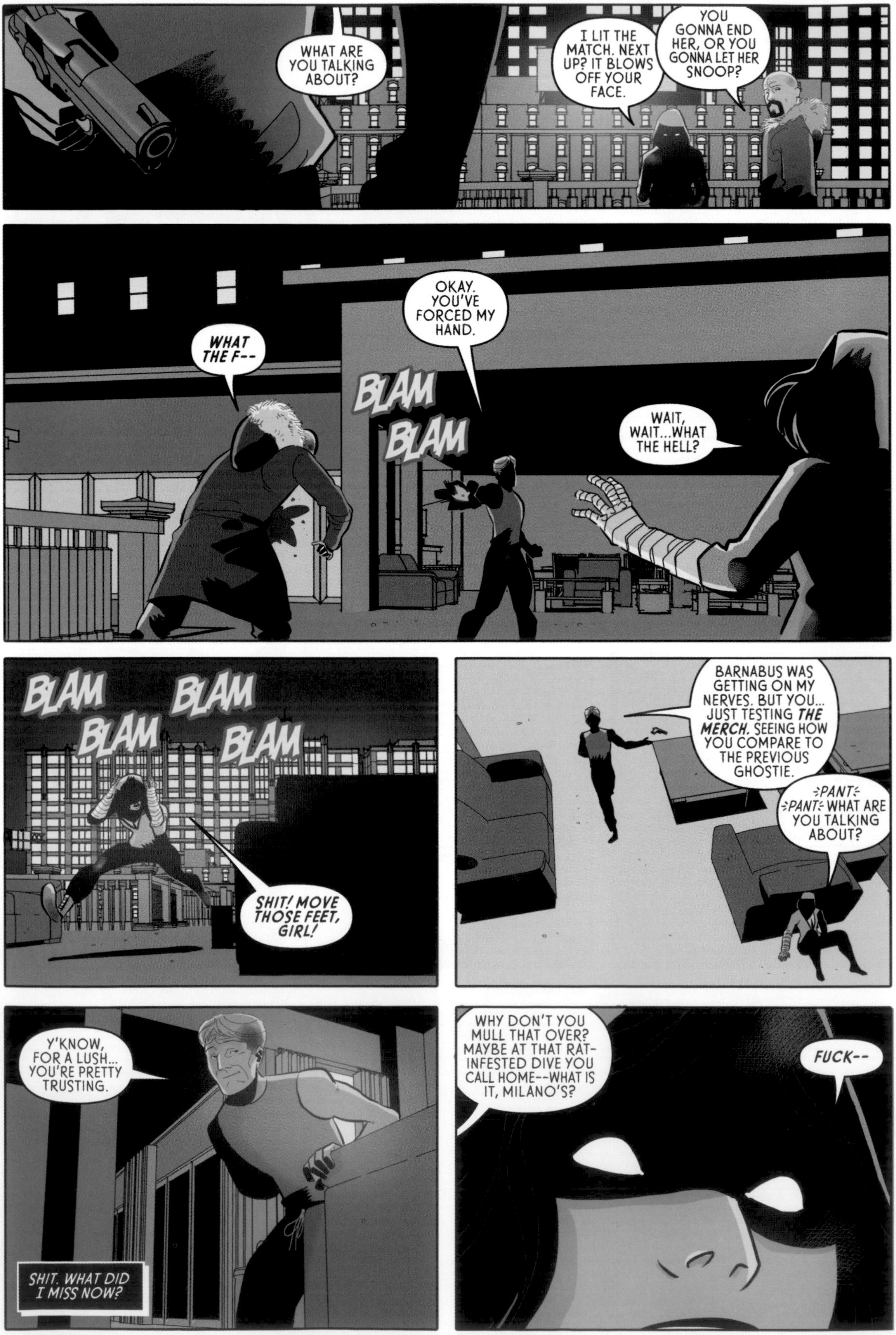
WHAT ARE YOU TALKING ABOUT?
YOU GONNA END HER, OR YOU GONNA LET HER SNOOP?
I LIT THE MATCH. NEXT UP? IT BLOWS OFF YOUR FACE.
WHAT THE F--
OKAY. YOU'VE FORCED MY HAND.
BLAM
BLAM
WAIT, WAIT...WHAT THE HELL?
BLAM
BLAM
BLAM
BLAM
SHIT! MOVE THOSE FEET, GIRL!
BARNABUS WAS GETTING ON MY NERVES. BUT YOU... JUST TESTING THE MERCH. SEEING HOW YOU COMPARE TO THE PREVIOUS GHOSTIE.
PANT PANT WHAT ARE YOU TALKING ABOUT?
Y'KNOW, FOR A LUSH... YOU'RE PRETTY TRUSTING.
SHIT. WHAT DID I MISS NOW?
WHY DON'T YOU MULL THAT OVER? MAYBE AT THAT RAT-INFESTED DIVE YOU CALL HOME--WHAT IS IT, MILANO'S?
FUCK--

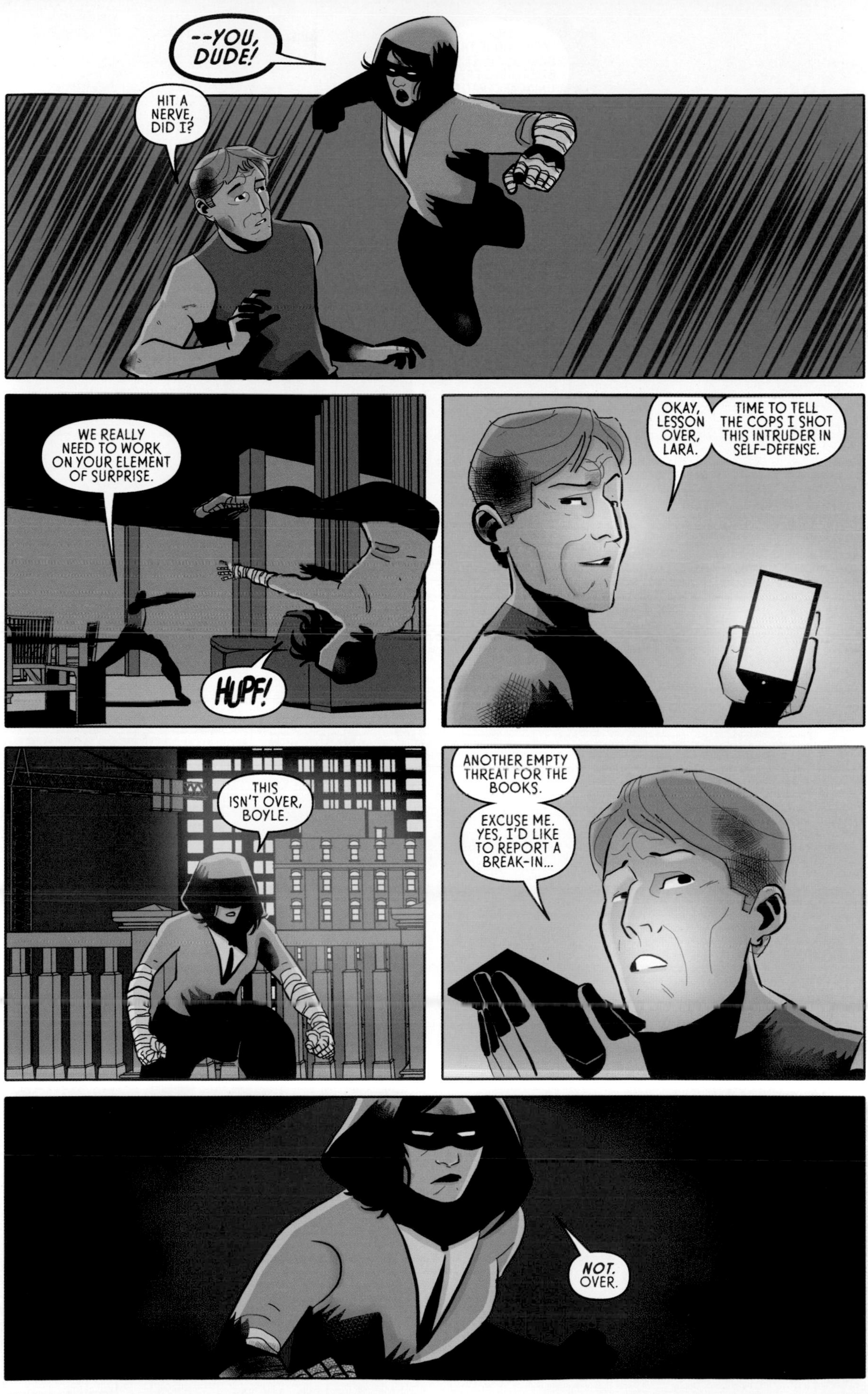
--YOU, DUDE!
HIT A NERVE, DID I?
WE REALLY NEED TO WORK ON YOUR ELEMENT OF SURPRISE.
HUPF!
OKAY, LESSON OVER, LARA.
TIME TO TELL THE COPS I SHOT THIS INTRUDER IN SELF-DEFENSE.
THIS ISN'T OVER, BOYLE.
ANOTHER EMPTY THREAT FOR THE BOOKS.
EXCUSE ME. YES, I'D LIKE TO REPORT A BREAK-IN...
NOT. OVER.

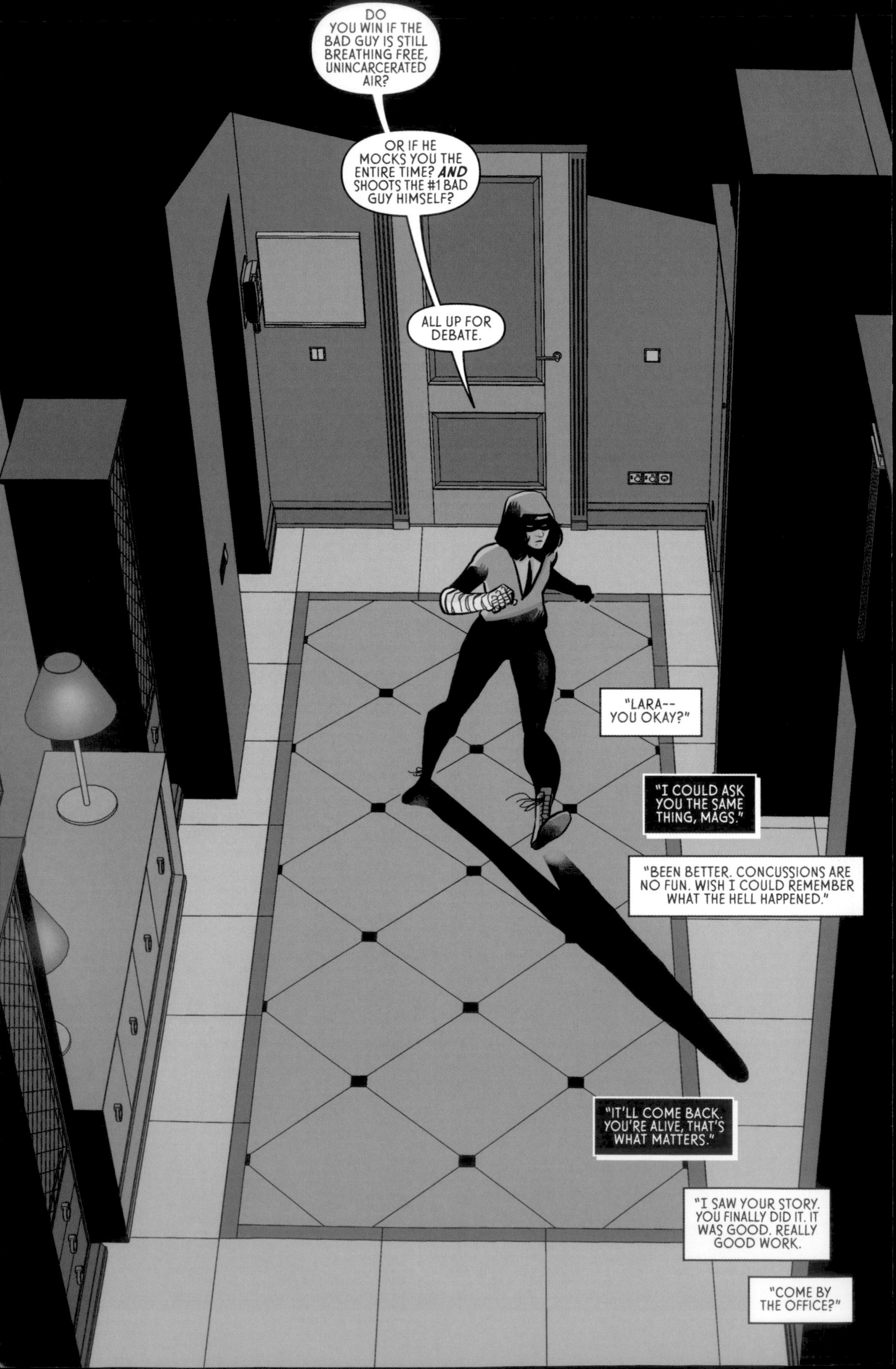
DO YOU WIN IF THE BAD GUY IS STILL BREATHING FREE, UNINCARCERATED AIR?
OR IF HE MOCKS YOU THE ENTIRE TIME? **AND** SHOOTS THE #1 BAD GUY HIMSELF?
ALL UP FOR DEBATE.
"LARA-- YOU OKAY?"
"I COULD ASK YOU THE SAME THING, MAGS."
"BEEN BETTER. CONCUSSIONS ARE NO FUN. WISH I COULD REMEMBER WHAT THE HELL HAPPENED."
"IT'LL COME BACK. YOU'RE ALIVE, THAT'S WHAT MATTERS."
"I SAW YOUR STORY. YOU FINALLY DID IT. IT WAS GOOD. REALLY GOOD WORK.
"COME BY THE OFFICE?"

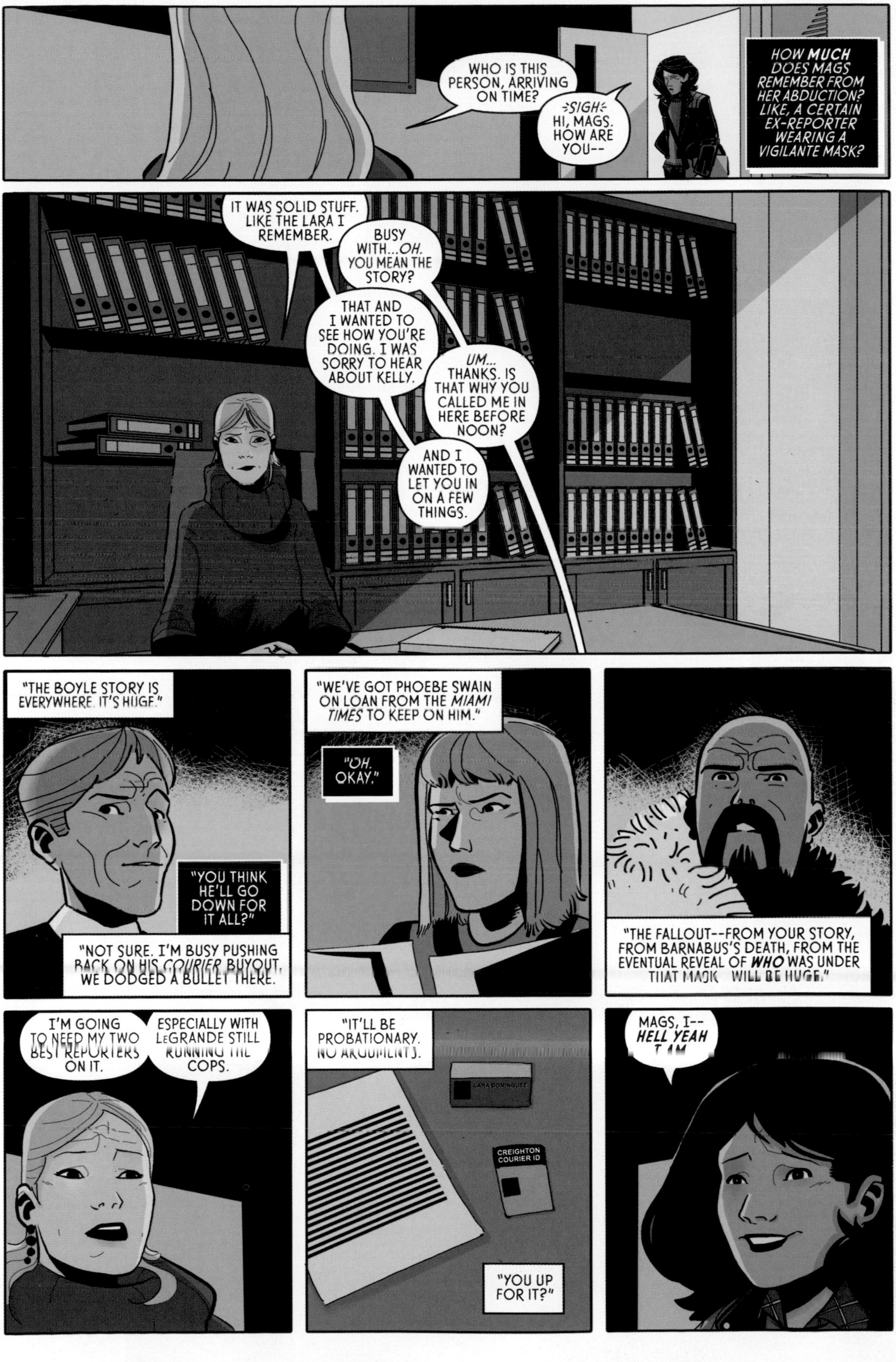
HOW MUCH DOES MAGS REMEMBER FROM HER ABDUCTION? LIKE, A CERTAIN EX-REPORTER WEARING A VIGILANTE MASK?
WHO IS THIS PERSON, ARRIVING ON TIME?
*SIGH* HI, MAGS. HOW ARE YOU--
IT WAS SOLID STUFF. LIKE THE LARA I REMEMBER.
BUSY WITH...OH. YOU MEAN THE STORY?
THAT AND I WANTED TO SEE HOW YOU'RE DOING. I WAS SORRY TO HEAR ABOUT KELLY.
UM... THANKS. IS THAT WHY YOU CALLED ME IN HERE BEFORE NOON?
AND I WANTED TO LET YOU IN ON A FEW THINGS.
"THE BOYLE STORY IS EVERYWHERE. IT'S HUGE."
"YOU THINK HE'LL GO DOWN FOR IT ALL?"
"NOT SURE. I'M BUSY PUSHING BACK ON HIS COURIER BUYOUT. WE DODGED A BULLET THERE.
"WE'VE GOT PHOEBE SWAIN ON LOAN FROM THE MIAMI TIMES TO KEEP ON HIM."
"OH. OKAY."
"THE FALLOUT--FROM YOUR STORY, FROM BARNABUS'S DEATH, FROM THE EVENTUAL REVEAL OF WHO WAS UNDER THAT MASK--WILL BE HUGE."
I'M GOING TO NEED MY TWO BEST REPORTERS ON IT.
ESPECIALLY WITH LeGRANDE STILL RUNNING THE COPS.
"IT'LL BE PROBATIONARY. NO ARGUMENTS.
LARA DOMINGUEZ
CREIGHTON COURIER ID
"YOU UP FOR IT?"
MAGS, I-- HELL YEAH I AM

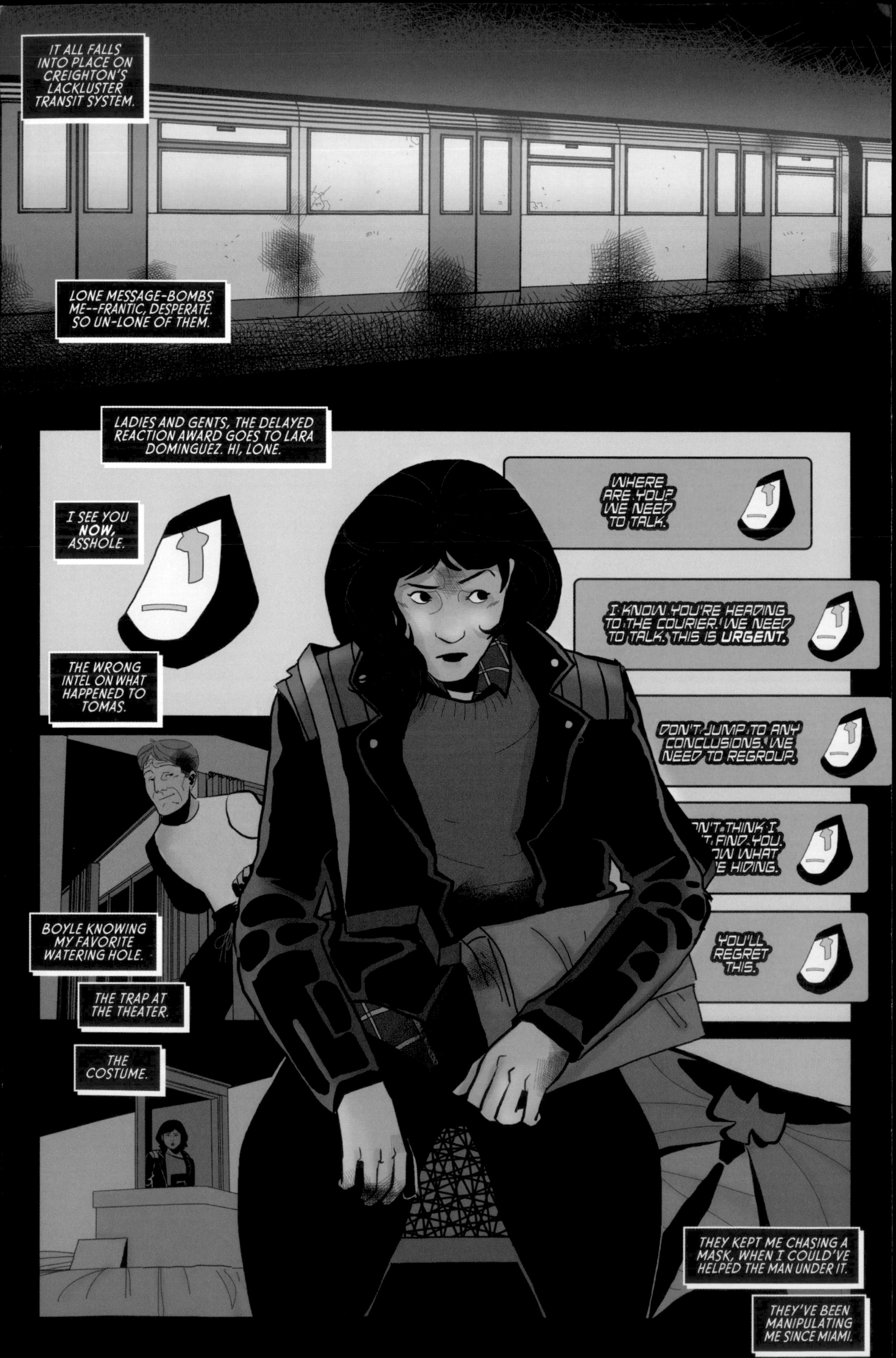
IT ALL FALLS INTO PLACE ON CREIGHTON'S LACKLUSTER TRANSIT SYSTEM.
LONE MESSAGE-BOMBS ME--FRANTIC, DESPERATE. SO UN-LONE OF THEM.
LADIES AND GENTS, THE DELAYED REACTION AWARD GOES TO LARA DOMINGUEZ. HI, LONE.
WHERE ARE YOU? WE NEED TO TALK.
I SEE YOU **NOW,** ASSHOLE.
I KNOW YOU'RE HEADING TO THE COURIER. WE NEED TO TALK. THIS IS **URGENT.**
THE WRONG INTEL ON WHAT HAPPENED TO TOMAS.
DON'T JUMP TO ANY CONCLUSIONS. WE NEED TO REGROUP.
N'T THINK I T FIND YOU. OW WHAT E HIDING.
BOYLE KNOWING MY FAVORITE WATERING HOLE.
YOU'LL REGRET THIS.
THE TRAP AT THE THEATER.
THE COSTUME.
THEY KEPT ME CHASING A MASK, WHEN I COULD'VE HELPED THE MAN UNDER IT.
THEY'VE BEEN MANIPULATING ME SINCE MIAMI.

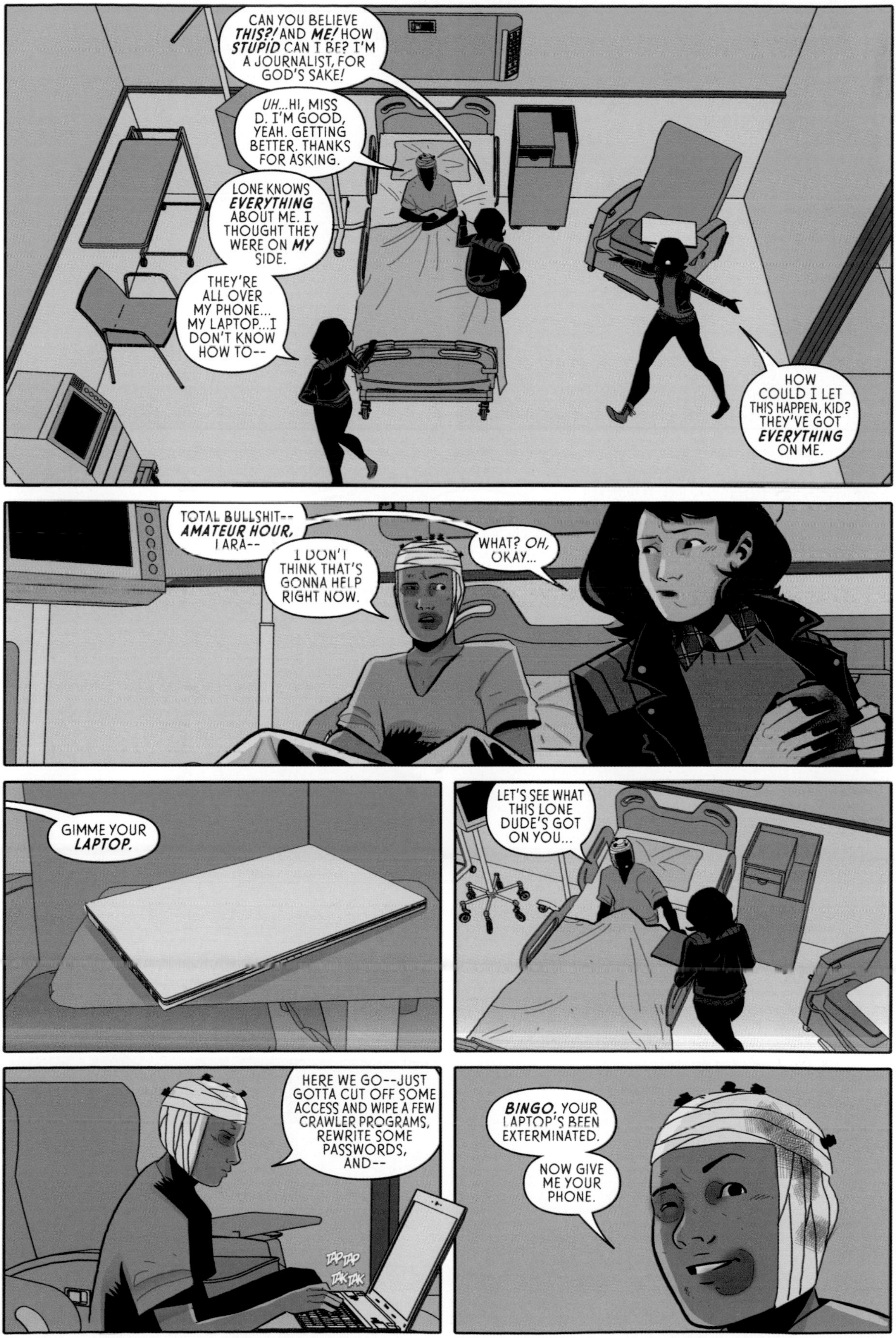
CAN YOU BELIEVE THIS?! AND ME! HOW STUPID CAN I BE? I'M A JOURNALIST, FOR GOD'S SAKE!
UH...HI, MISS D. I'M GOOD, YEAH. GETTING BETTER. THANKS FOR ASKING.
LONE KNOWS EVERYTHING ABOUT ME. I THOUGHT THEY WERE ON MY SIDE.
THEY'RE ALL OVER MY PHONE... MY LAPTOP...I DON'T KNOW HOW TO--
HOW COULD I LET THIS HAPPEN, KID? THEY'VE GOT EVERYTHING ON ME.
TOTAL BULLSHIT-- AMATEUR HOUR, LARA--
I DON'T THINK THAT'S GONNA HELP RIGHT NOW.
WHAT? OH, OKAY...
GIMME YOUR LAPTOP.
LET'S SEE WHAT THIS LONE DUDE'S GOT ON YOU...
HERE WE GO--JUST GOTTA CUT OFF SOME ACCESS AND WIPE A FEW CRAWLER PROGRAMS, REWRITE SOME PASSWORDS, AND--
TAP TAP
TAK TAK
BINGO. YOUR LAPTOP'S BEEN EXTERMINATED.
NOW GIVE ME YOUR PHONE.

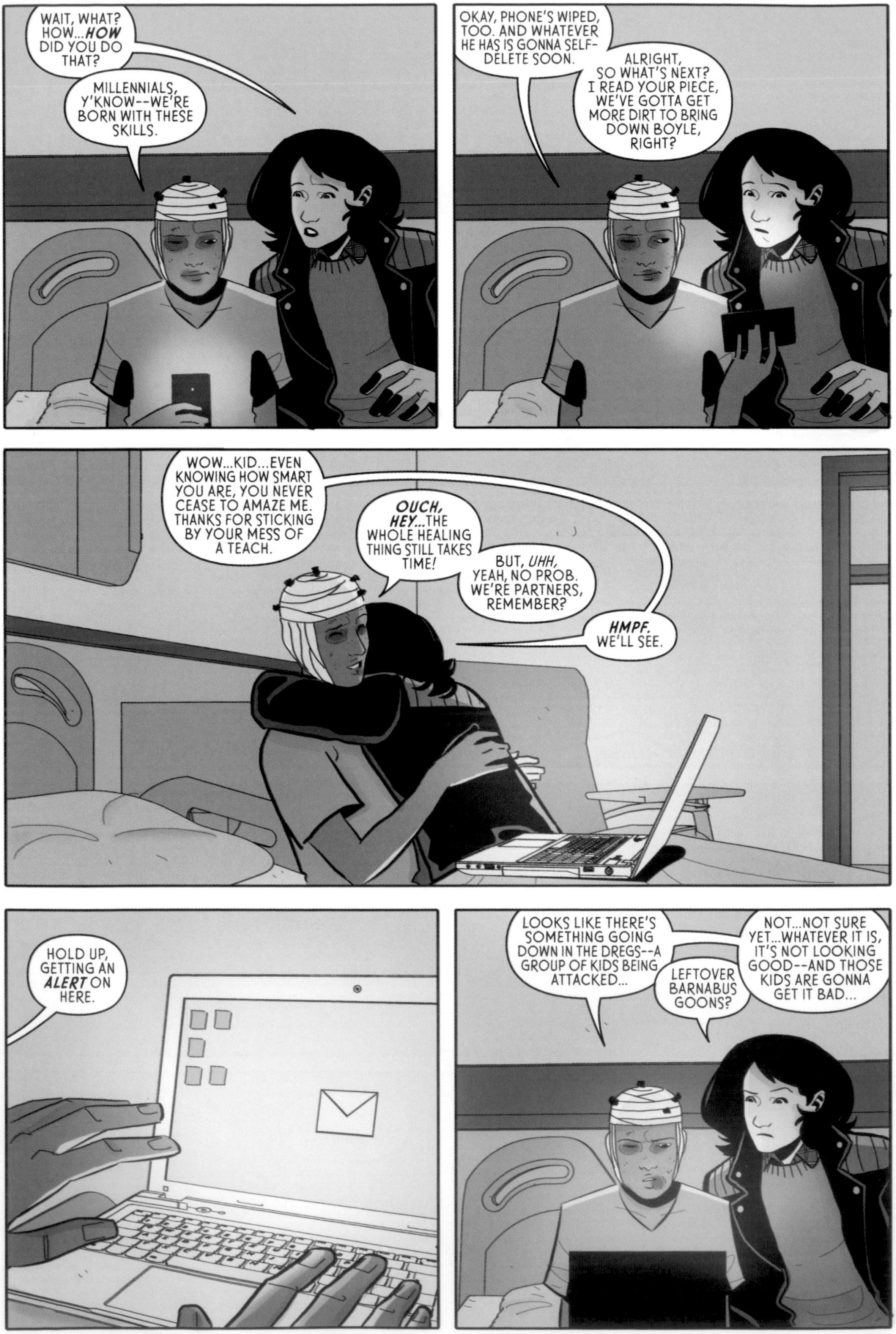
WAIT, WHAT? HOW...**HOW** DID YOU DO THAT?
MILLENNIALS, Y'KNOW--WE'RE BORN WITH THESE SKILLS.
OKAY, PHONE'S WIPED, TOO. AND WHATEVER HE HAS IS GONNA SELF-DELETE SOON.
ALRIGHT, SO WHAT'S NEXT? I READ YOUR PIECE, WE'VE GOTTA GET MORE DIRT TO BRING DOWN BOYLE, RIGHT?
WOW...KID...EVEN KNOWING HOW SMART YOU ARE, YOU NEVER CEASE TO AMAZE ME. THANKS FOR STICKING BY YOUR MESS OF A TEACH.
**OUCH, HEY...**THE WHOLE HEALING THING STILL TAKES TIME!
BUT, *UHH,* YEAH, NO PROB. WE'RE PARTNERS, REMEMBER?
**HMPF.** WE'LL SEE.
HOLD UP, GETTING AN ***ALERT*** ON HERE.
LOOKS LIKE THERE'S SOMETHING GOING DOWN IN THE DREGS--A GROUP OF KIDS BEING ATTACKED...
LEFTOVER BARNABUS GOONS?
NOT...NOT SURE YET...WHATEVER IT IS, IT'S NOT LOOKING GOOD--AND THOSE KIDS ARE GONNA GET IT BAD...

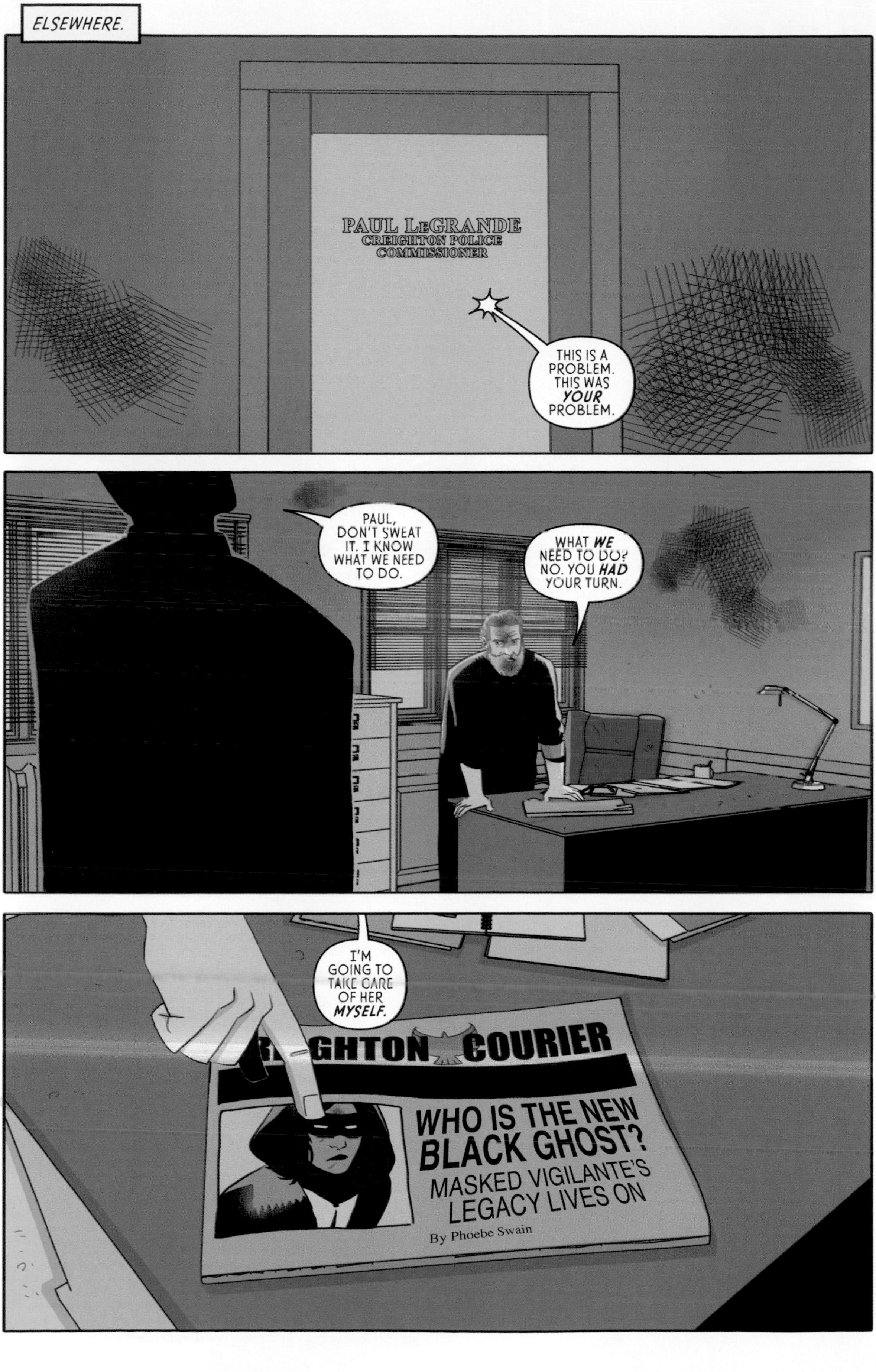
ELSEWHERE.
PAUL LeGRANDE
CREIGHTON POLICE
COMMISSIONER
THIS IS A PROBLEM. THIS WAS *YOUR* PROBLEM.
PAUL, DON'T SWEAT IT. I KNOW WHAT WE NEED TO DO.
WHAT *WE* NEED TO DO? NO. YOU *HAD* YOUR TURN.
I'M GOING TO TAKE CARE OF HER *MYSELF.*
GHTON COURIER
WHO IS THE NEW BLACK GHOST?
MASKED VIGILANTE'S LEGACY LIVES ON
By Phoebe Swain

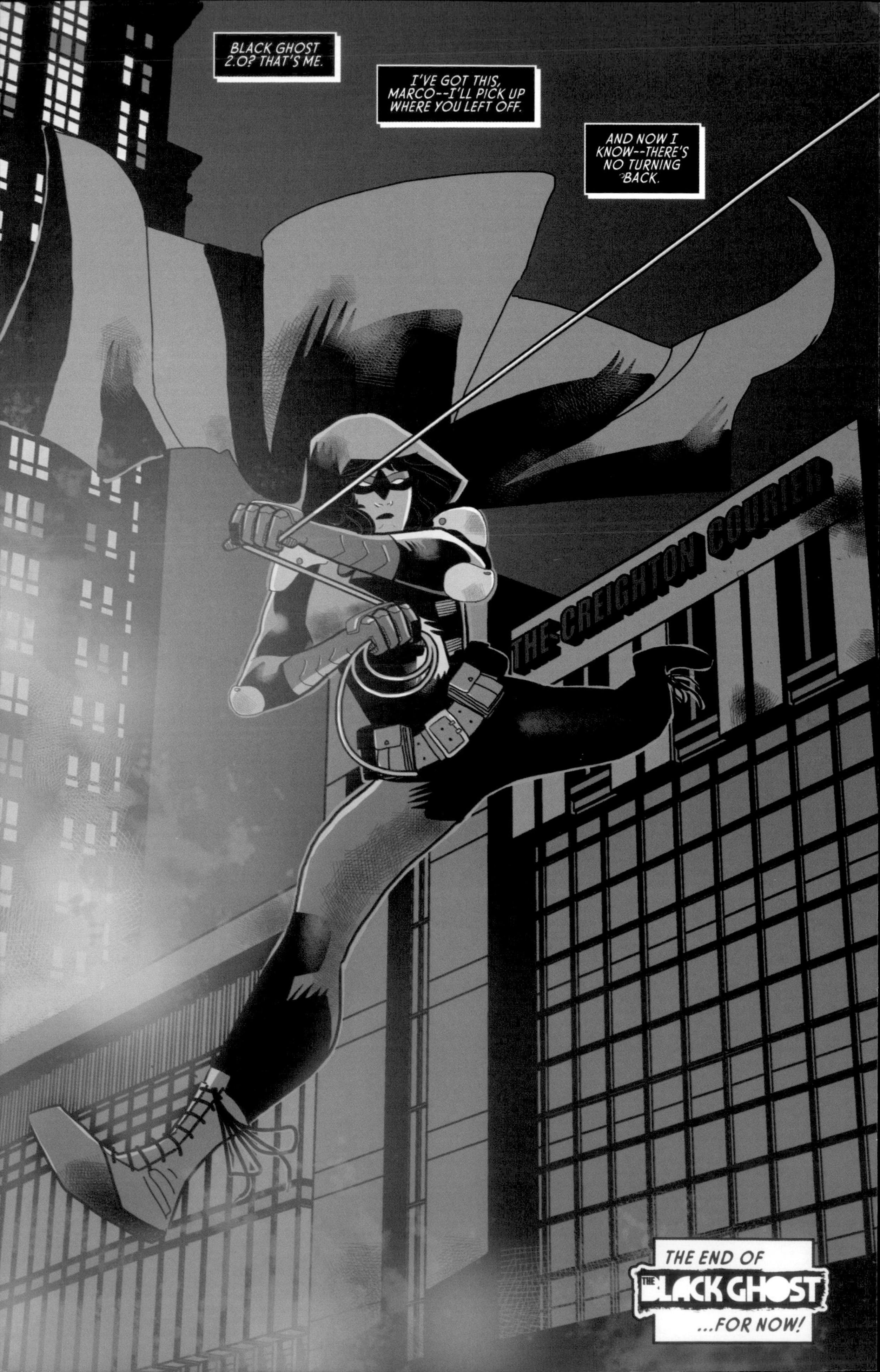
BLACK GHOST 2.0? THAT'S ME.
I'VE GOT THIS, MARCO--I'LL PICK UP WHERE YOU LEFT OFF.
AND NOW I KNOW--THERE'S NO TURNING BACK.
THE CREIGHTON COURIER
THE END OF THE BLACK GHOST ...FOR NOW!

# CHARACTER DESIGNS

## BY GEORGE KAMBADAIS

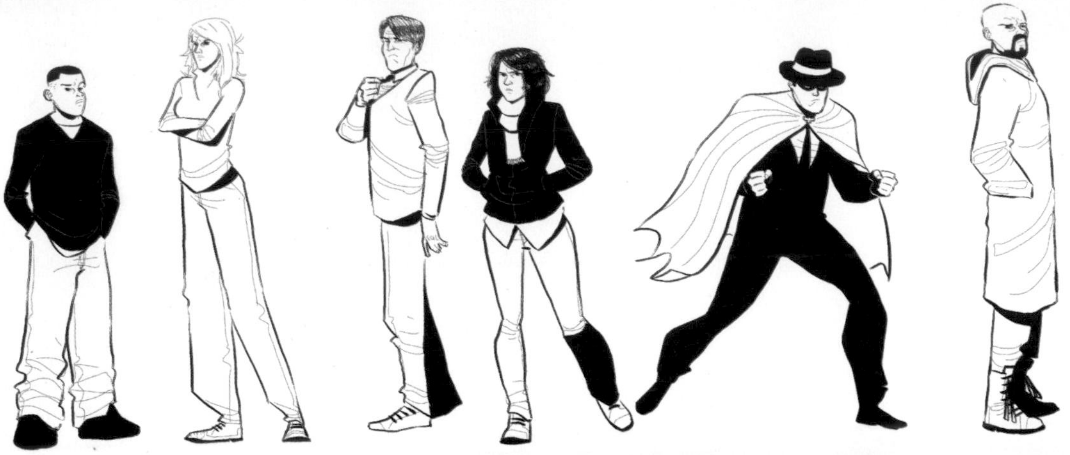

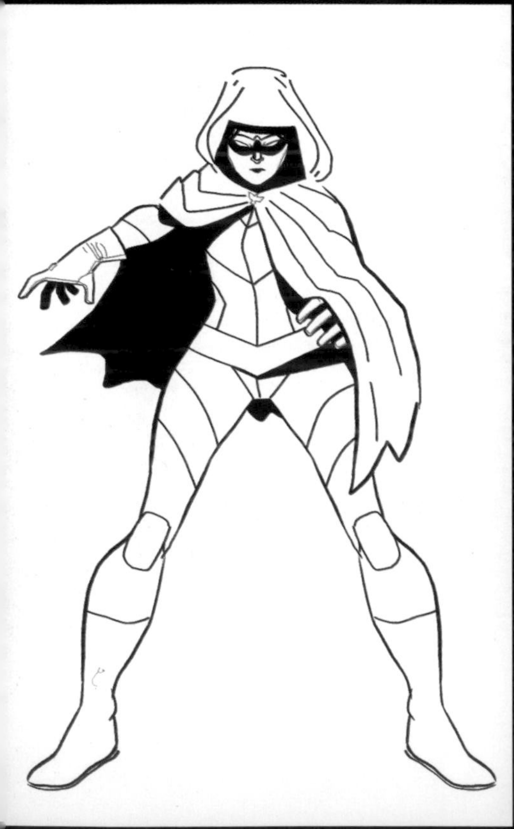

**Top**—*Artist George Kambadais's initial cast designs. From left: Ernesto, Maggie Braffet, Boyle, Lara, the "OG BG," and Barnabus.*

**Left**—*Original Lara as Black Ghost costume design.*

**Bottom**—*An early "DIY Black Ghost" design for Lara's early forays as the BG.*

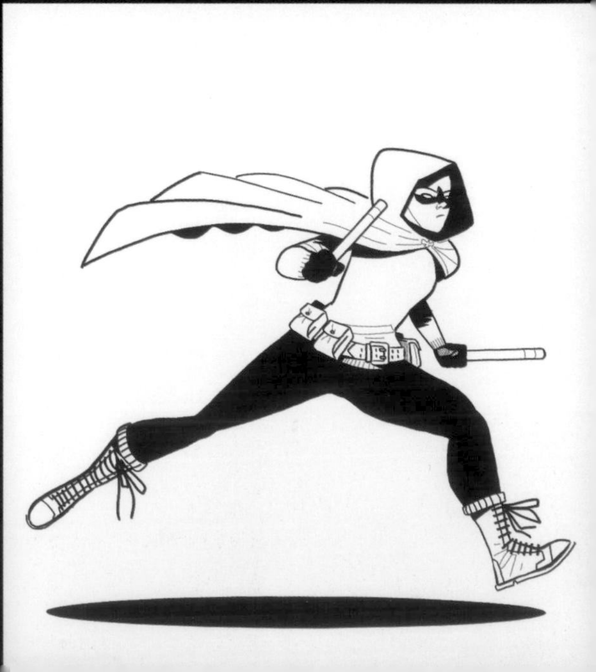

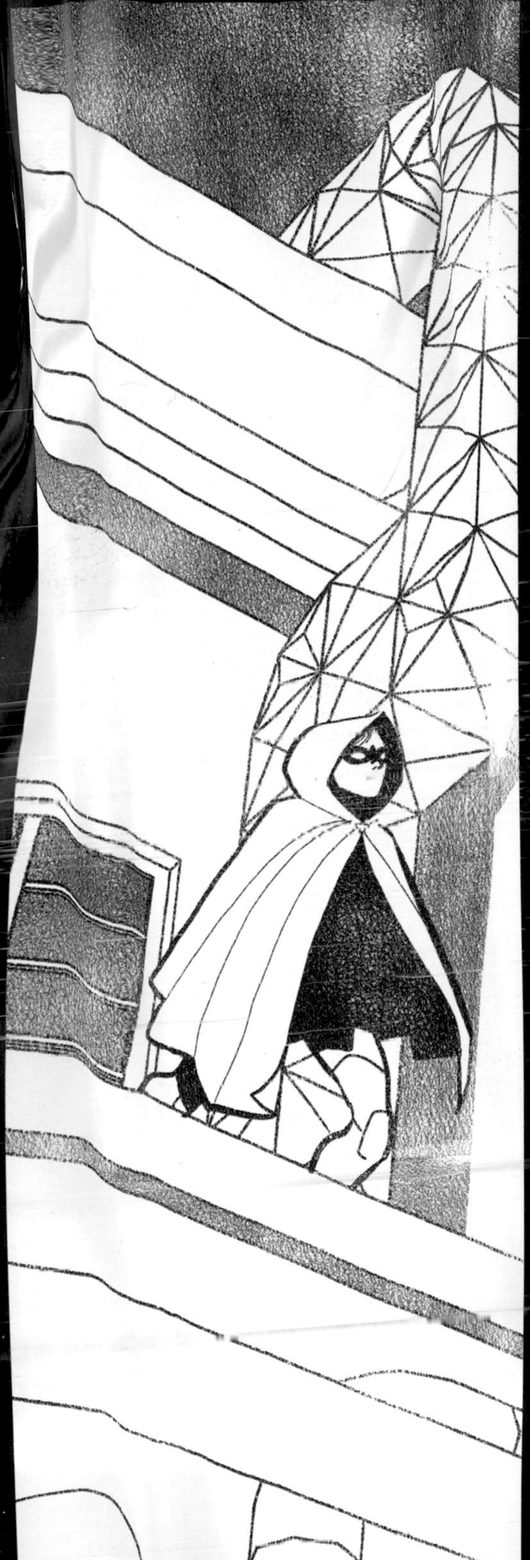

**Left**—*A moody, noirish take on Lara as the Black Ghost. One of the sketches that sold us on George as the artist for the series.*

**Bottom**—*A slight variation to George's "DIY Black Ghost" design.*

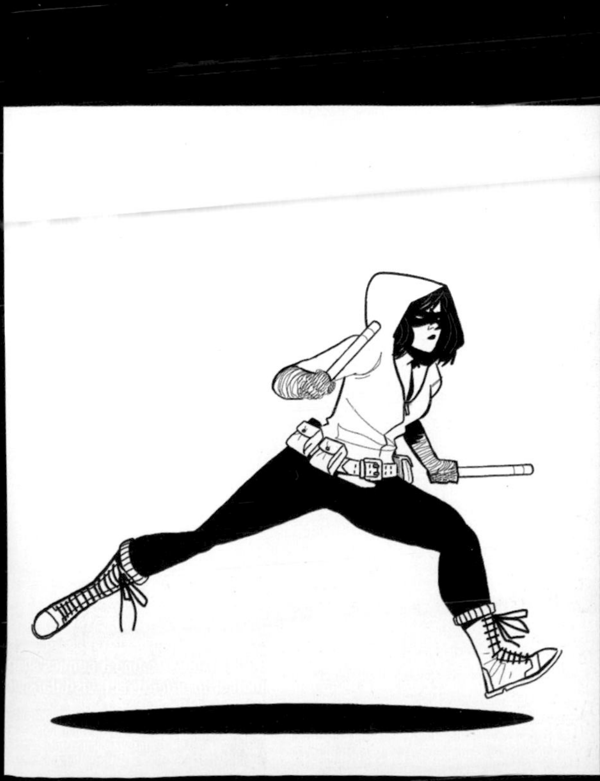

# COMIXOLOGY COMES TO DARK HORSE BOOKS

JASON LOO
CHIP ZDARSKY
AFTERLIFT

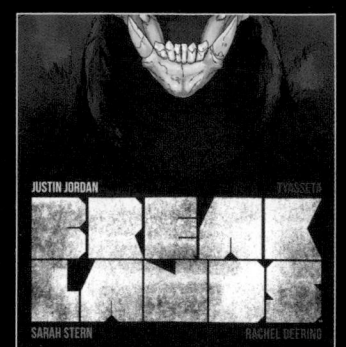

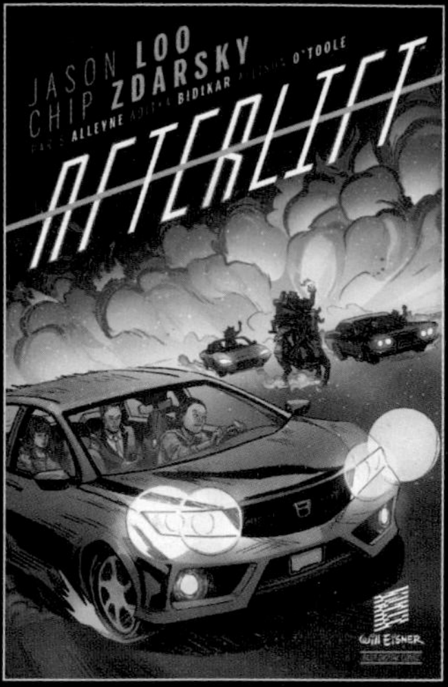

ISBN 978-1-50672-440-9 / $19.99

JUSTIN JORDAN
TYASSETA
BREAKLANDS
SARAH STERN
RACHEL DEERING
VOLUME 1: THE CHASE

ISBN 978-1-50672-441-6 / $19.99

curt pires
alex diotto
dee cunniffe
micah myers
Youth
Named One of "10 Comics to Celebrate Pride" by the New York Times
"Bold, genre-defying and heartfelt, Youth hits a reader like the meteor in its own pages: an angry, wondrous and transformative book." —Scott Snyder (Batman, Justice League)

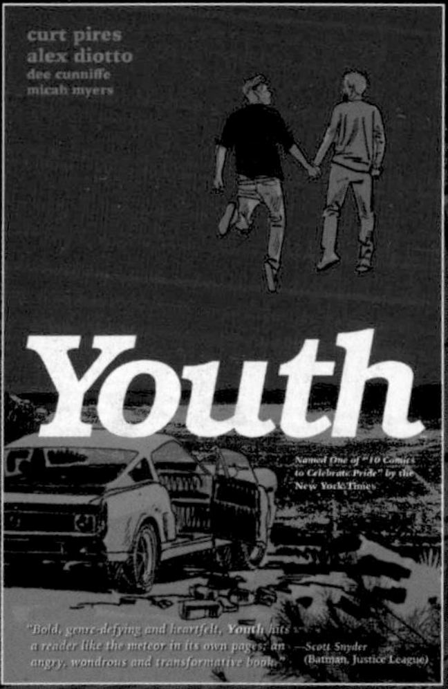

ISBN 978-1-50672-461-4 / $19.99

Named one of the "8 New Comic Book Series for the End of Summer" by the New York Times
BLACK GHOST
HARD REVOLUTION

ISBN 978-1-50672-446-1 / $19.99

THE PRIDE
OMNIBUS

ISBN 978-1-50672-447-8 / $29.99

JIM ZUB • MAX DUNBAR
STONE STAR
VOLUME 1:
FIGHT OR FLIGHT

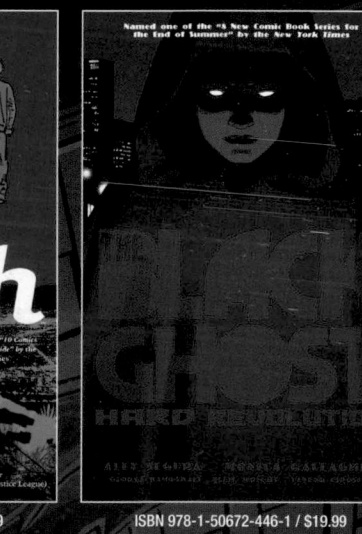

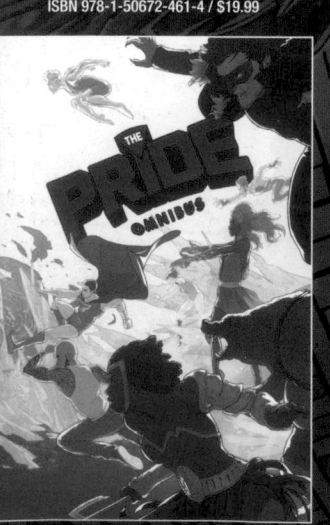

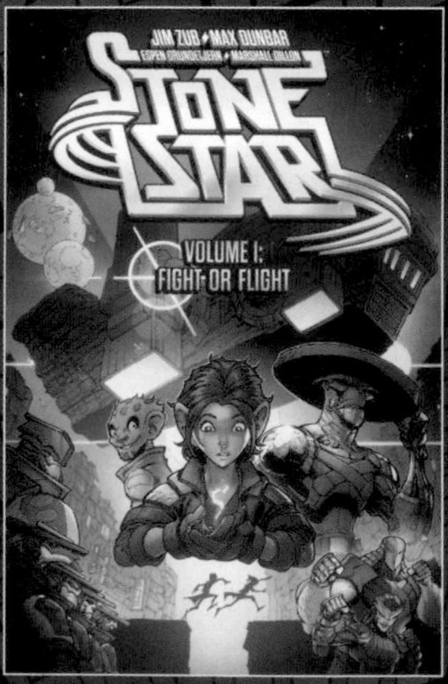

ISBN 978-1-50672-458-4 / $19.99

### AFTERLIFT

*Written by Chip Zdarsky, art by Jason Loo*

This Eisner Award–winning series from Chip Zdarsky (*Sex Crimin*... Daredevil) and Jason Loo (*The Pitiful Human-Lizard*) features ... chases, demon bounty hunters, and figuring out your place in ... world and the next.

### BREAKLANDS

*Written by Justin Jordan, art by Tyasseta and Sarah Stern*

Generations after the end of the civilization, everyone has po... you need them just to survive in the new age. Everyone ... Kasa Fain. Unfortunately, her little brother, who has the pote... reshape the world, is kidnapped by people who intend to do ju... *Mad Max* meets *Akira* in a genre-mashing, expectation-sm... new hit series from Justin Jordan, creator of *Luther Strode*, ... and *Reaver*!

### YOUTH

*Written by Curt Pires, art by Alex Diotto and Dee Cunniffe*

A coming of age story of two queer teenagers who run away from their lives in a bigoted small town, and attempt to make their way to California. Along the way their car breaks down and they join a group of fellow misfits on the road. travelling the country together in a van, they party and attempt to find themselves. And then . . . something happens. The story combines the violence of coming of age with the violence of the superhero narrative—as well as the beauty...

### THE BLACK GHOST SEASON ONE: HARD REVOLUTION

*Written by Alex Segura and Monica Gallagher, art by George Kambadais*

Meet Lara Dominguez—a troubled Creighton cops reporter obsessed with the city's debonair vigilante the Black Ghost. With the help of a mysterious cyberinformant named LONE, Lara's inched closer to uncovering the Ghost's identity. But as she searches for the breakthrough story she desperately needs, Lara will have to navigate the corruption of her city, the uncertainties of virtues, and her own personal demons. Will she have the strength to be part of the solution—or will she become the problem?

### THE PRIDE OMNIBUS

*Joseph Glass, Gavin Mitchell and Cem Iroz*

FabMan is sick of being seen as a joke. Tired of the LGBTQ+ community being seen as inferior to straight heroes, he thinks it's about damn time he did something about it. Bringing together some of the world's greatest LGBTQ+ superheroes, the Pride is born to protect the world and fight prejudice, misrepresentation and injustice—not to mention a pesky supervillain or two.

### STONE STAR

*Jim Zub and Max Zunbar*

The brand-new space-fantasy saga that takes flight on comiXology Originals from fan-favorite creators Jim Zub (*Avengers, Samurai Jack*) and Max Dunbar (*Champions, Dungeons & Dragons*)! The nomadic space station called Stone Star brings gladiatorial entertainment to ports across the galaxy. Inside this gargantuan vessel of tournaments and temptations, foragers and fighters struggle to survive. A young thief named Dail discovers a dark secret in the depths of Stone Star and must decide his destiny—staying hidden in the shadows or standing tall in the searing spotlight of the arena. Either way, his life and the cosmos itself, will never be the same!

**AVAILABLE AT YOUR LOCAL COMICS SHOP OR**
visit comicshoplocator.com / For more inform...



COMIXOLOGY ORIGINALS